MW01448237

LONE STAR PICTURE SHOWS

NUMBER TWO
Sam Rayburn Series on Rural Life

James A. Grimshaw, Jr., General Editor

LONE STAR

PICTURE SHOWS

RICHARD SCHROEDER

Texas A&M University Press

COLLEGE STATION

First edition

The paper used in this book meets the minimum requirements
of the American National Standard for Permanence
of Paper for Printed Library Materials, z39.48-1984.
Binding materials have been chosen for durability.

Library of Congress Cataloging-in-Publication Data

Schroeder, Richard (Morton Richard)
Lone Star picture shows / Richard Schroeder.—1st ed.
p. cm.—(Sam Rayburn series on rural life ; no. 2)
Includes bibliographical references and index.
ISBN 1-58544-097-3 (alk. paper)
1. Motion pictures—Texas—History. 2. Motion picture theaters—Texas—History. I. Title. II. Series.
PN1993.5.U78S37 2001
791.43'09764—dc21 00-010350

This book is dedicated

to the educators

who through the years

have helped me get to this point.

RICHARD L. SLAUGHTER
Arlington State University

MARGARET CAMERON
Arlington State University

DR. CURTIS L. POPE
East Texas State University

DR. OTHA C. SPENCER
East Texas State University

DR. JACK J. BELL
East Texas State University

DR. BOB L. TITUS
East Texas State University

Contents

List of Illustrations, IX

Preface, XI

Acknowledgments, XV

Introduction, XVII

CHAPTERS

1. Storefronts to Nickelodeons: The Beginnings to 1914, 3

2. Nickelodeons to De Luxe Theaters: 1908 to 1921, 27

3. Grand Movie Palaces: 1921 to 1929, 48

4. "Talkies"—Motion Pictures Learn to Speak: 1928 to 1941, 81

5. War to Wide Screens: 1941 to 1960, 110

Appendix 1: Texas Motion Picture Theaters, 149

Appendix 2: Texas Motion Picture Stars, 173

Appendix 3: Pioneers of the Texas Motion Picture Theater Industry, 175

Appendix 4: Theater Circuits in Texas in the 1930s, 177

Notes, 181

Bibliography, 189

Index, 195

Illustrations

Automobile advertising, Majestic Family Theatre, Waco, 5
Tyler movie letter, 1898, 6–7
Automobile and horse parades, Sulphur Springs, 10
Dixie Nickelodeon, Houston, 1911, 12
Nickelodeon, Austin, 1911, 12
Vitagraph display, Waco, 15
Bijou Nickelodeon, Austin, 1911, 16
Texas Nickelodeon, Austin, 1911, 17
Wednesday Book Club, Wills Point, 1907, 18
Crystal Nickelodeon, Waco, 19
Merchants' Matinee, Cozy Nickelodeon, Waco, 20
Washington Nickelodeon, Dallas, 21
Phillips's Egyptian Nickelodeon, Fort Worth, 22
Liberty Nickelodeon, Fort Worth, 23
Crescent Nickelodeon, Austin, 1911, 24
Yale Nickelodeon, Austin, 1911, 24
Air Dome, Mineola, 25
Palace light bulb, 1908, 26
Amarillo movie production, 29
W. Hope Tilley and camera, San Antonio, 1910, 30
W. Hope and Paul Tilley's workshop, 1911, 30
W. Hope Tilley, Austin, 31
Star Film Ranch, San Antonio, 1910, 34
Sunset Pictures studios, San Antonio, 36
Sunset Pictures location truck, San Antonio, 37
Opera House/Texas Theater, McGregor, 1912, 39
Isis Theater, Houston, 40
Isis Theater, Fort Worth, 42
Gerald Morgan operator, Lyric Theater, San Antonio, 42
Herald Robb and Ed Rowley, 43
Crystal Theatre, Dallas, 44
Martha Mansfield, *The Warrens of Virginia*, 50
Filming *Wings,* San Antonio, 1926, 52
Flying crew for *Wings*, 53
Wings head cameraman Harry Perry, 53
Wings officer wives extras, 54
Harlem Theater, Dallas, 55
Pastime Theater, Houston, 56
Teatro Zaragoza, San Antonio, 56
Teatro Obrero, San Antonio, 57
Box office, Teatro Progreso, San Antonio, 58
Theater row, Dallas, 58
Queen Theater, Galveston, 60, 61
Majestic Theater, Dallas, 1921, 62
Opening night audience, Majestic Theater, Dallas, 1921, 62
Olga Petrova, Majestic Theater, Dallas, 1921, 63
Ticket office, Majestic Theater, Dallas, 1921, 63
Stage, Majestic Theater, Dallas, 1921, 64
Majestic Theater, Houston, 1923, 66
Auditorium, Majestic Theater, Houston, 1923, 66
Entrance hall, Majestic Theater, Houston, 1923, 67
Stage, Metropolitan Theater, Houston, 1926, 68
Lobby, Metropolitan Theater, Houston, 1926, 69
Loew's State, Houston, 1927, 70
Stage, Loew's State, Houston, 1927, 70
Majestic Theater, San Antonio, 1929, 71

Ticket office, Majestic Theater, San Antonio, 1929, 71
Stage, Majestic Theater, San Antonio, 1929, 72
Silent movie music, 73
Auditorium, Palace Theater, Corpus Christi, 74
Organist, Plaza Theater, El Paso, 74
Cliff Queen Theater, Dallas, 77
Hippodrome Theater, Waco, 79
Auditorium, Hippodrome Theater, Waco, 79
Stage, Hippodrome Theater, Waco, 80
Iris Theater, Houston, 85
Ritz Theater, Houston, 86
Silent movie turntables, 88
Teatro Nacional, San Antonio, 90
Publicity, Isis Theater, Houston, 90
Village Theater, Dallas, 93
Knox Street Theater, Dallas, 94
Lawn Theater, Dallas, 95
New Liberty Theater, Fort Worth, 96
Gayety Theater, Fort Worth, 97
Truck display, Ritz Theater, Corpus Christi, 98
Bicycle advertisement, Ritz Theater, Corpus Christi, 98
Children's matinee crowd, Palace Theater, Corpus Christi, 98
Truck advertisement, Ritz Theater, Corpus Christi, 99
Mickey Mouse Club officers, Palace Theater, Corpus Christi, 99
Sidewalk display, *The White Rose,* Waco Theater, 100
Children's publicity parade, *Skippy,* Waco Theater, 101
Sidewalk display, *Monkey Business,* Waco Theater, 102
Lobby display, *The Vagabond King,* Waco Theater, 103
Window display, *Scaramouche,* Waco, 104
Bill Rast driving display truck, Waco, 104
Door handouts, six-shooter, Waco, 105
Mr. and Mrs. Karl Hoblitzelle, 109
Texas Theater, San Angelo, 111
Fort Sam Houston Theater, San Antonio, 112
Interstate's staff, Brownwood, 114
Capitol Theater, Dallas, 114
Aggie Theater, Arlington, 115
Demonstrating television, Wilshire Theater, Dallas, 1946, 116
Upton Theater, San Antonio, 117
Concession stand, Tyler Theater, 117
Star Theater, San Antonio, 118
Harling Theater, San Antonio, 119
Arcadia Theater, Ranger, 120
Palace Theater, San Antonio, 122
Ritz Theater, Weslaco, 122
Highland Theater, San Antonio, 123
Texas Theater, Austin, 124
Columbia Theater, Ranger, 125
Cine El Rey, El Paso, 129
Texas Theater, San Antonio, 130
"Mid-nite Ramble," 131
State Theater, Fort Worth, 132
Airline Drive-In, Houston, 132
Cactus Drive-In, Pharr, 133
Mission Drive-In, San Antonio, 134
Sidewalk display, *Bwana Devil,* Melba Theater, Dallas, 139
Sidewalk display, *House of Wax*, 140
Post card promotion, *This is Cinerama*, 142
Lambert Little, projectionist, Texan Theater, Hamilton, 146

Preface

I spent my childhood in the dark—at the Orpheum, Strand, Fox, Waco, 25th Street, Melrose, etc.

When I first started attending movies I knew that something very special produced those light beams thrown from that mysterious "black box" at the rear of a theater. I quickly determined that those were not real people up on the screen but merely images created in that "black box."

When I was old enough to "go to the picture show" alone, the Saturday afternoon matinee at the Melrose usually featured two "shoot-'em-up bang bangs," two cartoons, and a chaptered movie, or serial, if you like. I loved those things; I hated those things. I never saw the final chapter of a chaptered movie; I don't really think they made one.

I loved riding with Roy Rogers, Gene Autry, Hopalong Cassidy, Tex Ritter, and Marshall Reed, to name a few. We received this entire afternoon's entertainment, and sometimes a small door prize, for nine cents. Some Saturday mornings I substituted the "kiddies" matinee at the Waco Theater. Jones "Fine" Bread sponsored a talent contest broadcast over radio station WACO and hosted by Mary Holliday. After the broadcast, we saw a "B-Western." I am told that it was on this show that Hank Thompson started his singing career. If my family journeyed eighteen miles to Grandma's house on Sunday, mother slipped me a quarter, and I walked two blocks and spent another afternoon in the dark. The old Texas still stands just off Main Street in McGregor exactly where it has been since 1912.

While sitting on the left side of the left aisle of the Melrose about half-way down—I don't know why these particular seats had such a hold on me—I was often twisted around in my seat watching the light being thrown out of that box, that mysterious "black box," just wondering; "How is the magic created?" I learned from cousin Bill. He took me to the Skyview Drive-In in North Waco one Saturday evening. He showed me everything in the projection booth and how it worked. I learned how to thread the projectors and how to strike the carbon arcs. I was perplexed when Bill would strike the arc, shut it down, raise the side of the lamp house, and light his cigarette. It seemed a terribly complicated process to light a cigarette. The most important thing I learned that night was what the "cues" were, that they were located in the top right corner of the picture on the screen, what happened in the booth when the first one flashed at the end of a reel of film, and what a projectionist did when the second flashed nine seconds later. I even did a "change-over," changing from the reel of film that had just finished showing to the next reel. Afterward, when at the Melrose, I was always punching cousin Ronnie in the shoulder and pointing to the rear because now I knew how to "pick up" the first cue signaling that a change-over was eminent. Watching that beam of light instantaneously leap from one "peep hole" to the other was a never-ending thrill. I occasionally spot those cue marks in old movies on television.

I "expanded" my knowledge and experience in

junior high when I learned the subtle art of sneaking into a theater. I crawled through a hole in the back fence of the Westview Drive-In in Waco with Paul, the preacher's son. After moving to Dallas, I went behind the scenes, or screen, at a grand movie palace with Uncle Willie. His main job was opening and closing the curtain at the Majestic Theater and spotting and changing burned-out light bulbs in the theater's monstrous marquee. That was much more difficult than I would have thought.

During my years of studying and teaching in college, my fascination with the mechanics and skills of operating the equipment in a motion picture projection booth never diminished, although I did branch out. I started producing motion pictures. My master's thesis was a documentary film, the first ever at Texas A&M University at Commerce. I made films at Texas Tech University on grants from the Ranching Heritage Center and the U.S. Department of Health, Education, and Welfare. I produced experimental films and documentaries that were shown on public television and at experimental film festivals.

During my years of teaching I continued to observe and learn about motion pictures: 3-D, Cinerama, stereophonic sound, wide screens, etc. I proudly wear the mantle of "Projectionist." While a faculty member at Sam Houston State University in Huntsville I substituted a few weekends for one of my photography students who was the projectionist at the Dorothy Theater. I experienced first hand the "mysteries" of the projection booth during a film break on my very first night, and the graciousness and understanding of the audience when I "shut down" for five minutes in the middle of *Georgie Girl* while I untangled a neat little wad of film that had "piled up" in the sound box.

I have been a student and observer in many areas of mass communications for fifty years. My observations and studies in the field of radio and television resulted in my publishing in 1998 a historical preservation of broadcasting in Texas entitled *Texas Signs On*. *Lone Star Picture Shows* is the result of a fifty-year interest in motion pictures.

There are numerous books covering the history of this subject at the national level. Absent is that one single work concentrating on the industry in this state. Consequently, the scope of this project is the history of the motion picture industry in Texas from the beginnings to 1960. The most startling fact, which I had not previously realized when I started researching this project in 1996 was that the projection of a moving image in the state was *one hundred years old.*

Research took me to special collections, historical societies, libraries, archives, and individuals all over the state. I interviewed twenty-seven motion picture theater owners, managers, cashiers, projectionists, and an organist who spent their lives working in the business. To a large extent, their lives are this project. Without their remembrances, recollections, stories, experiences, and anecdotes to enhance basic facts, there would be little of interest to preserve. Although some written accounts by actors, producers, and directors were found, I found not one of those individuals available for interview.

Written accounts of the evolution and development of motion pictures through the period of this study, especially newspaper articles, are available but at best sketchy and incomplete in their coverage. Interestingly, the further back in history I looked, the more I found. There are sufficient accounts and descriptions of storefront theaters around the turn of the twentieth century, nickelodeons during the century's second decade, silent movie theaters after 1910 and through the 1920s, the coming of grand movie palaces in the 1920s, and the coming of "talkies" in the late 1920s, but written accounts of movie theaters in the 1930s, 1940s, and 1950s are virtually nonexistent. The majority of information concerning these decades came from those interviews. Motion picture personnel who worked in the 1920s and 1930s were also difficult to find. Actors, producers, and directors of early Texas-produced films were nonexistent. The managers, projectionists, organists, and others whom I interviewed were exciting, informative, and interesting: a treasure of knowledge. Scotty Davidson of Tyler, who started rewinding silent movie reels in 1919 to "get into show business," was senior. He, like many others, spent his life hibernating in those "black boxes," helping create the magic that brought so much pleasure to so many. He and the others have a story; it is the history of this industry.

There were limitations in researching and writing. This study was never meant to be a history of every motion picture theater in the state. It was never meant to be a dictionary of theaters or motion picture personnel. This could never be adequately researched, I would not care to write it, and you probably would not be interested in reading it. The history of most theaters in Texas was never recorded, or, if recorded, has literally been thrown away. Additionally, large amounts of information was not accessible. Many newspapers in Texas do not allow researchers access to their files or archives.

There were plenty of theaters in Texas through the first sixty years. Every town and city with a population of at least a hundred had at some period one or more motion picture theaters. Greenville, where I live, with a population of approximately ten thousand in the 1940s and 1950s, had seven. Dallas has had more than a hundred and thirty theaters or theaters of different names. I estimate that four thousand movie establishments have existed in this state before 1960. A list of all *found* theaters, approximately two thousand, is in Appendix 1. This list is terribly incomplete. I compiled it mainly from newspaper advertisements and directories of those cities and towns to which I traveled for research. Because I did not visit every community in the state and because most theaters did not advertise in newspapers or city directories before 1915 or 1920, I became convinced that possibly two thousand additional motion picture establishments, which I was not able to document, opened and operated.

Additionally, this preservation was never meant to be a sociological analysis of the effects of the coming and evolution of motion pictures on the people, towns, culture, and society of the state. This would be a worthy project; however, this study is not designed to accomplish this.

Another anticipated limitation was confirmed during research. Although African-American and Hispanic theaters have existed almost as long as other theaters, there was very little information concerning them. However, in one area there was more documentation than I had hoped. Information concerning Spanish-language theaters, especially in South Texas, was greatly expanded with the discovery of a small museum in Robstown, the project of Clifford Edge. The information he collected and made available concerning "Stout" Jackson was of tremendous help. Regrettably, there is not a museum with similar information on African-American Texas theaters.

It is believed this historical preservation successful. *Lone Star Picture Shows* presents the formation and development of motion picture exhibition, production, and distribution in the state of Texas. It illustrates how the projected image was first presented and how it evolved into store-front theaters, nickelodeons, grand movie palaces, neighborhood theaters, and drive-in theaters. It tells of the beginnings of the motion picture production industry, how it grew, the early stars, the studios located in the state, films made in Texas, and the declined of that moviemaking. It shows how motion pictures were first obtained and distributed and into what that part of the business evolved. *Lone Star Picture Shows* illustrates what effects the coming of sound, World War II, and television had on the industry.

If readers have never experienced watching a weak, flickering image on a stretched bed sheet in a formerly deserted building or vacant lot; trying to concentrate on the story of a silent motion picture while reading projected dialogue with a piano pounding their eardrums; the grandeur in a grand movie palace where the decor, spectacle, ambiance, and musical presentation were as much of the performance as the images on the screen; spending an afternoon in a "bloody bucket" watching a Texas-made "horse opera" where the hero in a white hat fired twenty-five shots from his six-shooter; the enjoyment of watching a film in a "passion pit" or drive-in; or ducking in their seats as objects were "thrown" at them through the "hole" in a 3-D motion picture screen, the people whose lives are contained in these pages have, and their stories may give readers insight and enlightenment as to what they have missed.

Acknowledgments

I could not publish this book without thanking the many people who helped me produce it. This includes the people who assisted me in all the libraries, archives, and special collections around the state. I do not know how a history could ever be written without their unselfish help and assistance.

I could never have written this history without the twenty-seven individuals who gave me their time for interviews about their lives working in the motion pictures industry in Texas.

I especially thank Mary Lou Morris, my "yell-across-the-fence" neighbor, who has always been available to assist me in proofreading both histories I have published, and my wife, Judith Katherine Hall Schroeder, who I believe is more proud of my two publications, if that is possible, than I.

Introduction

Thomas Edison is credited with inventing motion pictures, but it took many inventions, experiments, and innovations by many gifted people of science to allow him and others to bring movies into existence. There were contributions from physiology, chemistry, physics, photography, and mechanical technology.

Persistence of vision, without which motion pictures could not exist, had been known since 1824. Peter Roget, of thesaurus fame, published a paper that year stating that the image formed on the retina of the eye is retained for an instant after it disappears. The concept led to toys and gadgets such as the Thaumotrope. This coin-shaped disc, which rotated on a cord between a person's hands, had half its desired image on one side and half on the other. When spun, persistence of vision made the two sides form a complete image. The Mutascope and Kinematoscope created a perception of motion using a series of still images printed on cards that were rapidly "flicked" into view, one after another. Viewers looked through an eye piece, turned a handle, and a series of images with progressive steps of action flashed into view for a fraction of a second. The perceived motion was real, interesting, and entertaining. Except that these amusement park devices could not project that image onto a screen, the Mutascope and Kinematoscope made practical some of the basic ideas of early motion picture projectors.[1]

The magic lantern, or the principle of it, had been known since the seventeenth century. Athanasius Kircher described it in a book in 1646. The idea of having a light source, a drawing on transparent material, and a lens project an image onto a flat surface was used and refined during the next two centuries. One of the first "spectacular" uses of the magic lantern was for public showings around 1798 called Robertson's Phantasmagoria. Audiences were shocked and terrified by grotesque and macabre images that appeared, moved, enlarged, disappeared, and seemingly leaped out on a series of rear projection screens. During the early 1800s, lime light allowed a much brighter image from the magic lantern and another principle of the movie projector had been established.

The phenomenon that causes light coming through a "pin hole" on one side of a dark enclosure to create a reversed, recognizable image on the opposite side had been known and used since the 1500s. Artists used the "camera obscura" to augment their drawing skills by placing drawing paper on ground glass where the projected image formed. This device became the first photographic camera when a light sensitive plate was substituted for the glass. In the 1800s, while the camera obscura was in use, experimentation in the physics of light transmission and refraction developed lenses that replaced the "pin-hole." This created brighter images for the artist and shorter exposures for early photographic processes.

Nevertheless, photography was not ready to contribute to the birth of motion pictures. Early photographic emulsions had to become much more sensitive to light and be coated on a more suitable support base to capture the rapid series of still images needed in movies.

The Daguerreotype, developed by Louis Daguerre in 1837, was the first practical photographic method of capturing and preserving an image, but it resulted in a positive image formed in the camera on a highly polished metal plate. There was no negative, no practical method of easily making multiple positive prints. In 1839 Henry Fox Talbot developed the Calotype, later renamed Talbotype, which produced a negative from which positive prints could be made, but it used paper as a support base. These early photographic processes could never be used for motion picture film stock for obvious reasons—and their exposures were too long. A Daguerreotype plate was exposed fifteen to thirty minutes. Talbotype's exposures were not any shorter. Better lenses, improvements in emulsions, and post-exposure development reduced exposure times in both processes to a few minutes. The wet-collodion process used by Mathew Brady and other photographic historians in the 1860s to record the Civil War was likewise inadequate. It required several seconds to expose a "wet" glass plate that immediately had to be rushed to a nearby, light-proof tent and developed before it dried. Motion pictures required an emulsion sensitive enough to allow twenty or more separate exposures to be made continually each second.

What motion pictures needed was George Eastman. In 1888 his Eastman Dry Plate Company introduced "roll film" in its Kodak "detective camera," the first camera made to be used by amateur photographers. One of its main innovations was an emulsion sensitive enough to allow the taking of "snapshot" type photographs. Originally on a paper base, Eastman soon switched to a clear, flexible celluloid base for the round negatives produced in the first "hand camera." This more sensitive, clear roll film in subsequent years became the basis for movie film stock.

A practical motion picture process was almost conceived by Eadweard Maybridge. In the 1870s Maybridge became famous for producing the first photographic analyses of motion by sequential, still pictures using as many as twenty-four individual cameras. His first and most famous motion study was of a galloping horse to help determine if there was one single instant when all its hooves were off the ground. This led to numerous other studies, many of which he published. Maybridge utilized these motion series to make paintings on glass for use in a device called the Zoopraxiscope. It sequentially projected twelve images on a screen to produce motion. Audiences were amazed. He gave countless demonstrations of his motion-capturing and projection system throughout England and America but never produced a real motion picture system.[2]

Then Edison and his assistants adapted the principles of the Mutascope and Kinematoscope; took parts of Maybridge's Zoopraxiscope; integrated it with the principles from the magic lantern; interjected Eastman's flexible, transparent film; perfected the mechanics of transporting film through a camera obscura using sprocket holes; incorporated a shutter with the lens; and produced a motion picture process Edison named Vitascope. Other inventors used the same advancements and innovations to develop their own individualized "movie equipment." The Lumières brothers of France quickly followed Edison and introduced their system called Cinematographe.

Using Edison's Vitascope, movies were first projected for a paying audience at Koster & Bials Music Hall in New York City on April 23, 1896. Ten months later, on February 1, 1897, images from a Vitascope introduced movies to Texas at the Dallas Opera House. From this first presentation, the production, distribution, and exhibition of motion pictures evolved. The business of the moving, projected image in the state of Texas began in earnest—more than *one hundred years ago.*[3]

LONE

STAR

PICTURE

SHOWS

Storefronts to Nickelodeons

THE BEGINNINGS TO 1914

While passing through Waco in 1901, a cowboy entered the Winnie Brothers' Kinetoscope Parlor. He was fascinated by the peep shows with their flickering images and illusion of motion. He paid a nickel to "peek" at *Minnie Renwood in a Serpentine Dance* and *Sisters Leigh in Their Umbrella Dance.*[1] What he saw that day inspired him. Soon he helped instigate one of the most significant developments in entertainment history. This historical preservation concerns its instigation, development, and evolution in the Lone Star State.

Throughout the years this phenomenon, or where it happened, has been referred to by many different and unusual terms:

"Views"—in the late 1890s and early 1900s, the first type of films, which showed all kinds of normal, everyday scenes like trains coming down the tracks, people walking out of a building, fire engines leaving the station, women washing clothes, a mother feeding a baby, etc.

"Storefronts"—turn-of-the-century motion picture theaters created by converting any store, abandoned building, or deserted room into a motion picture viewing establishment.

"Sheets" or "Picture Sheets"—early reference to motion pictures or the place where they were shown; named for the use of a bedsheet as a viewing screen.

"Black Tops"—traveling tent shows that featured motion pictures as part of the entertainment and used a tent dyed black to reduce outside light.

"Shot-Gun Houses"—1940s and 1950s theaters that showed predominantly B-Westerns.

"Flickers" or "Flicks"—early motion pictures whose screen image had a bad or irritating flicker.

"Chasers"—a vaudeville term for poor-quality motion picture features placed last on the bill for the purpose of making people want to leave the theater or "to chase people out of the theater."

"Ozoners"—drive-in theaters.

"Rats"—term used by kids in Houston to refer to the Star Theater, being "Star" spelled backward; later, a generic term for any motion picture theater.

"Canned Theaters"—early sound motion pictures that were merely filmed stage presentations.

"Galloping Tintypes"—early silent motion pictures.

"Talkies"—early sound motion pictures.

"Grind Houses"—theaters that showed any type or quality of motion picture; usually double features, cartoons, serials, or short subjects—anything they could "grind out."

"Cow Pasture Theaters"—early drive-in theaters.

"Turns"—a vaudeville phrase used when projected images began to have a place or their "turn" on the bill.

"Oaters"—B-Westerns, motion pictures including many horses.

"Bloody Buckets"—motion picture theaters that showed predominately B-Westerns, a large amount of shooting and killing.

"Horse Operas"—B-Westerns in which lead characters were cowboys accompanied by their horses.

"Shoot Em Ups (Bang Bang)" or "Bang Bangs"—B-Westerns; many six-shooters and much shooting.

"Passion Pits"—drive-in theaters where couples could go and ignore the feature on the screen.

"Duals"—double features or reference to theaters that ran predominately double features.

"Town Houses" or "Downtowners"—theaters located in central business districts of cities.

"Open-Airs"—drive-in theaters.

Thomas L. Tally, the cowboy traveling through Waco, was so intrigued and excited by his experience in Waco in 1901 that when he settled in Los Angeles, California, a short time later he established Tally's Phonograph and Vitascope Parlor at 311 South Spring. He set up a projector and screen in the rear of the parlor. He separated the moving images in the back from the arcade in front by a partition with peep holes. The attractions seen through those holes proved more popular with patrons than the attractions in front. Later that year Tally opened the Electric Theater at 262 South Main. It was the first theater in the nation devoted exclusively to the commercial showing of the projected image.[2]

The first American showing of a motion picture to a paying audience took place on April 23, 1896, at Koster & Bials Music Hall in New York City.[3] The images were projected by Thomas A. Edison's Vitascope. Within a year, Texas had moving images being projected in Dallas, Waco, Gainesville, Galveston, Tyler, and many other towns.

A public demonstration of the Vitascope occurred in Dallas on February 1, 1897. The Opera House showed scenes of a Mexican duel, a lynching, a fire rescue, and Niagara Falls. In early 1897, a two-reel comedy flashed from a projector mounted on the balcony rail at the Majestic Family Theater on North Fourth in Waco. A bedsheet hung above the stage. Crowds at the infrequent showings were so large that many people had to sit on the stage behind the sheet and view the image in reverse. That same year people in Gainesville viewed their first motion picture, *Serpentine Dance*—flickering images of dancing girls tinted red, blue, and pale green.[4]

In early April of 1897, an ad in the *Galveston Daily News* announced that "Edison's latest and greatest wonder, 'The Vitascope'" was to be shown at the Grand Opera House. It proclaimed:

> Greatest wonderment. Excites enthusiasm. The universal wonder of the age. Direct from New Orleans after 100 nights of the greatest success. Change of Programme daily.
>
> . . . The pictures were photographed on Kinetoscope films "and are no bigger than the nail of one's little finger." Each of these films . . . is 50 feet in length and the Vitascope utilized an arc light of 2000 candle power and the picture thrown on the screen "is magnified 600 times."[5]

The motion picture venture did not succeed. On April 15, the newspaper announced, "The Edison Vitascope gave its last performance at the Grand Opera House last night. The audiences were not sufficiently large to make it profitable to the company, and

Figure 1. The first projected, moving images in Waco were shown at the Majestic Family Theatre.
Courtesy The Texas Collection, Baylor University, Waco

Manager Fred White released them from their contract. They go to Orange where they show tonight."[6] These showings were the earliest documented projections of a moving image in the state.

The next year, on February 28, 1898, Mrs. M. B. Adams of the Church Circle at the Marvin Methodist Church in Tyler mailed a letter to parishioners inviting them to see "this wonderful new invention which has so startled and interested the public for the past few months." Those who bought tickets and attended on March 7 received a printed program titled, "The World's Latest Sensation. Edison's Startling Invention . . . THOSE IMMENSE LIVING, MOVING PICTURES . . . ," which explained:

If your own family photographs were taken by this new process you would all appear alive and full size on the large canvas, not sitting still as in ordinary photographs but actually walking back and forth, full life-size, laughing and shaking hands as if really alive. Thus every variety of living moving scenes both on land and sea have been lately photographed hundreds of miles away by this new system and will be shown on the immense canvas in real life movements so natural you would feel that horses and men would actually leave the canvas and come dashing into the audience as they gallop by. . . . It is nothing like the stereopticon or magic lantern, but a new invention called, "Vitascope,"

Tyler, Texas, Feb. 28th, 1898.

From Mrs. M. B. Adams,

Church Circle,

Marvin M. E. Church.

Would you kindly mail the enclosed postal card, saying if you would like to see this wonderful new invention which has so startled and interested the public for the past few months, and stating how many tickets you wish.

Note.—We are allowed to keep forty per cent. for the Church, on all tickets we sell by means of enclosed postal card before date of entertainment, without one cent of expense. We are mailing a letter to all our people and wish to know by enclosed card how many tickets you will buy of us. The Company pays for everything, the postage, our printing, and all other expenses; and if you will buy tickets of us at once, we will clear a nice sum.

Date and Price.—Monday evening, March 7th, lecture room. Admission 35c, reserved seats 50c, children 25c. Reserved seat plan opens at Harris Bros' Drug Store, Friday at 9 o'clock a. m., where all tickets bought of us will be honored. Read explanation of entertainment on program enclosed.

Please mail the postal at once as we must sell the tickets before date of entertainment, and wish to deliver them before reserve seat plan opens. We will send you the tickets.

Signed: Mrs. M. B. Adams,

Tyler, Texas.

Figures 2 and 3. The letter announcing a demonstration of projected, moving images on March 7, 1898, at the Marvin Methodist Church in Tyler and the program listing scenes to be shown. Courtesy Smith County Historical Society, Inc., Tyler

"Biograph," "Projectoscope," etc. The pictures are very large, clear and bright, and steady in motion. The principle will be explained. . . .[7]

The program's reverse side listed the scenes to be shown or "views," as they were called. Admission was thirty-five cents, plus fifty cents for a reserved seat. The church received half the proceeds. About this time, the first movies in Honey Grove were shown on the second floor above the Piggly Wiggly on the west side of the square.[8]

The first movie establishment in San Antonio "was a vacant store on Alamo Plaza where someone hung up a sheet to serve as a screen and placed a blanket over the front door to keep out the light." The year was 1898. "The pictures were one-reelers, and the folding chairs were so uncomfortable that cowboys would remove the saddles from their horses and take

PROGRAM.

SELECTIONS FROM THE FOLLOWING:

Black Diamond Express.	Lone Fisherman.
Storm at Sea.	Fire Rescue Scene.
Infantry Manœuvres.	The Little Mischief.
Morning Fire Alarm.	The Burning Stable.
Police Making Arrests.	Just Before the Wedding.
Tub Race on River.	Clarks Thread Mills.
Feeding the Doves.	Children's Pillow Fight
Switzerland R. R. Scene.	Society at Rockaway.
Whirlpool Rapids.	Mother's Morning Task
Babies' Swinging Day.	Milker's Mishap.
Buffalo-Chicago Flyer.	McKinley's Inaugural Parade.

EXCELLENT MUSIC INTERSPERSED.

EXPLANATION.

IF your own family photograph were taken by this new process you would all appear alive and full size on the large canvas, not sitting still as in ordinary photographs but actually walking back and forth, full life size, laughing and shaking hands as if really alive. Thus every variety of living moving scenes (as on preceding page) both on land and sea have been lately photographed hundreds of miles away by this new system and will be shown on the immense canvas in real life movements so natural you would feel that horses and men would actually leave the canvas and come dashing into the audience as they gallop by. The rolling billows of the ocean, express trains at full speed, fierce dashing fire brigades, and many such scenes are so thrilling that persons in the audience often say they feel like moving from their seats lest the monstrous waves dash over them or the passing trains leave the track. Many other scenes are beautiful and humorous, and large audiences are perfectly amazed and delighted. It is nothing like the steriopticon or magic lantern, but a new invention often called "Vitascope," "Biograph," "Projectoscope," etc., etc. The pictures are very large, clear and bright, and steady in motion. The principle will be explained. No one who has not seen this masterpiece of the great Edison can afford to miss the opportunity.

SEE TESTIMONIALS OVER.

them inside to sit on. There were 50 seats at a nickel each."[9]

"I saw my first motion picture in the Peterson Theatre here in Paris," stated A. W. Neville, a long-time resident. "A traveling dramatic company had a couple of two-reelers that were shown between acts. They were a railroad train in motion and a fire department bringing its horse-drawn apparatus out of the station to answer an alarm. The projection machine was turned by hand and was rather jerky, besides the scratches on the films giving them the appearance of a fine rain falling."[10]

E. E. Taylor, an optometrist, opened an establishment for projecting images in Houston. It was situated on the east side of Main between Rusk and Capitol. "I recall going to the movie back in 1898," remembered A. E. Amerman, later mayor. "Mr. Taylor has told me that when he operated it, the movie was the first in Houston." Joseph Hornberger remembered going to the movies in Houston in 1900:

The first one I attended was on Congress Ave. . . . The picture was supposed to have been very funny, and I saw it four or five times. It was about a fisherman who was sitting on a plank projected over a small stream. Along came a fellow in a covered wagon. He stopped the team, slipped over and picked up a big rock. He threw it at the opposite end of the plank. Up in the air went the fisherman, coming down in the water.

This film looked like one of the slow motion pictures of today. This caused a great deal of laughter and applause, and that's all there was to the show until the house got filled up again. In those days, when a picture was finished, the house was cleared. If you wanted to see it again, you had to pay again.

In order to make the room dark, they had black-painted canvas stretched around the room. The room had a few chairs, and a sheet was used as a screen. A Ward and Alster projector was used. Admission was 10 cents.[11]

Another early movie establishment of Houston was operated by optometrists. P. W. Cain and his brother T. E. opened a theater in 1902 in the 300 block of Main. When this location did not succeed, the brothers tried a "free" open-air theater, called an air dome, on a lot at Elysian and Carter. They sold advertising to Houston merchants. According to Cain, this theater was successful:

> Cooperation of the merchants insured our success. We were there several weeks and later moved to a site on Congress for an additional several weeks. It was a tough section over there near the roundhouse in those days. The neighborhood boys thought it was great fun to toss rocks through the screen and perpetrated other bits of their brand of humor which proved embarrassing at times. We were forced to employ a special officer to maintain order and keep the rock throwers in their places.
>
> One night one of the playful lads brought in from the woods one of the striped-back kitties and turned it loose in the crowd. There was no more shows that night.[12]

According to Louis Wolfin, motion pictures were first shown in Amarillo in the late 1890s. As a child, Wolfin attended a presentation of a moving image in 1900:

> I can remember riding in the surrey with my parents out to the railroad yards—somewhere to see some pictures of Spanish War events. Our destination was . . . a large freight car parked on a siding. On the end of the freight car was a large screen of some kind of white canvas or sheet. We saw pictures projected on this screen of the Spanish American War cavalry . . . fording this stream and then riding up the opposite bank, and the picture actually moved. Who was responsible for this showing? I don't know, but it could have been the Santa Fe Railroad since their freight car and siding was used for the entire show. There were probably two dozen buggies and surreys parked around the end of the car. As far as my knowledge—this preceded actual moving pictures [theaters] by a considerable time.[13]

Edison's Cineograph Company used a 1900 model Edison machine, "the finest and most scientifically constructed picture machine of today," to present moving images to El Paso for the first time. The show, at the Opera House on May 10, 1900, presented "thirty interesting and historical pictures such as the arrival of Dewey on board the Olympia in New York harbor, charge of the Rough Riders, Spanish bull fight in Madrid, railroad scenes, driving scenes, and numerous others taken from incidents of the day all over the world." The evening's performance concluded with "a true-to-life reproduction of the great Jeffries-Fitzsimmons Fight at Coney Island."[14]

The first projection of a moving image in Austin was in a tent show on January 10, 1900. The first movie in Fort Worth was outdoors. In 1903 Joe S. Phillips used a bedsheet to show *The Great Train Robbery* in "Fort Worth's old Rosen Park located at the end of the long-past Rosen Heights streetcar line. I had to draw current for the projector off the trolley wire," stated Phillips. "To reduce this from 500 volts to 110 volts, limit of the projector, we ran the current through a barrel of salt and water. This served as a rheostat."[15]

John H. Sparks became a projectionist in 1904 and later showed the first movie in the stockyards area of Fort Worth.[16] Winston O. Sparks of Fort Worth recalls his uncle's fascination with moving images:

> While he was in St. Louis, he had run into a man who ran hand-cranked silent movies—hand-cranked projector. He was fascinated with them and found out all about them. My uncle was "hot" for theater.

. . . He found a theater that was for sale. He bought it. Some of the relatives thought he bought it for the beautiful ticket taker that worked there. . . . He married her.

There was a fellow here on the North Side who had a little "dog and pony show." It is like a small miniature circus. He had several tents, and every spring he would go out into Central Texas. . . . He had borrowed money from Mr. Tidball and Mr. Van Zant. One winter this man moved into Fort Worth and set up his winter quarters, and went to Tidball and Van Zant and says, "It's not working. All the big circuses are taking away my money."

Included in his stuff was a little tent, maybe ten by ten, a movie projector with an arc lamp, and maybe folding chairs—maybe a big piece of white canvas. Mr. Tidball started saying, "What are we going to do with this—this movie projector? I think maybe we might put that to use. Why don't we try it. . . . Let's see if we can adapt this thing to a building."

. . . They put ads in the paper, and my uncle said, "Hey, maybe I can do that. . . ." They got in touch with him. He knew exactly what to do with the projector.

So they said, "Let's try it and see if it will work." They got all the chairs and they covered up all the windows to make it dark inside. . . . They advertised it by putting billboards up here and little bulletins around, and they showed the first movie in that building. . . . He was probably using the movies left over from the "dog and pony show." It started out and showed promise; that's when they built the Isis Theater around the corner on Main Street.[17]

The first movies were brought to Ballinger on a wagon by Earnest Buchwald; "Old Buchwald" as people called him. That was before electric lights so the projector used a carbide light much like that used in the circus and early automobiles. Carbide powder was placed in a cylinder. Water dripped onto the powder, forming gas. This moved through small rubber tubes to a point that was ignited. The screen was the white wall of a building. The first images were of a train rounding a bend and coming toward the audience. This scared the audience so badly that many jumped and ran. In Odessa the first "morally clean" movies were shown at the Opera House by R. E. Piper. Then, a Mr. Cross tried, unsuccessfully, to build an air dome over his garage for use as a movie house.[18]

The Great Train Robbery was the first motion picture experience for Greenville residents. The movie was part of the performance in the traveling tent show of E. J. Lamkin. These shows, which had a movie as part of the bill, were referred to as "black tops."

Lamkin was impressed by the patronage and returned in 1904 to open the city's first permanent storefront picture establishment, the Empire, situated on the northeast corner of the square on the ground floor of the Odd Fellows Building. He was not without competition for long. Five other theaters, some owned by Joe Urquhart, Ed Williams, and the Bond family, quickly opened. Landon C. Moore, chemist for the soap factory of the Texas Refining Company, opened a storefront theater at Lee and Oak. "It never had over a handful of people in it," stated W. Walworth Harrison of Greenville, "and sometimes showed to a dozen."[19] Harrison recalled attending the first theater in Greenville: "One of the first pictures shown at the Empire was *The Chicken Thief,* which like *The (Great) Train Robbery,* involved a lot of action, chases, falls, spills, climbing fences, and the like. It was then believed that action was about all that could be conveyed through the pictures and in the beginning no one probably realized that drama could be pantomimed successfully. The Empire also had some vaudeville, usually just one bill a week and often it was a magician or an animal act, like trained rats."[20]

Harrison remembered the early ballyhoo the Empire used to attract an audience: "Lamkin thought it necessary in the beginning to use ballyhoo out front

Figures 4 and 5. Two early forms of ballyhoo in Sulphur Springs: an automobile parade publicizing the Air Dome and a horse parade promoting the Lyric. Courtesy Hopkins County Historical Society, Sulphur Springs

before the matinee performance, and shortly before two-thirty a small band formed in front of the theatre composed of local musicians who left their regular work temporarily for the fifteen minute 'build up.' Rufe Turner laid down his soldering iron to play bass horn. Allie Obenchain quit tuning pianos to play trumpet. Fred Rogers, an employee of Lamkin, played the drums. George Dennis came from the messenger office and sometimes John Gipson left his barber shop and filled-in."[21]

Movies started at the armory at 701 Ohio in Wichita Falls in 1904. Two transient businessmen first offered local people a chance to see "pictures in motion." Audiences viewed persons walking toward the camera or up a set of stairs. The projector's light source was a combustible gas produced by dropping a liquid on a solid substance, like the old carbide lamp. The first moving picture in Giddings was a short reel included in a "lyceum" program. When circus ponies and elephants were shown performing, people exclaimed, "Isn't that true to life? How in the world do they make such pictures?"[22]

What had begun in New York City in 1896 within a few years had rapidly spread throughout the nation and Texas. Movies were being shown in many different locations. Referred to as "storefronts," an enterprising individual could lease an old store or building, rent some chairs—possibly from the local mortuary—hang a sheet on the back wall, place a rented hand-crank projector on a table or platform, and be in the motion picture business. The "flicks" entertained audiences at vaudeville houses, churches, tent shows, amusement parks, public parks, empty buildings, unused rooms, organization or civic meetings, local store, penny arcades, town squares, and vacant lots.

Equipment to start a movie establishment was readily available. The Southern Talking Machine Company, situated at 347 Main in Dallas, carried "everything needed." They offered "Moving Picture and Stereopticon Outfits ready for prompt shipment."[23]

The projected image was not always used to fascinate audiences. In the early 1900s, movies became one item on the bill of many tent shows, traveling vaudevillian troupes, and live entertainment theaters. The image quality was so poor—with weak, spotty lighting and scratches that made pictures look "rainy"—that movies became known as "chasers." The motion picture feature was placed last on the bill. Managers used it to drive or "chase" people out of the theater.[24] After image quality improved, movie features still remained the final act. Managers' attitudes had changed, however. They now believed that the higher-quality images left patrons with a favorable or positive attitude as they left the theater.

At the Majestic in Dallas in 1907, the last act on the bill was often "Edison's Kinetograph." By 1910, this feature, still the last item, had been renamed "MAJESTOGRAPH."[25] As quality improved and movies became increasingly popular, they steadily took over the program at live-performance theaters until some started featuring entire evenings of exclusively motion pictures. Projected images started to monopolize the program, but live acts were kept on the bill and placed between movie features. Known in the trade as "coolers," these acts were intended to entertain while the projectors cooled down. Soon enterprising Texans were operating motion picture establishments in practically all empty spaces available in downtown districts.

Nickelodeons

On June 15, 1905, motion pictures took a major step toward becoming a viable business. John P. Harris and Harry Davis of Pittsburgh, Pennsylvania, opened a motion picture gallery.[26] Instead of scheduling performances only in the evenings, "Harris and Davis began showing a program of movies which ran continuously from 8 A.M. until midnight, in the tradition of continuous vaudeville. Charging five-cent admission, they called this new format a 'nickelodeon.' ('Nickel' for the admission and 'Odeon,' Greek for theater.) The ninety-six-seat theater, originally

THE DIXIE THEATRE
MOVING PICTURE
MILANO PRODUCTION
A POET'S VISION OF HELL
DANTE'S INFERNO
DIVINE COMEDY
THE MASTERPIECE OF MOVING PICTURES
A POET'S VERSION OF HELL
HELL
THE WORLD'S GREATEST ALLEGORY
MOTION PICTURES
TODAY YOUR LAST OPPORTUNITY TO SEE THIS $100,000 PRODUCTION
WHY NOT? GO NOW.
A Continuous Performance. Admission 25¢ 15¢
DIXIE THEATRE 7-DAYS-7
THURS., DEC. 28
PRICES

D.W. GRIFFITH
Pippa Passes
THE NET OF INTRIGUE
"GRANT, POLICE REPORTER"
Helen Gibson
THE HAUNTED STATION
TODAY
THE DEATH SIDING
IS MARRIAGE SACRED?
HEARST-PATHE NEWS
U.S. TRANSPORT WRECK
GERMANS RENEW RUTHLESS SEA WARFARE
NEW AUSTRIAN ENVOY
INTERNATIONAL ICE FUND
GENERAL FILM SERVICE

Figure 6. (left) *The Dixie Nickelodeon at 603 Main in Houston in 1911. Courtesy The Institute of Texan Cultures, San Antonio*

a storeroom, was cheaply redecorated with stucco, burlap, and paint to convey a sense of pseudoelegant interior design. Opera chairs arranged in rows served as seating, and a white linen sheet as a screen."[27]

With Edison's showing in 1896, random showing in various locations, storefront theaters, and the founding of the nickelodeon in 1905, the number of motion picture establishments grew rapidly. In the first few years after Harris and Davis's entrepreneurship, "nickel madness" erupted. Quickly, every city and town in the nation and Texas had movie businesses lining both sides of its main downtown streets. Many of these "poor man's shows"—called that because the first patrons were predominately tramps and drunks—were on side streets just off the main street where the rent was cheaper. By 1907, just two years after they began, there were three thousand nickelodeons in the United States. One year later there were eight thousand.[28] Chicago had three hundred. This explosive growth continued until around 1914 when their decline was equally rapid.

Although the exact number of Texas nickelodeons is not known, estimates can be drawn by considering the known nickelodeons in certain cities. In Galveston in 1910, the Parisian, the Fortunia, the Orpheum, and the Marvel operated on the south side of the 2300 block of Market. More than ten were situated along that street. By 1911 San Antonio had seventeen just on Houston Street between Alamo Plaza and Main. These included the Bijou, the Lyric, the Imperial, the Ideal, the Gem, the Electric, the Dixie, the Crescent, the Big Tent, the Marvel, the Picture Show, the Star, the Royal, and the Wigwam #1, among others.[29] (A list of motion picture establishments *found* in Texas up to 1960 is in Appendix 1.)

Figure 7. (left) *A nickelodeon in Austin in 1911. Courtesy Austin History Center*

Clara Boelhauwe, a San Antonio resident, saw her first movie at the Wigwam near Alamo Plaza. The movie was preceded by a vaudeville act in which a woman sang several songs. The pictures shown in these nickelodeons, as remembered by W. J. Lytle, an Alamo City resident, were "'all of the running kind,' showing a mad chase or a train in motion."[30]

Although there were variations, the basic nickelodeon consisted of a small store, building, or room; a box, later a box office, located at the entrance to collect the nickels (no tickets); seating for fifty to two hundred consisting of folding or ordinary kitchen chairs, generally so few as to require some patrons to stand; bare walls painted red or with some kind of black cloth hanging around the inside of the room; a muslin sheet, plain or sized, hanging on the back wall; and a hand-cranked projector on a table or platform near the entrance with the film running into a basket, cotton picking sack, or trash can. A cheaply decorated front usually employed some form of "ballyhoo" like a carnival-style barker or anything to create music or noise to attract customers. A pianist or an (automatic) player piano operating at full volume provided music during the show. Nickelodeons offered twelve to eighteen performances a day, seven days a week, from 8 A.M. to 10, 11 P.M., or midnight. For the admission price of one nickel, patrons enjoyed one or two features from one-thousand foot reels lasting twenty to thirty minutes after which they had to leave. Especially if the program was two reels, a singer located beside the screen or near the projector performed an illustrated song, giving the projectionist time to rewind the film and change reels.

Moving images returned to El Paso on May 28, 1906. L. M. Crawford and Frank Rich used "some good moving pictures" as part of the bill at the air dome, a one-thousand seat enclosure at the east side of city hall at San Antonio and Myrtle Streets. The theater was a roof garden and bleachers with a large level garden space directly in front of the stage for chairs and tables. Refreshments were served during the performance by uniformed waiters.[31]

In 1906 Houston's first nickelodeon opened on Texas Avenue across from the Rice Hotel. On January 1, 1907, George Kenneth Jorgensen opened the city's second nickelodeon in a small store at 410 Main. Jorgensen owned a "movie machine" and had earlier toured the state with carnivals, and then on his own journeyed to different towns and projected movies on the sides of buildings or any place where people were interested enough to watch. In Houston:

> He rented a vacant store building, filled it with 200 folding chairs, installed his "Little Edison" picture machine, hung a sheet across the opposite wall, set up his ticket office out front, and, at a cost of $85, he was in business.
>
> The first day, a Sunday, he collected $40 from the 800 people who came to see his two-reel show. The next day, 1200 people dropped in to see the "flickers."
>
> He did everything—selling tickets, grinding out the film and, of course, rewinding it by hand. He had to turn on the house lights at the end of each reel, giving his patrons a five-minute intermission while he rewound the film.
>
> A month after he opened his Nickelodeon, he sold it for a profit and moved to Galveston where he opened the Crystal Theatre with an investment of $180.[32]

Quickly, other nickelodeons opened in Houston, including the Gem, Star, Rex, Scenic, Vaudette, Dixie, Pastime, Crescent, Happy Hour, Theato, Crystal, Key, Crown, Strand, Zoe, Liberty, Rialto, and many, many others. The *Houston Chronicle* reported the growth of nickelodeons in that city:

> There were dozens of these little theatres scattered up and down Main, all showing one-reel and two-reel pictures and charging only one price, a nickel. . . .
>
> Another early-day theatre was the Scenic at 507 Main. The Vaudette, operated by Mr. [Moye] Wickes from 1910 to 1912, in the 400 block of Main was a tiny thing with less than 100 seats for which he paid $350 a month rent. Other theatres, all of them in small store buildings, would seat or accommodate between 250 and 300 persons.
>
> Programs changed at the discretion of the theatre operator. Usually he got seven reels a week, but would run two reels to a program, which would bring in about three changes a week.
>
> Sometimes the programs would be filled out with illustrated slides. . . . When the illustrated slides were flashed on the screen, the audience was not asked to sing, as they are now, but a singer in the operator's booth sang. If he didn't know the tune, he would play a phonograph record for an accompaniment.
>
> Many of the first pictures were made in Europe, the Pathé Studios being in France, the Tureno and the Milano in Italy. . . . There were no stars in the old days. The exhibitor bought his picture from posters. If the posters pleased him, he bought the film, not knowing what it would be about. Sometimes he leased the reels, sometimes bought them outright, or sometimes traded them with other operators.
>
> Newsreels first came into being about 1911. Pathé and Universal made the first newsreels, and an exhibitor never knew what he was going to show. He merely ordered a reel and took what they sent him, but some of the more ingenious ones would order an illustrated magazine from New York and post some of the news pictures outside the theatre to advertise the newsreel.
>
> Players in the movies were not given names until about 1911 or 1912. There were several reasons for this. One was that most of the films were foreign made, and the names would be hard to pronounce. Another was that producers realized the star system would develop, and featured players could demand larger salaries.

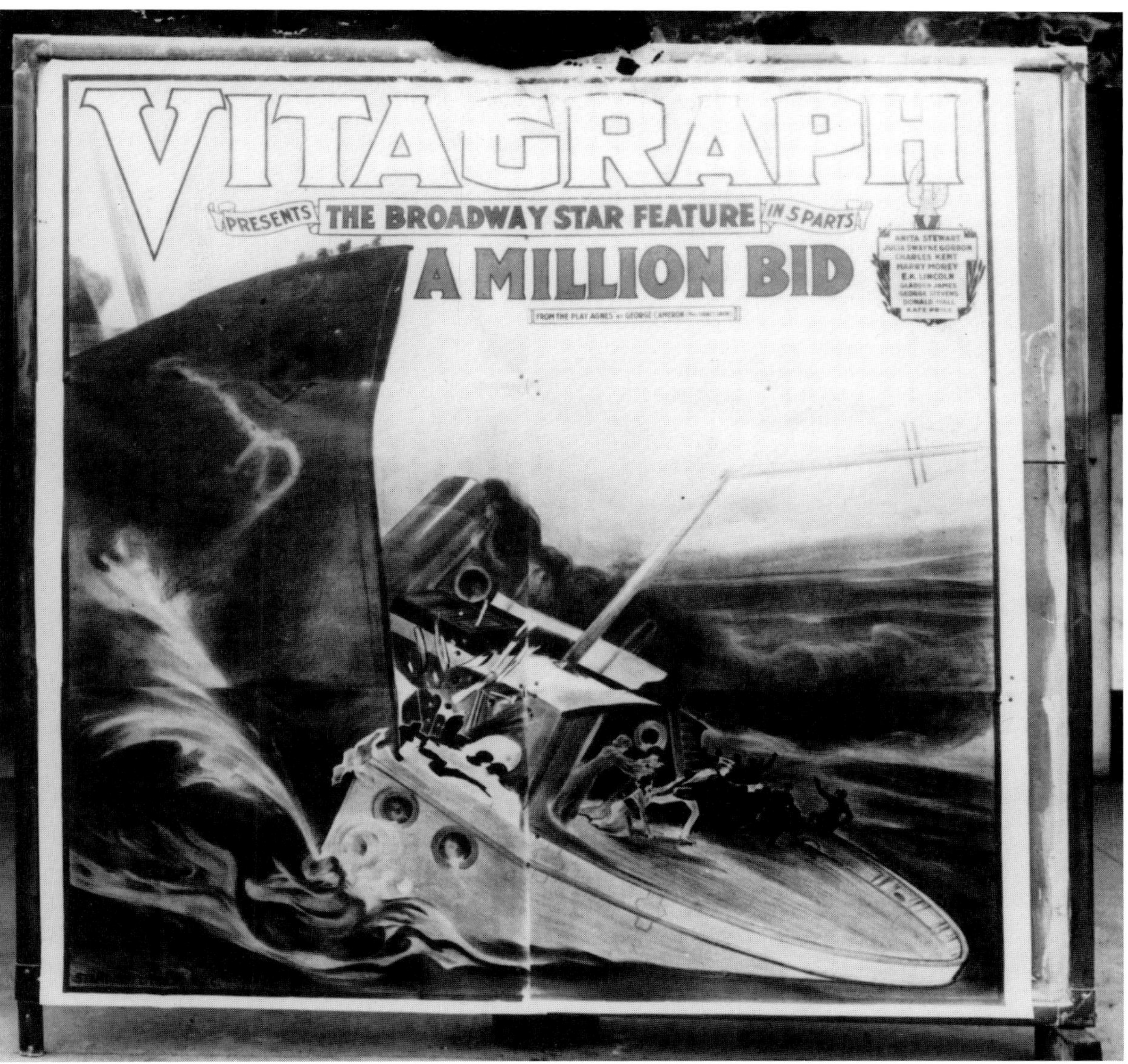

Figure 8. Sidewalk display in front of the Hippodrome in Waco. Courtesy The Texas Collection, Baylor University, Waco

> In the early days, all players were paid the same, a flat rate of $5 a day. . . . Florence Turner, one of the first stars, was known simply as "The Vitagraph Girl," Mary Pickford as "Little Mary," and Marian Leonard as "The Biograph Girl." The old Vitagraph was the first to use names.[33]

In the spring of 1910 a fire destroyed the Theato in Houston. Although no lives were lost, an ordinance was passed requiring all theaters that had no rear exits to have their seats facing the doors that led to the street. This caused many nickelodeons and future theaters to reverse the usual arrangement.[34]

When Jorgensen moved to Galveston in the summer of 1907, he opened the Theatorium, situated at 411 Tremont—Galveston's first nickelodeon. He later opened the Crystal, sometimes called the Theatorium-Crystal, at 405–407 Tremont next to the Theatorium. He also started a nickelodeon in old Electric Park on the beach front. To open the Theatorium:

A projection machine had to be bought; folding chairs had to be provided. Films had to be purchased. There were no film exchanges in those times. . . . The first film to be shown to a Galveston audience . . . a Pathé hand-colored, one-reeler, was labeled *The Hen that Laid the Golden Egg.* Next came *The California Train Robbers,* a thrilling, sensational hair-raiser, a two-reeler, by gosh. . . .

Among the early producers were Essanay, Sinclair, Pathé and Biograph. Rotund John Bunny and the beauteous Marguerite Snow were among the first film stars. Most of the early pictures were made outdoors, and producing concerns made their headquarters in loft buildings in New York and Chicago. . . .

In those days the exhibitor purchased his film outright, ran it for about a week, and then tried to sell it to someone else. Mr. Jorgensen made an exchange agreement with a Houston exhibitor, and the two traded films until an exchange was opened in Dallas by J. D. Wheelan. . . .

A full program lasted about forty-five minutes after which the film which had been run through the projector and into a sack was rewound. This rewinding operation sometimes lasted 10 or 15 minutes. The lights were turned on; and the customers were left to their own devices. Usually they talked, argued, or criticized the management while small boys ran whooping up and down the aisles or threw spitballs at each other.

Musicians were hired to entertain the audience while the film was being rewound and to provide sound effects during the showing of pictures. Sometimes as many as eight or nine musicians were employed. They were grouped in the darkness behind the screen where they

Figure 9. The Bijou Nickelodeon in Austin in 1911. Courtesy Austin History Center

Figure 10. The Texas Nickelodeon in Austin in 1911. Courtesy Austin History Center

could watch the picture. Their purpose was to interpret in sound the action on the screen. In the early days the drummer had perhaps the hardest job of all as he made the battle noises when the cavalry arrived in the nick of time and slew [Native Americans] by the dozen. . . . Most of the early pictures were Westerns.

In the quarter century since the first theater was established here, ballyhoo methods have improved as much as the motion pictures themselves. A clown, performing his foolish antics in front of the theater was Jorgensen's first ballyhoo medium. Next, a large phonograph, or perhaps they were gramophones in those days, was set up in the lobby. "We played that instrument continuously . . . until people got sick and tired of the racket. . . ." Next came those tinny, nerve-shattering automatic pianos.[35]

When Jorgensen opened the Theatorium he opened a vaudeville theater on the second floor above it. To help promote the movie, Jorgensen put the entrance to the vaudeville theater on the first floor inside the movie theater. To see the upstairs show, a patron had to first buy a ticket for the movie and enter through its auditorium.

Jorgensen also owned and operated the Beach Crystal, at Twenty-third and Boulevard; the Casino, 2111 Market; the Vaudette, 2103 Market; the Leader, 2211 Market; and the Crystal, 1608 Elm in Dallas; and others out of state.[36] By 1907, Galveston also had the Colonial, the Globe, the Majestic, the Marvel, the O'Donnell Jacob, the Fortunia, the Orpheum, the Parisian, the Star, the Lyric, the People, the Cozy, the Dixie One, the Leader, the Ruby, and many others.

Harold and Yuill Robb's family operated the first nickelodeon in Big Spring. They used benches as seats, the screen was a plaster wall, and "the piano was mounted on large rollers so it could slide into a large box when rain interrupted the program." Harold operated the noisy projector and then climbed down from the tin booth and announced the name of the next feature through a megaphone. They had slides for transposition stating "Please Be Patient," "Ladies Please Remove Your Hats," and "Just a Moment Please While We Change to the Next Reel." Because of competition, the brothers moved to San Angelo where they started an "open-air" nickelodeon over a feed and grain store with Ed Rowley forming the beginnings of the Robb & Rowley (R & R) Theater circuit.[37]

Movies in Tyler continued to be shown at churches as well as nickelodeons after their establishment. On July 6, 1906, the ladies of the First Baptist Church conducted a benefit movie night at the Grand Opera House. The crowd saw *Penny O'Milk Please, Presence of Whales, Pipe Dreams, Sausage Factory, Troubles of a Hobo,* and *Cavalry Fording a Stream.* The feature presentation was *Revolution in Russia* showing the military bombardment of Odessa.

On March 20, 1906, J. L. Urquhart opened the Empire, situated on the south side of Tyler's square. The first movies were *Postman's Christmas Box, Impracticable Voyage,* and *Fire Cascades.* The illustrated songs for the evening were *Bright Eyes Good Bye, Bathing in France,* and *Washing Clothes in Sicily.* The 3:30 and 7 P.M. performances had to be rearranged so they would not interfere with the services of local churches.

Figure 11. Karl Lybrand showed the first motion picture in Wills Point in 1907 at the Wednesday Book Club Opera House. Courtesy Karl Lybrand, Majestic Theatre, Wills Point

In the summer of 1907, the Tyler Roller Rink started showing movies three times daily. Opening night features were *San Francisco, At the Dentist, A House of Another Color,* and *The Bank King.* Movies shown in other local nickelodeons were *Tale of a Tenement, Sporty Dad, Saved by the Tide, Hanson's Folly, The Aviation Meet at Los Angeles—California, Baby's first Tooth, Eavesdropper, Suicide Club, His Masterpiece, Man with Three Wives, Saved from Conviction, Girl Sweet, Road to Love,* and *Wheels of Justice.*[38]

The quality of the motion picture features steadily improved, according to W. Walworth Harrison of Greenville:

> Gradually the scope of the films broadened; but for many years they were brief sketches, and several different pictures were shown on one program. Travel and scenic films were new additions, and the French manufacturers began to turn out novelty pictures based upon optical illusions and photographic tricks. The French also began very early to experiment with color. . . .
>
> The movie bill for May 28, 1907, . . . indicates the progress the pictures had made since the primitive "chase" pictures of a few years before. The Lyric display ad carried the slogan "Catering to ladies and children especially . . . ." The feature picture was . . . *Bethrothed's* [*sic*] *Nightmare.* . . . Following this came *A Horrible Adventure. Ascending Mt. Blanch* was next and it was evidently a travel picture. The fourth number was *A Wonderful Flame,* and the last movie was entitled *Amateur Night.* Following this list were two titles in quotations: "Down at the Baby

Figure 12. The Crystal Nickelodeon in Waco. Courtesy The Texas Collection, Baylor University, Waco

> Store" and "Good Old U.S.A." These were evidently illustrated songs. . . . An "Illustrated" song was a regular feature without which no movie theatre was complete at that time. Colored slides were projected on the screen illustrating the saccharine story told by the song, and meanwhile a soprano sang the words, accompanied by a pianist.[39]

Movies in Wills Point originated in 1907 at the Wednesday Book Club Opera House. Karl Lybrand helped found the business with a hand-powered machine that "spewed and spluttered." He renamed it the Home after becoming manager. "The theater was just a little metal building that ran silent pictures," recalled grandson Karl. "It was not a permanent structure. I think that the Home came out of the same building as the Wednesday Book Club." When a new theater was built in the 1920s, it was named the Majestic. Starting with the Wednesday Book Club in 1907, this line is the longest continuously owned and operated theater by a single family in the country. The single-screen Majestic still operates every day except Wednesdays.[40]

The Dreamland in Amarillo was a large barn-like structure in the 700 block of Polk. Originally a skating rink owned by H. Joe Isaacs and managed by Gus Hollander, in 1907 it started showing collections of news films, brief story reels, and short comic "turns." The screen was a "stretched" bedsheet; admission, five cents. Films were shown between skating ses-

Figure 13. The "Merchants' Matinee" at the Cozy Nickelodeon in Waco. Courtesy The Texas Collection, Baylor University, Waco

sions. The projection booth was a cage covered with asbestos suspended above the skating floor. The single projector was stopped every few minutes as a reel "ran its course" and a new reel loaded. Each reel contained one or more separate subjects each announced by the projectionist.[41]

That year the Dreamland experienced an event that was to become all too common in early motion picture establishments. One evening, a hundred patrons were watching a movie when the film broke. The spectators moved around waiting for the movie to start again. Suddenly the operator leaped from the projection cage carrying a blazing reel of film. After throwing it into the street, he returned to the theater and assured the patrons that there was no danger of the fire spreading. Then he and an assistant returned to the booth and tried to fight the fire, but it spread and eventually burned down the theater. The Dreamland was never rebuilt.[42]

By August of 1907, Wichita Falls had three nickelodeons. The Casino, a large tent at Eighth and Indiana, was owned by Dr. Waller, a dentist. The air dome was at Tenth and Indiana and the Majestic at 712 Ohio. When the Majestic burned, a Mr. Tritch built the Gem, "Wichita Falls' first all-enclosed, permanent structure for the exhibition of motion pictures. A big electric sign hung above the sidewalk and a double-row of incandescent bulbs over each of the three arches ornamented the facade." Admission was five cents for children and a dime for "grownups."[43]

In 1908 a magic-lantern show played the opera house in Huntsville. It was a curiosity to the audience because the pictures actually moved. People marveled when they saw a dog "jerkily" run down the road, and laughed at a fisherman sitting on a bridge who spilled into the water when a plank he sat on became loosened. A few years later, Robert Philips, a roof tinner, opened the first theater.[44]

Waco's first nickelodeon, the Dixie, opened in 1908 at 407 Austin. Owner William L. Terry was one of the first to have a popcorn machine and an electric, automatic-changing player piano. The success of the Dixie led others to start converting many of the city's downtown stores into nickelodeons. By 1910 Waco had seven. The Box Brothers' Vendome; the Ideal at 505 Austin, converted by Mrs. Henry Lingsweiler from a millinery shop; the Huaco, operated by Paul C. Negroponte; the Cozy at 604 Austin, owned by Paul Jacobs; and J. A. Lemke's Elmo were a few of those that lined Austin Avenue. The Cozy and the Elmo, situated at 604 and 606 Austin, had a common connecting lobby. Herschel F. Dunn, who was employed there as a teenager, was first an usher. Later he ran the music machine and the player piano. He "learned the business" at the age of ten at a storefront theater in Smithville. The owner agreed to school Dunn if he would "sweep out" each day.[45]

Waco had two open-air theaters, the forerunner of the drive-in. Air domes usually consisted of four walls, seats or benches placed on the ground between the projection platform and the screen, and no roof. They were summer operations that made patrons endure the heat and mosquitoes but not the stale air from the closely packed patrons of indoor theaters. Air domes were cheap to build and operate, requiring only a vacant lot with a fence; minimal construction. They were less a fire hazard so did not require all the fire proofing in the projection booths as did enclosed theaters. The air dome at 120 North Sixth and the Air Dome Royal at 513 Franklin were operated by the Box Brothers, Doc and Pat. The Royal was considered a "swank" operation by patrons; it had "backed seats nailed to the boards."[46]

The first motion picture shown in Lubbock was filmed on the Lindsey Ranch situated twelve mile west of town. Frank Barclay played a Mexican villain and Clifford Lindsey a Texas cowboy. The one-reeler was filmed by a "man from California." It premiered in the Opera House, which had motion picture equipment installed in 1909 by owner E. McElroy. Barclay and Lindsey were the first ushers. This type of performance being new, when a matinee was planned, the light company had to be notified so more power could be generated. In 1916 Lindsey built the first theater in Lubbock after admiring one in St. Louis.[47]

One of the first permanent movie establishments in Dallas was the Dixie, established in 1905. In the next ten years, dozens of nickelodeons joined storefront theaters—the Bioscope, Candy, Colonial, Favorite, Feature, Grand Central, Happy Hour, Star, Roseland, Nickelodeon, Queen, People's, Orpheum, Newport, Mammoth, Old Mill, Washington, and many, many others. The Grand Central was possibly the first nickelodeon in Dallas for black audiences.

The Washington was lavish compared to generic nickelodeons. It had an extremely large bronze and

Figure 14. The elaborate Washington Nickelodeon on Elm Street, theater row, in Dallas. Its façade was the largest theater front in the Southwest. Courtesy Texas/Dallas History and Archives Division, Dallas Public Library

marble ornate front with a huge arch, the largest in the Southwest. Ten-foot high figures adorned the top and sides of the arch. The façade was ablaze with a thousand lights and fronted Elm Street, which became "theater row." "Theaters used to be all over main streets," recalled Bob Baker, a Dallas projectionist for fifty-eight years. "The beautiful Washington opened at 1615 Elm . . . it was the first Dallas theater with a pipe organ. No posters up front to detract from the beautiful sculptures. The only sign announced, 'Organ music from 11 A.M. to 11 P.M.' We'd pack them in." When the Washington closed during the depression, the admission was still ten cents.[48]

According to Virginia Cooper, a long-time Dallas resident, all the lighting and decorations at the Washington did not impress her when she attended a movie there as a child:

As I recall, the Queen and the Old Mill were not too bad, but the Washington was a narrow tunnel of a building, never well-lighted, and, according to reports, rat-infested. The management specialized in serials and shoot-'em-up Westerns. Popular hero of the latter was that strong, silent, two-gun man, William S. Hart. Most little boys worshipped the characters he portrayed.

My favorite stars were Charlie Chaplin and Mary Pickford. Mary was my ideal. Her long blond curls started a style that swept the country. How I longed to look just like her. . . .

The films we saw were silent, of course, with written subtitles. Music throughout was supplied by a piano player who sat just below the screen and executed selections suiting the action—the cop and robber type tunes, sentimental ballads,

Figure 15. Phillip's Egyptian Nickelodeon at 712 Houston in Fort Worth. Courtesy North Fort Worth Historical Society

Figure 16. The Liberty Nickelodeon in Fort Worth. Courtesy North Fort Worth Historical Society

> love songs, etc. When the film broke, which was often, the person played on and on, usually a medley calculated to keep an impatient audience from walking out. In my way of thinking, the pianists that played in the movie theaters of that day were very much underrated and unappreciated. Surely, their unsung performances took imagination, steady nerves, and pliant neck muscles.
>
> The first words that flashed on the screen were usually, "Ladies, please remove your hats" and then, "Please read the titles to yourself. Loud reading annoys your neighbors." In spite of this, we often got stuck behind a wide, feathered hat or had to listen to the murmur of a parent reading to a child.[49]

Main Street was where nickelodeons clustered in Fort Worth. There were the Orpheum at 1511 Main, the Philips at 710 Main, the Odeon at 1004 Main, the Hippodrome at 1108 Main, the Gem at 1404 Main, the Queen at 1410 Main, the Blue Mouse at 1010 Main, the Gayety, the Rex, the Pershing, the Liberty, the Rialto—addresses unknown but most likely on Main—and Phillips' Egyptian, "close by" at 712 Houston. By 1915 Fort Worth had fifteen.[50]

"Most of them were merely store buildings fitted with screen, seats, projector and box office," remembered Jack Gordon, newspaper columnist. "Those were the days when kids could get in for a nickel. The other dime parents gave children for street-car fare to town and back was saved for popcorn and a second movie. Most of the kids walked. But it was different back when old Bill Hart rode the screens at the Odeon, Blue Mouse, Rex, etc. The kids would cheerfully walk a mile for Saturday movie-going."[51]

"The Queen Theater on lower Main had the dis-

Figure 17. The Crescent Nickelodeon in Austin, 1911. Courtesy Austin History Center

Figure 18. Wishert and Marshall's Yale Nickelodeon in Austin in 1911. Courtesy Austin History Center

Figure 19. The Air Dome in Mineola in 1910. Courtesy Select Theater, Mineola

tinction of showing the first film ever raided by police," recalled Gordon. "It was *A Fool There Was,* starring Theda Bara. The late A. Zuccaro, owner, foiled the cops by jumping into the theater box office and locking the door. They took the film, but not Zuccaro. That was in 1911. Someone had always been trying to hang movies out with the wash."[52]

J. S. Phillips, who showed the first film in the city in Rosen Park in 1903, built the Odeon in 1910, the first nickelodeon designed specifically to be a movie house. Admission to view the one-reel pictures was five cents. A year later his theater started showing French color movies, in which each frame had been painstakingly tinted by hand. Color in movies had started almost as early as movies. One of the earliest, in 1895, *Annabelle's Butterfly Dance,* had color that shifted and blossomed as a vigorous young lady shook the folds of her flowing costume. The historic *Great Train Robbery* had a gunshot as a burst of red. There were many such experiments. Individual artists followed stenciled outlines to hand paint on black and white film, frame by frame.[53]

A traveling picture show came to Cooper in 1909. Two boys were hired to clean the feed store so the movie could be shown. Interested viewers sat on sacks of feed, and a bed sheet was hung so they could see the *Harry K. Thaw and Stanford White Tragedy—Madison Square Garden, New York.* The action was "amplified" by a man standing behind the screen telling what was happening. This prompted John D. Jones to borrow money and open the Empress in Greenville in 1911. He soon sold it and moved to San Angelo. Jones became partners with Harold Robb and Ed Rowley to form the Concho Theater Group, the corporate name Robb and Rowley chose for theirs and Jones's eight San Angelo movie houses. Jones bought the Crystal Theatre Movie and Vaudeville House located on the north side of Concho Avenue between Chadbourne and Oakes Streets from Noah Smith in July of 1920. Smith had operated the first open-air picture show, or air dome, in that city. It was located one door south of the Chadbourne Building. Additionally, Smith built the first airplane ever flown in San Angelo.[54]

The first moving picture in Lampasas was at the Hannah Springs Opera House in 1910. The features

Figure 20. This light bulb, which started burning at the Byer's Opera House in September of 1908, still burns at the North Main Historical Society Museum at the Stockyards in Fort Worth. Courtesy North Fort Worth Historical Society

were a major boxing bout and a "very dramatic comedy."[55]

One of the longest-lived items in Texas theater history still "shines." While nickelodeons were showing short movie "turns," large theaters were being built for vaudeville and live performances. When the Byer's Opera House of Fort Worth was being readied for its September 21, 1908, opening, Barry Burke, stagehand, climbed a ladder and screwed a small, low-wattage light bulb into a socket near the stage door. The little bulb became famous decades later as theater personnel realized that it had been the same all those years.

After the bulb's longevity was recognized, care was taken to keep it burning. In the 1920s, the theater was converted to a full-time movie house and renamed the Palace. During the remodeling, the electric company installed a special line so the bulb's power would not be interrupted. On one occasion the bulb stopped burning when the electricity for the theater failed; but when power was restored, the bulb again burned. Eventually they installed a meter solely for that light and "footed" the bill.

Whenever he visited Fort Worth, even into the 1950s, Burke would go backstage to see if the bulb was still burning. "I can't help but feel," stated Burke, "that when the lamp finally goes out, I'll go with it." The future of the bulb was in jeopardy when the Palace was razed, but it was rescued and still burns at the North Main Historical Society Museum at the stockyards in Fort Worth.[56]

In less than two decades, motion pictures had evolved from a novel gadget used to amaze, bewilder, and frighten audiences to a growing, financially stable industry. Major steps had transformed "flickers" into "movies." Other steps were poised to advance it even further. During coming years, technical experimentation in color and sound would lead to their incorporation into standard movie usage in the 1920s and 1930s. The storefront theaters and the improvements and advances of the nickelodeons eventually instigated the constructing of downtown, suburban, and neighborhood movie houses and those magnificent de luxe grand movie palaces of the 1920s.

The presentation of movies consisting of everyday scenes like a trolley going down the street, fire trucks leaving the station, or a person washing clothes, had evolved with the help of films like *The Great Train Robbery* into features with story lines and plots told through cuts, variation of shots, pacing, inter-cutting, etc. Edwin S. Porter's film established the idea of the narrative motion picture. After its release, images of just something moving quickly became unacceptable. During the following years, the industry discovered, experimented with, and refined every type of movie theme and plot: comedy, Western, adventure, romance, etc., all except the one format that required sound: the musical.

Americans had accepted the idea that "going to the movies" had become a permanent and important part of their culture and personal lives. In this short period, the gadget had become an industry; gadgeteers had become businessmen. As "nickel madness" eventually "ran its course," it was quickly replaced by built-for-purpose theaters established exclusively for the presentation of longer and more sophisticated films, viewed by a more demanding and sophisticated audience.

Nickelodeons to De Luxe Theaters 1908 TO 1921

As the nickelodeon craze peaked, it was challenged and slowly, systematically replaced by an industry entering a new phase of expansion. Certain individuals endeavored to establish a moviemaking industry in Texas, and even sought to make Texas the motion picture production center of the nation. Film business pioneers built "de luxe" theaters for everyday, comfortable and pleasurable movie viewing by repeat patrons. Booking, promoting, and more serious efforts in filmmaking hoped to promote and maintain regular movie attendance. Trained professionals, especially projection booth operators, helped theater owners run a more professional entertainment establishment.

During the coming decade, Texas would develop a strong industry in production, distribution, and exhibition of motion pictures. The Tilley Brothers, Star Film Ranch, Essanay Company and numerous other studios in San Antonio and El Paso would make Texas a main production location. With fifteen or more studios in the 1910s and 1920s, San Antonio nearly became the production center of the nation until Hollywood established itself. Dallas became a major film distribution center. San Antonio and El Paso established centers for Spanish-language films. Just as importantly, Texans started building de luxe theaters to replace the crude nickelodeons. The Opera House/Texas Theater in McGregor built in 1912 was one of the first.

Early Filmmaking in Texas

The first shooting of motion picture footage in Texas was in 1900. Cameraman G. W. "Billy" Bitzer of the New York–based Biograph Company arrived in Galveston on September 13 and during the next few days filmed the destructive aftermath of a hurricane that had recently struck that city. Photographers from the Edison Company shot the Galveston disaster on September 24. Segments were used in the movies *Panorama of East Galveston; Panorama of Orphans Home; Galveston, Panoramic View;* and *Wreckage along Shore, Galveston.* Both groups disregarded the wishes of city authorities who did not want the devastation publicized.[1]

The first company in Texas established for the purposes of making and/or distributing motion pictures was the Wheelan-Loper Film Company of Dallas and San Antonio. Wheelan started July 18, 1908, the representative of the monopolistic Motion Picture Patents Company. Wheelan was renamed the General Film Company and later the Mutual Film Corporation of Texas. Although primarily a film distribution business, Wheelan carried an inventory of cameras, lighting apparatus, and reels of unexposed film stock, and promoted itself as a production company.[2]

The first motion picture feature made with a Texas theme was *Texas Tex* produced in Denmark in 1908. The Great Northern Production Company, headquartered in Copenhagen, used real Native Americans from a touring wild west show.[3]

Essanay Film Manufacturing Company

The earliest motion picture feature filmed in the state was in El Paso. On November 19, 1909, *The El Paso Herald* warned citizens not to be disturbed by unusual happenings they may observe in the downtown area during the next few weeks. "If you see a hatless man rushing 'madly' down San Francisco Street with six, burly policemen in hot pursuit, do not become excited or alarmed. There is no danger." G. M. "Broncho Billy" Anderson, actor and secretary of the Essanay Company, a Chicago-based film company, had established winter headquarters in El Paso and was using the streets of the city for feature film production. Jesse J. Robbins was the cinematographer or "the expert at the machine." The company was headquartered at the Angelus Hotel and used Washington Park to build scenery for indoor settings. Essanay was expected to be in El Paso one month.

Five years later, on August 26, 1914, Essanay announced plans to establish a studio and moving picture city near El Paso. P. Flex visited the city looking for fifteen hundred acres for "the making of western pictures." The company, consisting of 210 employees, a tribe of Native Americans, and 300 head of horses,

Figure 21. An early filmmaker in Amarillo shooting fire engines leaving the station. Courtesy Amarillo Public Library Photo Archive

Figure 22. W. Hope Tilley hand cranking a movie camera in San Antonio about 1910. Courtesy James R. Buchanan

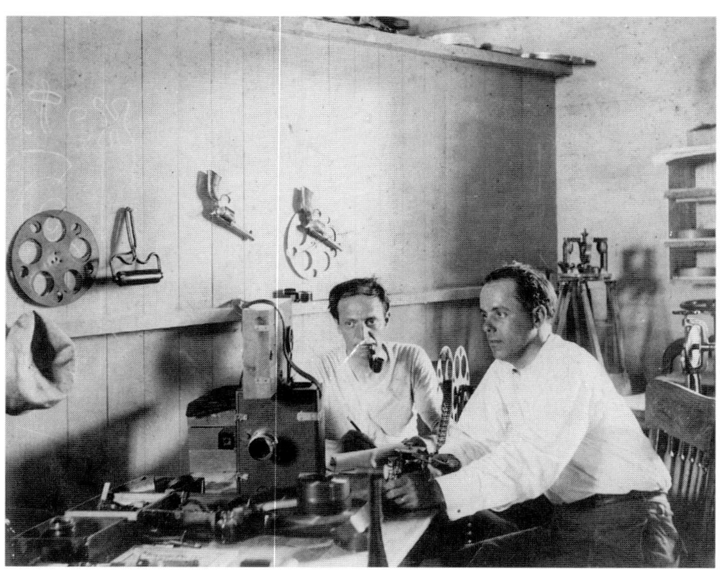

Figure 23. W. Hope and Paul Tilley in their Austin studio workshop, 1911. Courtesy James R. Buchanan

was then located in Niles Canyon, California. Flex stated that the entire outfit would be moved to El Paso if a suitable location could be found. The company intended to erect a concrete indoor studio, developing room, dressing room, outdoor western setting, and fifty or sixty houses, barns and other buildings to form a film city. The company decided to move to El Paso when company executives were shown pictures of Hueco Tanks, Cloudcroft (New Mexico), the Franklin Mountains, the El Paso county roads, and numerous other photogenic sites.[4]

The Tilley Brothers

While "nickel madness" spread throughout the state, W. Hope and Paul W. Tilley started a production company. The Tilleys built their own movie camera and started shooting news footage in the Houston area. Their first story was of a whale, in an advanced state of decomposition, which had washed up on a beach near Port Arthur. Unbeknownst to the Tilleys, another pair of photographers were filming news in that area. King Vidor, future Hollywood film director, and Roy Clough, future Texas radio station owner, started their own production company working out of Galveston.

In 1910 the Tilleys moved to San Antonio to live with their grandfather, a city physician. Behind his home they converted an old servants' quarters into a film-developing and printing laboratory. They named their business "Satex," short for "San Antonio, Texas." They developed their own and other moviemakers' footage because theirs was the only film processing lab south of St. Louis. The first sale of their footage was of army maneuvers on the Texas/Mexican border. They also sold footage titled *Army Life,* featuring President Teddy Roosevelt on tour at Fort Sam Houston in San Antonio; footage of the U.S. Army's first airplane, which was built by the Wright Brothers; and a feature titled *The Texas Prison Systems.*

To supplement their production income, the Tilleys worked as projectionists in local theaters.

Figure 24. W. Hope Tilley filming for Satex Film Company of Austin. Courtesy James R. Buchanan

They learned the job in Charleston, South Carolina, in 1906. Paul had been laid off from the Gaskill and Munday Carnival, and with another jobless band member obtained a couple reels of motion picture film, rented a house, bought a second-hand projector, borrowed a roomful of chairs, and opened for business. They showed "Pauline overcoming all her perils for a couple of weeks and went broke," reflected W. Hope. Their business philosophy was "You had to change the picture, not change the audience."[5]

That year the brothers also traveled to Central Texas towns showing theirs and other companies' films. They "set-up shop" wherever they found a likely location and audience. At the Alamo they built an outdoor screen on a pole and showed slides, movies, and advertisements. Business was good until another promoter painted the entire end of the Bexar Drug Company building white and placed a projector on top of an adjacent structure. The Tilley's business "wandered off" around the corner.[6]

After their grandfather died in 1911, the Tilleys moved to Austin and started a production company on the second floor above the Casino Theater. "The main reason we had to leave San Antonio," remembered W. Hope, "was the fact that the Motion Picture Patents Corporation was putting all filmmaking out of business by agreeing with the major film supply company not to sell perforated film to anyone who did not have a license from them. We had to order film from France and then ran the risk of being caught."[7]

The Tilleys named this business "The Kinema Company," renamed it "The Tilley Brothers," and then "The Texas Bioscope Company." Texas Bioscope advertised itself as Austin's very own movie studio "doing our bit to put our town on the movie map.

Children's movies made on contract, 25 feet made quarterly. The only real way to record the little one's antics for future viewing."[8]

The Tilleys continued to support their Austin-based business as projectionists:

> I remember how we used to fight the other operators for our favorite films. The one who grabbed the Chaplin film was the happiest. Then came the Keystone Kops, Fatty Arbuckle, and all the others. In those days we turned the projector by hand, rewinding one reel, and turning the crank to put the other one on the screen at the same time.
>
> We did try inventing a motor driven machine, a Rube Goldberg affair put together by the operator of the Texas Theater. It didn't last long. The Austin Fire Department called it a fire risk and we went back to building muscles .... Those were the days ... no Sunday shows, top salary of $10 a week, and no income tax![9]

During summers, W. Hope pursued a career of producing music for traveling carnival shows. In the winter the movie business had priority. Soon the Tilleys were making their own cartoons, titles, slides, advertising, newsreels, and some small comedy features, called "turns." One feature had bank robber "Skinny Pryor come sprinting out of the American National Bank at Sixth and Congress and lead a chase up Congress to the Capitol grounds."[10]

On January 25, 1913, papers of incorporation for Satex Film Company of Austin were filed with the secretary of state. The partners were the Tilleys, who contributed their production business and equipment; Ed Besserer, owner of the Casino, who contributed his business reputation and money; and one "silent" partner, Charles Pyle, a promoter and self-proclaimed "film production expert," who received a salary of $50 a week as manager. A production studio was established on the corner of Thirteenth and Lavaca. Filming took place on an open-air stage using muslin screens overhead to diffuse the sunlight. Pyle was producer and director, W. Hope was cameraman, and Paul was film technician and gofer. Pyle immediately signed Martha Russell, billed as a former leading lady with Essanay Pictures, at an unheard of salary of $150 a week. Other company members were Valentine Felton, scenario editor, who had been with Biograph Film Company more than a year; Robert Kelly, actor and leading man, formerly with Henry W. Savage, William A. Brady, and Kiaw & Erlanger Productions; Virginia Duncan, formerly with David Belasco's "Girl of the Golden West"; Herman Lewis, who was associated for several years with large film manufacturing concerns in the East; and William and George Talbot, scenic artists, who had built and painted sets for some large Eastern production centers.[11]

In early February of 1913, the Satex company went on location in Mexico to start production of their first film, *Their Lives by a Slender Thread.* "The Satex Company," stated Pyle, "specializes in themes that might be described as sensational—or highly dramatic—stories . . . with lots of action, spice and ginger. Those are the kind that devotees of the picture show like." During the filming of scenes containing large amounts of gunfire, the crew was arrested and jailed. Mexican authorities demanded the movie's footage be forfeited. Pyle agreed, but forfeited not the film of the movie but cans of nonessential film. The crew was released and quickly returned to Texas.

Victor E. Martin, Austin newspaper reporter, observed a Satex production:

> What perfectly sane person could fancy circumstances under which a party of friendly people, unless indeed they might have escaped from a certain institution at the northern edge of the city, should drive out into the country, and as this party of motion picture makers are known to have done? They placed two of their men in road wagons, who on meeting one another appeared unwilling to share the road and so locked wheels and engaged in hand-to-hand

> combat. Presently a wheel of one of the wagons is wrenched off and the nag goes tearing down the road—a real runaway—while the crowd by the roadside rolls around the turf in glee. One fellow, the strangest of all, stands solemnly eyeing the whole proceeding and grinding some sort of a new fangled sausage mill."[12]

Pyle and the Tilleys edited *Mexican Conspiracy Outgeneralled, Their Lives by a Slender Thread,* and *The Kentucky Feud* and printed twenty copies of each for distribution. The three-reel features were released in April, May, and June of 1913, respectively. In July, Pyle and Russell quietly left Austin, "motoring to Chicago in their new Haynes Touring Car" leaving three "drastically over budget" films in production and numerous "hot" checks. An audit of the company books showed that Pyle had spent $5,300 on *Their Lives by a Slender Thread,* which was budgeted for $3,000. The company abandoned plans to film a "race" (automobile racing) picture and a Galveston beach story, and four partly completed productions titled *Laska, Divorcé Evil, Shadow of the Virgin Gold,* and *The Arm of the Secret Service.* W. Hope later tried organizing another production company, The Tilley Film Company, but eventually gave up and returned to his music. Paul worked with King Vidor in Houston and Hollywood.[13]

The Star Film Ranch

Wallace McCutcheon and Paul Méliès, son of Gaston Méliès, brother of one of cinema's founding fathers, Georges Méliès of France, traveled south from Brooklyn, New York, in 1910 for two reasons. They wanted to find a location for winter film production and they were looking for a place that had not already been seen numerous times in previous motion pictures. They found San Antonio.

After reporting back to Brooklyn, McCutcheon and Méliès picked the location for their new studio. "San Antonio was selected by our firm," announced McCutcheon, "because we learned it was the land of sunshine and would afford us a great deal of scope for our operations. We were informed of Fort Sam Houston and one of our aims is to secure here a number of pictures of the soldiers." McCutcheon and Méliès leased a large house and twenty acres across from the Hot Wells Hotel. They hired a cook and house maid and purchased a Pianola. The Star Film Ranch was established.[14]

The company arrived in early 1910 and immediately began preparations for their first feature, *Cyclone Pete's Matrimony,* a Western comedy, followed by *Branding the Thief.* Critics claimed that the first two films of Star Ranch showed "genuine western atmosphere." The production company included William Clifford, playwright and authority on Shakespeare; Edith Storey, who had been making Westerns at Vitagraph for a year; Anne Nichols, who had been acting with the Méliès Company; Francis Ford, brother of director John Ford, who had been with the Edison Company since 1907; Francis Storey; and William Carroll. William Haddock was the company director and William "Daddy" Paley, an active cameraman since the 1890s, was cinematographer. Company officials hired authentic local cowboys Ben and Sep Cooper, Otto Meyer, John Ortega, Joe Flores, and Bill Giddinger to portray wranglers and to bring realism to the company's productions.

Ideas for films were accepted from anyone. Star Ranch usually paid $10 for an acceptable idea, story, or script. Jessie Gulledge, secretary-treasurer of the Hot Wells Hotel, wrote the script for *The Girl of the Alamo.* She was paid $30.

The Star Film Ranch drew people in entertainment. Sarah Bernhardt came in her private railroad car, which was parked on a siding near the hotel. Bernhardt was a cousin of Gaston Méliès's wife, Hortense. Cecil B. De Mille visited the company hoping to learn moviemaking. De Mille had been engaged to direct his first motion picture, *The Squaw Man.*[15]

Star productions did not construct sets if a large painted backdrop would suffice. Backdrops were

Figure 25. The Star Film Ranch crew filming In The Hot Lands *at their Hot Wells Studio's exterior, sun-lit set in San Antonio. The camera is being hand cranked by William Paley; Gaston Méliès sits on his left. Edith Storey is at the head of the bed with William Clifford attending a sick woman on the bed. Francis Ford stands between the two. Cowboy extras watch from off camera on the left. Courtesy of the Academy of Motion Picture Arts and Sciences, Beverly Hills, California*

nailed to the outside of the ranch production house. This L-shaped, sun-lit area was consistently used for every type interior scene: from barrooms to bedrooms. Films were shot outdoors if possible; it was faster and cheaper. Props were equally simple. Photographs of pretty girls and metal signs advertising local breweries were the decor on numerous saloon sets.

In producing a feature, just enough film was exposed to fill one 35mm motion picture reel, about 950 feet. The director rehearsed the cast carefully so scenes could be filmed in one but no more than two takes. No dialogue was furnished. Actors acquainted themselves with what script or scenario was available, then, on screen improvised what they apparently should be saying. To capture the look and feel of San Antonio, a film might include actual locations. The most frequently used were the missions in the San Antonio area. The city's oldest, San Antonio de Valero, the Alamo, was not used until *The Immortal Alamo*, the most expensive, most important, and one of the last features, was made. It was difficult to film around the people and the tourists, and the company never received permission to film inside the mission grounds.

Other missions were used extensively. The feature *Tony, the Greaser,* filmed in December of 1910, featured the Mission San Jose. In June of 1911, *The Kiss of Mary Jane* was filmed at Mission Espada, and Mission Concepción was the setting for *The Honor of the Flag.* Mission San Juan Capistrano was used extensively for interiors in many Star films.

The company was obligated to produce and release at least one single-reel feature a week. Some weeks it produced as many as five. At first prints were "struck" only on receipt of an order from a film exchange. Selling twenty prints of a feature guaranteed that the company recovered its cost of production. With a later distribution agreement, ninety to one hundred prints of each feature were sold. A laboratory, editing room, and screening room were constructed at the ranch. Prints were viewed by the entire company and if something needed to be corrected, it was re-shot the next day. The Méliès Company produced approximately seventy-one features during the year it was located in San Antonio. On April 22, 1911, while *The Immortal Alamo* was in distribution, Gaston Méliès moved his company's operations to Santa Barbara, California.[16]

The Essanay Film Company, the Tilley Brothers, and the Star Film Ranch were the beginnings of an extensive history of production companies in the Lone Star State, a majority being situated in El Paso and San Antonio. At one period, San Antonio boasted seven.

In 1911 the Vitaphone Company came to San Antonio to take advantage of the city's locations. Scenes for *The Fall of the Alamo* used the ruined and unrestored San Jose Mission. In 1913 a group of Texans, including Fidelio G. Chamberlain, Sr., formed The Siege and Fall of the Alamo Motion Picture Corporation. They wanted to produce a series of movies about the Texas shrine. They received a charter and sold stock. The corporation never produced any features, and the franchise was canceled by the state in 1916.[17]

Two gentlemen, a Mr. Blackwell and a Mr. Stanford, announced on December 30, 1915, that they would establish a motion picture studio in El Paso. In 1916 Charles Goodnight, a cattleman in the Panhandle, staged a buffalo hunt. He invited Kiowas from Oklahoma to his J A Ranch. The Native Americans chased and killed buffalo from Goodnight's herd with traditional bows and arrows. Eleven thousand spectators witnessed the hunt. Two months later, Goodnight restaged the hunt and filmed it. The Wiswall Brothers from Denver, Colorado, were at Goodnight's ranch two months shooting footage used in the movie *Old Texas.*[18]

The Excel Fotoplay Company made motion pictures in San Antonio in 1915. For one, Marjorie Stinson, the youngest licensed pilot in the nation, almost killed herself, an actress playing a child, and the company's cameraman. While filming a scene at Fort Sam Houston, Stinson flew too low and close to the camera and operator, overturning both.

Another studio was built six miles south of San Antonio in San Jose in July of 1917. P. S. McGeeney started the Shamrock Photoplay Corporation specializing in two-reel Westerns. The company had indoor studios covered with canvas that could be rolled back to admit natural daylight. Some Shamrock features were *Jim of 3C Ranch, Down the Apache Pass,* and *Down at the 4C Ranch.*

The San Antonio Photo Plays Studio was erected in the 1910s in the south part of the city. John B. Carrington, secretary of the local Chamber of Commerce, was one of the backers. House actors were Billie Bauer, Arthur Deagen, John M. Edwards, and Daisy Sinclair.

Frank Powell shot a motion picture entitled *The Heart of the Sunset* in San Antonio in 1917 for an out-of-state company. He returned a year later, leased a bankrupted bath house and hotel in the 5200 block of South Flores in the Harlandale District, and started The Sunset Picture Corporation. The rooms of the bath house were remodeled into movie sets. To create the background needed for cowboy pictures, a small western set was built, containing a saloon,

Figure 26. The Sunset Picture Corporation filming at their outdoor, sun-lit stage in the Harlandale District of San Antonio. Courtesy James R. Buchanan

hotel, and various small businesses. The first feature was started in May of 1919. House Peters, the actor featured in practically all Sunset productions, starred in *The Forfeit* and *You Never Know Your Luck.* The studios were open to the public. Visitors were allowed to move around the lot as long as they did not interfere with filming.

In 1918 William "Big Bill" Steiner built a studio in south San Antonio on Hutchins Avenue. Steiner intended to produce Westerns with a touch of comedy, thus its name, Jester Comedy Company. He hired Aubrey M. Kennedy to direct. Kennedy had produced the popular *The Perils of Pauline* series, starring stunt actress Pearl White. Steiner selected San Antonio because of the mild weather and good natural lighting.[19]

Two production companies established themselves in El Paso in 1918. The Ziegfeld Cinema Corporation advertised for "extras" to be used in a production to begin "within weeks." A charter for the Pasograph Company of El Paso, which was to "manufacture" motion picture films and stories, was filed in Austin in June of 1918. The incorporators were Nat P. Wilson, Harris Walthall, and James Kenne.[20]

Two other production companies were formed in that city in 1920 and 1921. Brenon-Alvares Productions was an "association of some of the most prominent leading men, leading women and heavies in the picture industry." Maurice Brenon, production manager, stated:

> I served with the cavalry division on the Mexican border in and around El Paso and I know the country thoroughly. I state unqualifiedly that there is not another such location in the United States for making motion pictures. It has actual year round sunshine—no "high fogs"; it has an ideal winter climate for working outdoors; the valley of the Rio Grande between El Paso and Yaleta is fertile enough to be rural New England; we can get all the pines we want and snow, too, up at Cloudcroft [New Mexico]; there's one of the largest military posts in the country including an aviation field; across the border is Juarez with its actual Mexican atmosphere; in fact there isn't a phase of outdoor composition that we can't get. . . . I'm sure we are making no mistake in selecting El Paso.[21]

The company planned to film three or four "superfeatures" during the 1920–21 season starting August 15, 1920. George Foster Platt would direct the first features, taken from Brooke Sawyer stories.

Another company, The Service Film Company, formed in El Paso in February of 1921 for the purpose of making films featuring Charlot Molina, a comedian who staged comedy bullfights. R. H. Mullineaux was to be president, Bennie Sosland, secretary, and L. S. Davis, vice president. Marion A. Kent, formally of Vitagraph Productions, was to be cinematographer, and "Duke" Reynolds was to direct. Service Film also planned to produce *Sugar Man Ben* and *The Missing Link,* a story of a local country club golf course featuring El Paso's society.[22]

Figure 27. Sunset Picture Corporation's location filming truck with cast and crew. Courtesy James R. Buchanan

Town-Booster Films

While professional filmmakers in Texas were establishing studios meant to produce professional motion picture features, movie producers of another type were "working the state." These entrepreneurs shot motion pictures specifically for local audiences. These roving companies produced "town-booster" films. Itinerant producers would come into a town; shoot everything of interest; concoct a story using as many citizens, dignitaries, and well-known locals as they could, or use a standard story line that they used in many towns; film these local "actors" in action scenes with wild chases and exciting visuals; quickly process and edit the film, sometimes within a week; and show it to the local audience, their friends, and any viewers who could be enticed into the theater. They also sold promotional items connected with the venture. After a couple of quick showings, the film was abandoned, and the producer moved to another town. Other producers came into a town, shot anything scenic, historical, or pictorially attractive, made some kind of travelogue feature from that footage, premiered it, and moved on.[23]

Students at the Agriculture and Mechanical College of Texas at College Station appeared in a local production in 1913. The Smith Brothers Studio, representing the Gaumont Picture Company, was contracted to film the physical equipment and student activities at the college. The studio would distribute a series of films to various theater circuits in Texas to acquaint patrons with the work of the students.

On December 13, 1914, a four-part locally produced movie titled *The Tangle* was shown at the Queen in Galveston. On July 22, 1915, *Sky Eye,* which used the Galveston Cotton Carnival, the Hotel Galvez, beach front, and other scenic sites, played the Dixie One.[24]

The local newspaper reported that a local theater owner would produce a town-booster film at the 1913 summer picnic in Commerce: "A. W. Lilly, 'the picture show man,' has engaged a motion picture photographer to come to Commerce on Wednesday, July 10, the first day of the picnic, for the purpose of making a moving picture of the decorated automobile parade. One thousand feet of film will be used showing the complete parade, Commerce street scenes, picnic scenes . . . . If you want to see how a moving picture is made and later see yourself in a moving picture, be on hand Wednesday morning."[25]

In Greenville in 1914, Charles L. Hilger wrote and produced a movie with an all-local cast titled *A Heart of the Hills.* The movie's program boasted a cast of Lucile Boydstun, E. C. Bracken, W. Walworth Harrison, Richard Porter, Sara Carddock, Mrs. William Bacon, and thirty others. Audiences viewed the finished film at the Colonial on November 16 and 17.[26]

In 1915 the Paragon Feature Film Company established a studio in Austin and made a movie using local residents as actors. *A Political Touchdown* was filmed near the governor's mansion. The climax was to show the mansion burning to the ground, a feat that presented some difficulty for the company's staff. The film premiered in Austin on December 15, 1915.[27]

El Paso boosters made a number of attempts to publicize that city. The Texas Good Roads Association shot "three hundred feet of 'movie' film" on January 25, 1915. J. E. Williams journeyed from El Paso to San Diego shooting the footage. L. J. Burrud promoted another film advertising El Paso in October. Local residents acted all parts. *The El Paso Herald* awarded $25 for the best film scenario.[28]

Another producer came to Greenville in February of 1920. J. R. "Jack" Dugger recruited stars from the repertory company at the King Opera House. Frank Marion portrayed the hero and Charles Harmon the villain. Mrs. Burgess Collier was cast as the leading lady because a film test showed that she photographed exceptionally well. *His Reward* used local extras and locations. School Superintendent L. C. Gee arranged for the film to include Greenville students and their schools. On February 11, Dugger filmed a scene of the heroine trapped in a burning office building. Hundreds of spectators watched as smoke billowed around the beautiful damsel. Fire trucks raced to the rescue. The heroine was carried down a fire ladder to safety, the villain foiled, and happiness ensued. A week later *His Reward* was part of a double feature at the Colonial.[29]

"If you're not in the picture, you'll see some of your friends" was the promotion used to entice people of San Antonio to see a booster film. *Twin Stars* was shown at the Texas on February 19, 1928. The film, sponsored by the theater and the *San Antonio Light,* was made from a scenario by hometown writer Jean De Hymel. The Berkova Motion Picture Company selected a cast of local actors for the all-city, two-reel production. Jewel Miller, Xelpho Joslin, J. S. Kelly, J. W. Hamilton, and J. W. Ollermann starred. *Twin Stars* was publicized as "an hilarious, laugh-producer from start to finish" that included "no scene but what provokes a riot of laughter."[30]

Wichita Falls's *Weekly Pictorial* premiered at the Strand in 1922. Only movie footage shot in that city and the surrounding area was used. These homemade newsreels continued into the 1950s. Numerous town and cities in Texas had similar newsreels to supplement national news films and to attract the local audience. In 1956 Mel Barker Productions filmed a black and white movie in Waco entitled *Kidnappers Foil.* Barker used local children in his standardized plot about two ruffians kidnapping a wealthy young woman. The kids organized search parties to try to find "Betty Davis" and collect a reward. Barker charged $20 to include a child in the movie.[31]

De Luxe Motion Picture Theaters

After 1910, the motion picture industry in Texas stood poised to take a major step. As nickelodeons jammed virtually every empty and unused space in a city's main business district, certain individuals started planning and building theaters to show longer and more sophisticated movies. Nickelodeon proprietors ran patrons "in and out" in the shortest possible time, sometimes at thirty- or forty-minute intervals; a quick turnover was more profitable. The new theaters were meant to be more comfortable than nickelodeons where just the physical viewing of a movie could be a challenge. Theater owners realized that audiences could not be expected to attend longer features under nickelodeon conditions. They designed the new theaters, also located in downtown districts, to be permanent and comfortable and used by more critical, demanding, and discriminating patrons.

Figure 28. The Opera House/Texas of McGregor is possibly the oldest theater in existence in the state. Built before marquees, movies titles were written on the front plateglass window. They proclaim the day's features as "His Uncle's Will—His Night Out—A Laugh to Every Foot of Picture—Bob Leonard—Ella Hall—5 and 10." The Texas still stands today just off Main Street where it was built in 1912. Courtesy Margaret Smith

Twenty-five-year-old Jake Smith moved from Atlanta, Georgia, to McGregor in 1900. He farmed and worked in a lumber company, but in 1912 he opened one of the first "built for purpose" motion picture theaters in Texas. His daughter-in-law, Margaret Smith, recalled why Jake built the Opera House, its first name:

> I heard him say that these tent shows would come in and they would put this advertising on his buildings and stuff, and he just got interested . . . just decided to build one. Jake Smith, my husband's father, built the theater from the ground up. His mother sold tickets from the time it opened until the night before she died—1943—seven days a week . . . .
>
> It was all glass [front], and he just wrote it [the movie titles] on there. The ticket office was in the lobby, closed in, and it was . . . to the back, and we could pull a curtain and look at the movie from the ticket office. . . . When . . . they had trouble, they would put up a slide. One slide said something like, "Wait a minute, the operator is having a fit."
>
> My half sister played the piano for the silent movies. She got married in 1916 and they bought a player piano. After they went to talkies, the player piano was out in the lobby. . . .
>
> He did not really seem to worry about profits, he was making a living somewhere else. When the Ritz came in here—it was some Dallas show people. They decided that since he was not really interested, they would come in and run him out of business; they would take over. So they came in and converted a store building and had Mr. McGennis run it. Mr. Smith just remodeled his show, fixed it all up, called it the Texas, and kept right on going.[32]

From the first day of operation, the Texas had a special balcony so minorities could attend, said Smith. "It was built originally with a (black) balcony. . . . There were two stairs to the balcony. One went right up the west side of the building and it went right into the black balcony. The other one went from the lobby up to the (projection) booth and the other side. The picture went through the center and separated it. . . . When they changed the law in the 1960s, he (Henry Smith, Margaret's husband) closed the balcony, and the blacks threw a fit because it was a great place to watch the movie. We used to go up there with hamburgers on Sunday night and watch the movie."

In 1982, Henry Smith closed the theater. The Opera House/Texas in McGregor is possibly the oldest motion picture theater in the state in its original structure. It stands today just off Main Street where it was built in 1912.[33]

Herman Fitchenberg built the first de luxe theater in Houston in 1913. The Isis was situated on Prairie Street close to Main. The next year E. H. Hulsey built the Queen in the 600 block of Main, the second in Houston. The Queen was the first theater in Houston to install an organ. A rivalry developed between the two theaters, resulting in the Isis installing a larger pipe organ and later employing a ten-piece orchestra.[34]

The Grand was the first permanent theater in Longview, but not very "de luxe" according to Lawrence Birdsong. "It was a storefront converted to a theater. Just a dry goods store with a front nailed to the front and some seats inside. . . . There was a little man, Mr. Star . . . and he was in front of the theater, and he was famous for his popcorn." The Grand was a "shotgun" operation—very cheap and very economical. It was "just awful," remembered Birdsong. The first motion pictures in Gladewater came with a traveling tent show during the oil boom. The first permanent theater was "Payne's Palace."

Birdsong became interested in motion pictures and got his first projector by selling perfume. He read an ad in a catalogue for a company called "Johnson Smith." He received his supply of perfume and tried to sell it door to door:

Figure 29. Promotion at the Isis in Houston. Courtesy Houston Metropolitan Research Center, Houston Public Library

I don't remember any other premium that I wanted other than a projector. . . . I said, "I want a movie machine!"

So my mother gave me the money and said, "Go buy the thing!"

I got one free reel of film. It was a six-inch reel of 35mm film. . . . It had a short story. I had that, and then when the theater in Gladewater opened I got carried away . . . I would have a picture show. . . .[35]

One of the first theaters in El Paso was the Alhambra, which opened August 1, 1914. Earlier that same year the first theater on the north side of Fort Worth had opened. The Isis was on North Main near the stock yards. "I thought I'd fool around with the theater for a few months just for fun . . . ," recalled owner L. C. Tidball. Opening night, May 21, 1914, was memorable for John H. Sparks, projectionist. There were no motors to run projectors and no sound, or so the audience and Sparks thought. He was hand cranking the first feature showing a tremendous storm and flood. "When the storm scene went on the screen, it was raining cats and dogs outside," recalls Sparks. "Lightning flashed. Thunderclaps shook the theater. . . . We had the best kind of sound for the storm on the screen—by nature itself. The effect was unforgettable."[36]

Tidball booked movies in the manner typical of most owners of that period: "We would go to Dallas once a week to buy pictures. We never took the trouble to look at the films; we just looked at the posters. If the lobby three-sheet for a particular film was flashy and showed somebody shooting, we'd buy the picture. Some of the films we bought in those days didn't even have titles on them. Suddenly one guy would be shooting at another on the screen and the picture was on. I guess movies haven't changed much at that."[37]

Tidball's ticket office "took in" $5.30 the first day. Receipts of this amount were typical for early theaters. The Dorothy in Huntsville had ticket receipts of $14.90 on January 23, 1923, while showing *Black Panthers Club* and a *Fox News* feature: $5.50 for the matinee and $9.40 for the evening. The Dorothy's income for that month was $1,300; a profit of $320. Although World War I had ended years earlier, the Dorothy, like every theater in Texas, still had to pay a monthly war tax. The Dorothy's was $140. Other movies listed in the Dorothy's booking ledger for that month were *Human Hearts, Beauty Shop, Flaming Horse, Good Provider, Little Wildcat, Wild Irish Rose, If Only Jim, Lavender Bath Lady, Over The Border, You Never Know, Kentucky Derby, Enter Madam, Scarlet Dear, Da And Dare, Youth Must Have Love, Jungle Goddess #1, The Bait, Ghost Patrol, Queen Of The Turf, Who Are My Parents,* and *Jungle Goddess #2.*[38]

During this period, one of the best-known theater circuits was formed. Harold Robb got his start in motion pictures in 1906 from his father I. J. Robb, who owned the power plant in Geary, Oklahoma. One of his customers was the local theater, which was having trouble paying its bill. The owner signed the movie business over to Robb as settlement. The business's inventory basically consisted of a few planks for seats laid across beer kegs. I. J. soon moved his family to Carlsbad, New Mexico, and then to Big Spring, where he opened the Lyric. It was here that I. J.'s two sons, Yuill and Harold, developed an interest in movie theaters and met Ed Rowley. He and the Robbs became partners on August 21, 1916, when Rowley paid $2,000 for a half interest in the Roof Garden Theater in San Angelo where the Robb brothers had moved because of stiff competition in Big Spring. The group called themselves "the Country Boys." The Roof Garden succeeded, and the partnership continued to grow by purchasing or constructing numerous theaters across the state. By 1939, Robb and Rowley (R & R) United, Inc., operated 150 theaters in 35 towns in Texas, Oklahoma, and Arkansas.[39]

John H. Rowley recalled how his father and Harold Robb started their circuit of theaters:

He [Rowley] was working for the Orient Railroad that runs between San Angelo and

Figure 30. L. C. Tidball's Isis was the first theater on the north side of Fort Worth. Courtesy North Fort Worth Historical Society

Figure 31. Gerald Morgan, age sixteen, was owner and operator of the Lyric at 2501 Buena Vista Avenue in San Antonio in the 1920s. With his portable projector, Morgan ran a one-man movie theater for children. Courtesy The Institute of Texan Cultures, San Antonio

Abilene. . . . So while he was working in San Angelo, one day a friend of his that he met in high school in Big Spring . . . wanted to talk to him about putting in a theater. I've always thought it was 1915.

Mr. Harold Robb—his parents operated a theater in Big Spring, Texas—had learned a little about the operations of a theater. He came down and asked Daddy to go in with him on a theater in San Angelo. . . . Robb was a bright person and very conservative. He wanted someone to go in with him to give him some encouragement. . . . They decided that they would put in a theater in San Angelo on the roof of a feed store. It had a booth on one end and a screen on another end, benches in between, and nature's air conditioning for them. It cost a nickel admission to get in; features were ten

Figures 32 and 33. Harold Robb and Ed Rowley of R & R Theaters. Courtesy Hoblitzelle Foundation

minutes long. They hadn't heard of popcorn or other concession items, and just operated at night. It worked well for my father because he could keep his job at the railroad in the daytime, do his share in the partnership at night—R & R Roof Gardens.

They made a go of it. They expanded into Lubbock, Sweetwater, Hillsboro—over a period of time. They didn't build any more open air theaters. . . . They found that their money went further if they only bought a half-interest in an independent operation—in Del Rio and Laredo, and Corpus Christi, which helped them expand faster.[40]

Motion Picture Operators and Employees

"We were crazy to go into the business in the first place," stated W. C. Shaver of Wichita Falls. "It's a good old man's job." He and S. F. Weidman were projectionists for fifty years. Both joined the International Alliance of Theatrical Stage Employees and Motion Picture Machine Operators Union on February 15, 1915. Shaver worked in an air dome early in his career. "I can remember people sitting in the rain with newspapers over their heads to watch a show."[41]

Bob Baker's first job in motion pictures was at the Crystal in Dallas in 1912. "A friend and I were walking by and the manager called me in from the street and asked me to relieve the ticket taker. I caught on and later he sent me up to the booth to relieve the projectionist." Baker and fellow projectionist John Hardin got tired of cranking those old machines he used when he moved to the Washington Theater. The two attached an electric motor to one. "This was great," recalled Baker, "but the city electrician blew his stack. He said it was unsafe and told us to take it off. Maybe that law banning motor-driven movie projectors is still on the city books."[42]

Frank Longoria went to the Amuse Theater in

Corpus Christi on October 13, 1917. The thirteen-year-old had just taken a seat near the projection booth to see a silent Western when the projectionist, Ponciano Mendoza, emerged from the booth clutching his chest. After getting the stricken man help, the manager and Longoria operated the equipment, keeping the theater open. Unwittingly, Longoria had just chosen his life's work. After Mendoza recovered, he taught the teenager how to be a projectionist, which Longoria was for the next sixty-two years. There were years he worked 365 days with no relief. "There's no such thing as getting sick on the job," said Longoria. "You have to be here. The public comes here to see a performance and we must give them a performance."[43]

Wylie York of Dallas wanted to be a projectionist since he was seventeen:

> I went to the manager of the old Bluebird Theater at Tyler and Jefferson [in Dallas] and asked if I could learn to be an operator. He said, "You go up and talk to Mr. Barrett, and if it's okay with him it's okay with me." So I did, and Mr. Barrett was kind enough to let me stay up there with him. He'd teach me a little as we went along, and it wasn't long before I could make a changeover as well as he could. I stayed there until I was 21. . . .
>
> In the latter twenties I said there was one theater I never would work in, and that was the Joy, a burlesque house on lower Elm Street. But the depression hit, and they hired me for $15 a week. That was for 80 hours, and I was glad to get it. I never saw the sun go down for six months.[44]

Figure 34. The Crystal on theatre row in Dallas. Courtesy Texas/Dallas History and Archives Division, Dallas Public Library

"I started in this business because it fascinated me, not because I thought I'd get rich," remembered Scotty Davidson of Tyler, "and it still fascinates me."[45] Davidson was "hooked on show business" when he saw his first motion picture in 1914:

An old fellow came through the country and stopped at the school and got permission to project some movies. . . . He drove a hack-like vehicle and on the side he had "Fuzzy-Wuzzy's Movies. . . ." I knew it because it had been announced at school. I ran home all excited, and I suppose they [parents] were all excited . . . . There were kids in the country that wanted to see the movies. I had never seen a movie in my life; I did not know what they were.

It was a night after school as best as I can remember. He had a projector that he cranked by hand . . . 35mm movie, and for a take-up arrangement he had a sack that the film unwound in—and then he rewound it. . . . I don't know what he had as a light source . . . because we had no electricity out there. . . . I would say [it was something] like a gas lamp or Coleman lamp. . . . To me and everybody else it was terribly bright. For his screen he had a sheet that he fastened on the wall with thumbtacks. I think he charged 10 cents. . . .

He had two reels: about 30 minutes in all of entertainment. One was a comedy . . . it had to do with Western action. . . . We kids, we hurrahed and everything else. It was something new for the grown persons. . . . What I was concerned about were these images of characters or people who would ride a horse and ride on off the screen—I wanted to know where they went. A cowboy comes along and goes off like this . . . where does he go? I was concerned about that. . . .

1920—My dad sent me to Childress, Texas, to go to high school. I became acquainted with a projectionist, or operator as we called it. He worked on weekends at the old Grand Theater and Opera House, and the Monogram which was a movie house. . . . I had never been in a projection room. . . . I kept wondering about it. So one evening he said, "Tell you what you do. You wait . . . until old man Phillips gets busy in the box office, slip in, and go to the projection room."

I said, "How do you get up there?" He told me how. . . . It was an impression that has lasted all these years. I wanted to be a part of it. So that was all I could think about. . . . I came down here [Tyler] as a junior in high school. . . . I was coming from high school one evening—by the old Queen Theater where the old Arcade was . . . Mr. and Mrs. Shields owned the theater. I walked up to the box office. . . . I told him that I was a high school boy and I wanted to know how to be in show business.

He looked me over and said, "Son, what are you doing now, going to school?"

"Yes, I'm going to school. I just came from school."

He said, "What part of show business do you want to get in?"

I said, "I want to be where they run the machines."

He said, "You need to talk to Mr. Frank McKeel."

I said, "Where do I see him?"

He said, "He's down at the Broadway."

. . . I go down to the Broadway Theater, and I inquire if they had a man named Frank McKeel working there. The cashier told me, "Yes, he's in the projection room." So I ambled up there; . . . . didn't know what he looked like; didn't know what kind of person he was; and that projector and the noise. I can still hear it; "Chukka, Chukka, Chukka. . . ."

I said, "Boy! Boy! This is for me."

He asked me some questions, and I told him that I was going to school. He said, "You don't need to be fooling around the theater while you're going to school."

. . . I said, "I want to get into the theater business. I want to get into the movies. . . ."

"First," he said, "you go to school. When you get out of school, I'll start you out rewinding film by hand." . . . You had a hand rewind . . . with a crank. I worked for him a while. I just couldn't wait to get out of school to get down there. . . .

He was a pretty hard task [master]. If you made a mistake once he would show you, "Don't make the same mistake twice!" The third was just too bad. Well, you don't work in a projection room without making mistakes.

He said to me, "I want to try you out on slides. . . ." I was a little nervous because I hadn't done anything but rewind some film; I hadn't even threaded the machine. He said, "You see that stack of slides over there?"

I said, "Yes."

"I'll show you how to handle them," he said. "The slides will be turned down like this. There is a dot, and the slide goes in upside down. . . . Be sure that you put it in upside down; you know that it will be reversed down yonder." I picked the slide up, he showed me how, put it in the slide carrier, and it was upside down. "I told you where to put your thumb and how to put the slide up. Do it again!" . . . I did it again, and I did it right. He said, "Make note of that."

Glass slides—that was our advertising then—we showed them at the end of each movie. Slides lasted about ten minutes. You did not leave it on very long . . . there were carbon arcs then and you would crack a slide—give people time to read it. We had a "This Machine is Operated by Union Operators." That was the last slide you put on there.

We had hand-fed arcs. You had to watch it all the time. . . . In the silent days, the carbons were at an angle; they weren't horizontal. You brought your carbons down to make contact. Then you had a knob to move the carbons horizontal; you had a knob that would raise it. . . . If it was too much to one side, you could move it over and line it up. . . . You could move your knob so it was clear out of line. They moved to horizontal carbons in the 1930s.

The first color movie was *The Wanderer of the Wasteland* over at the Electric Palace in 1924: Billy Dove and Jack Holt. The first Technicolor film was splotchy. It wasn't sharp; it was kind of sticky. . . . Back in the silent films, part of the film would be color and part would be black and white; same print. Then they came out with what they called "Sepia Color."[46]

When James Dear of Mineola started working at a motion picture theater at the age of twelve, "I did not even know what a movie was":

My brother Sam, who was six years older, he got a job running the projectors at the Select Theater. Well they needed a part-time cashier so my sister who was fifteen got the job of selling tickets. I was just a little general flunky. . . . I would sweep the lobby out here; I would change the advertising. I was paid a buck a day; fifty cents for an afternoon.

They opened up the Palace Theater. . . . This was back in the silent movie days. . . . We were running a Tarzan serial—I think it had thirteen chapters. . . . When it came time for the serial, we had to play a piano. . . . I had to go down there and sit on the front row. I would watch the screen and as soon as the end [of the movie] came up and the cast, it was time to "plug in" so we would have music going while Tarzan swung through the trees. The chaptered movie . . . would run about thirteen or fourteen minutes and I would sit there and then pull the plug. That was my job for Friday night and Saturday. I was director of music. . . .[47]

Bob Baker remembered a hot, summer night in 1915. He was hand cranking the old Simplex projector in the Princess at Elm and Akard in downtown Dallas: "The movie may have been the brand new 'Champion,' a comedy starring young Charlie Chaplin. The image flickered and jerked on the screen in the fashion of the times. Suddenly the highly flammable nitrate film caught fire. The projection room was not too high above street level. . . . I grabbed the burning film off, threw the tangled mess out of the window. It landed under a horse and buggy hitched to a post."[48]

"Nitrate film in the old days," stated Scotty Davidson, "made a projection room a 'deathtrap.'" Projection booth fires in early theaters were not rare. Movie prints made on cellulose nitrate film stock were highly flammable. Very little had to go wrong in early projectors before the film would ignite. Because of this hazard, projection booths were specially constructed, and projectionists had to be licensed. One of the first theaters to make improvements to aid in fire prevention was the Crawford in El Paso. On July 13, 1916, manager E. F. Maxwell announced, "The Crawford theater will have the safest moving picture booth in the city. We are making changes that are necessary for the absolute safety of the public. A fire wall is being erected between the theater and the flats on Main street, and while we are doing this we are installing a picture booth that will comply in every respect to the requirements of the city authorities." Even though many theaters in the state made improvements in fire prevention, many motion picture establishments burned.[49]

The 1910s had been a strong period of growth and advancement for the motion picture industry in Texas. The horribly uncomfortable nickelodeons had been replaced by the more comfortable de luxe theaters. The product on the screen had improved. Feature films were more serious in their efforts at moviemaking and storytelling. The "chase" films of the nickelodeons quickly became unacceptable.

"Going to the picture show" in a de luxe theater became a family activity. The audience's acceptance of and attendance to the new theaters perpetuated the planning and building of more elaborate and luxurious movie establishments, the grand movie palaces. The "supers," as some people called them, of the 1920s would become the ultimate in going to the movies.

Grand Movie Palaces
1921 TO 1929

The Texas motion picture industry of the 1920s produced some tremendous losses and magnificent gains. Although some local film studios in Texas would continue into the 1930s, the number was declining. Most major film production was now firmly established in California. Texas would continue as "locations" for major Hollywood studio productions like *Wings,* and some minority productions.

The state did become the home of numerous theater circuits such as Robb and Rowley (R & R) and Interstate. R & R Theaters would eventually operate more than one hundred theaters in the state. Interstate's founder Karl Hoblitzelle, from his corporate headquarters in Dallas, built and operated some of the most magnificent grand movie palaces in the nation. Interstate's Majestic in Houston was the first "atmospheric" theater in the nation—the first built on this internationally famous architectural design. The Majestic in San Antonio was the second-largest theater in the country. Loew's State Theater in Houston, although not a part of Hoblitzelle's empire, was crowned by many journalists as the most beautiful motion picture theater in the nation.

Filmmaking in Texas

Texas film production, which started in 1908, continued into the 1920s, especially in San Antonio. Maclyn Arbuckle, a San Antonio native, established the San Antonio Pictures Corporation in 1923. The studio, situated on South Presa, was a barn-like structure that had previously been an amusement park. Arbuckle remodeled the buildings into movie sets. L. D. Wharton was vice president, and Theodore Wharton was supervising director. They commissioned Irvin S. Cobb to write a screen play for the first production, *The Sheriff of Bexar.* The company's second film, *The Wildcatter,* concerned the life of an oil driller. Arbuckle's business venture was financed in part by Will Hogg, son of James S. Hogg, governor of Texas from 1891 to 1895.[1]

In June of 1922, the Benroy Motion Pictures Corporation of Dallas planned to produce motion pictures for national distribution. At that period there were only four companies producing movies for African-American audiences. Motion pictures specifically for and starring blacks were for years called "race movies." *The Homestead,* made in 1918, and *The Flying Ace,* made shortly after, were considered some of the very first. Between then and the 1950s, approximately five hundred such movies were made, many in Texas.

Benroy, situated at 1931 Main Street in Dallas, solicited investors in the *Express.* "You have a chance to help supply your race with Colored Motion pictures," wrote Ben D. Wilson, director. "There are 1100 Colored theaters in the U. S. that want a Colored picture every day, there are only ten Colored pictures on the market, this means that 1090 Colored theaters have to run white pictures each day when they would much rather have a picture with an all-colored cast." Benroy planned to make its features in Dallas. Wilson promised a picture with an all-colored cast by June of 1922.

The first Benroy film premiered at the Grand Central in Dallas on June 1 and 2. A second feature, a five-reeler entitled *The Man From Texas,* was promised no later than July 15. Wilson stated, "We are picking our cast from our shareholders. You may not think you are an actor, maybe you're not, but we have men who are judges of that." Wilson, who claimed fifteen years of motion picture experience, was selling 2,500 shares of stock at $12.50 a share.[2]

Another San Antonio studio that made one- and two-reel Westerns in the early 1920s for general audiences, but with no published name, was described as having a "death-row type" atmosphere in its movie plots. The first motion picture to make use of the armed service bases around San Antonio was *The Big Parade,* filmed in 1925 by a California studio. King Vidor directed John Gilbert and Renee Adoree.

The Fox Film Company from California shot the exteriors for *The Warrens of Virginia* at Brackenridge Park in San Antonio in 1923. The seven-reeler starred Martha Mansfield and Wilfred Lytell. Mansfield had been a Ziegfeld beauty and had co-starred with John Barrymore, Harold Lockwood, and Eugene O'Brien.[3] *The Warrens of Virginia* was, tragically, Mansfield's last movie:

> Since the movie was set in the Civil War period, Miss Mansfield was required to wear a frilly crinoline dress when appearing before the cameras. . . . On November 29, 1923, Martha stepped into the rear of a rented car and was whisked out to the park.
>
> While sitting in the car waiting for instructions, she was heard to scream loudly that she was on fire. She jumped from the car with her dress ablaze and ran away in panic. Her chauffeur and co-star in the picture both ran after her, and when she was caught, they beat out the blaze with their coats. She was immediately rushed to the . . . hospital where the doctors who examined her announced that her burns were not too serious. . . . Miss Mansfield died the next day. . . .[4]

In 1926 Out West Pictures Corporation established a permanent studio in the Alamo City. George La Dura was the general manager. Just as sound was about to come to motion pictures, H. W. Kier, Ray Kier, and A. A. Phillips established the National Pictures Gulf Coast Studio in North San Antonio at Cunningham and Brahan. For the next thirty years National produced numerous Westerns and religious films, including *The Passion Play, Border Fence,* and the biblical costume drama *Tubal Cain.* Although an acting "name" was occasionally used, a Kier feature generally used unknowns and local talent. The 1933 production staff consisted of Josh Binney, production manager and director; Malcolm McCarty, chief sound engineer; Jimmie Zintgraff, head of the laboratory and camera department; Jack Britton, chief electrician; William Rogers, property master; and Lester Kentner, publicity manager. In 1938 National filmed *The Fall of the Alamo,* one of its biggest productions, in two weeks. Coates Gwynne, director of the Mission Players in San Antonio, was cast as William Barrett Travis, and Florence Griffith, co-director of the San Antonio Civic Opera, was Mrs. Dickinson. The film was all pantomime, because the company could not afford

Figure 35. Martha Mansfield and Wilfred Lytell filming The Warrens of Virginia *in San Antonio. Ms. Mansfield is wearing the dress in which she was fatally burned. Courtesy James R. Buchanan*

sound equipment. *The Fall of the Alamo* was never distributed.[5]

Paramount Studios' production of *The Marching Herd,* starring Gary Cooper and Frances Dee, was filmed at the La Motta Ranch of J. R. Bell and Jack W. Baylor. That same year, 1926, J. Douglas Travers became director of film for the Alamo City and planned a motion picture centered on its civic and social life as soon as a cast of eight principal, forty supporting, and many "atmosphere" performers were assembled. About that time, Neal Hart starred in several Westerns made in another "nameless" studio situated on San Antonio's South Presa Street. William Farnum starred in one of the studio's Westerns, which, although silent, was in color.[6]

Color in silent movies was not unusual. Most feature films were printed on tinted stock. Different colors were used to enhance different scenes. Amber was used for daylight, dark blue was night, red for fires, green for sea sequences, etc. In 1922 Technicolor introduced a practical two-color process. Blue and orange were photographed separately and printed together on a single strip of film. The combination produced a limited range of hues but a reasonably good skin tone. Full color Technicolor started about 1934. Other processes used at that time were Agfacolor, Kodachrome, Sovcolor, Pathecolor, Supercinecolor, Ansco Color, Rouxcolor, Trucolor, Fujicolor, Gevacolor, and DeLuxe Color.[7]

Several studios utilized the Alamo City as a location for filming chaptered movies. In 1916, Vitagraph filmed *The Secret Kingdom,* starring Dorothy Kelly. Another San Antonio studio made two-reel "horse operas" starring Harry Myers. During filming, Myers was attracted to a young, petite blonde actress named Allene Ray. Using her in his features lead to a contract with Pathé Studios in Hollywood. When Pearl White and Ruth Roland retired from chaptered movies, Ray became the new "serial queen." In 1930, she and Tim McCoy starred in *The Indians are Coming,* one of the first talking serials. Ray was possibly the first Texan to become a Hollywood star. Between 1923 and 1935, she appeared in twenty segmented productions.[8]

In the 1920s, numerous short news features were staged and filmed in Texas using aircraft. Two such features used a self-proclaimed barnstormer, bootlegger, stunt pilot, and ladies' man named Slats Rodgers:

> Back in those days some fellows made a business of cracking ships on purpose, mostly for the movies. I tried it once. Some ex-army man in Dallas, I don't remember his name, said if I would crack up a ship and let him make a moving picture of it, he would give me $600. I looked around and found an old Jenny I could buy for $150, so I said it was a deal.
>
> I had heard a lot about Dick Grace and the big money he got for cracking up ships, and about some of the other dare devils. I figured I might as well get in on that easy money, since I was cracking up ships free anyway.
>
> I cracked the ship at a field about eight miles northwest of Dallas. We put a bunch of posts in the ground, sort of loose so they would knock down easy when I hit them. Then we moved an old sheep shed near the posts so that after it hit the posts I'd hit the sheep shed. We were going to make it look fine—air full of flying sheep shed.
>
> We had kept it pretty much a secret. There were only four or five people out there when I got ready to bust hell out of her. The ex-army man had his camera all ready. I took off and flew around a little, came in on a glide with the ignition off, and headed for the posts. They tore hell out of my right wing and threw me around. But I kept on going fairly straight long enough to stack her up in the sheep shed.[9]

Rodgers was not injured. Not long afterward, Ralph Clark from Temple approached him to help stage a fake train robbery that he would film and sell for "big money." "We'll put a long rope ladder on your landing gear and somebody will ride the blinds on the train," stated Clark. "When we get to the place I'll climb up on top and you come down and pick me up. I'll have a man about two cars back taking the pictures."

They selected a place between Bellville and Sealy: a long, straight track with no telegraph poles. Rodgers got an old Standard with an OX-5 engine, which had the reputation of "you can walk there faster." The first time they tried to film the scene there was a thirty-mile-per-hour head wind, and, according to Rodgers, "Well, that's one time a train out ran an airplane, and without even trying." A few days later Rodgers got a faster aircraft, and they filmed the scene without any problems, except that when the train and plane arrived in Sealy, the police "hauled" Rodgers, the actor, and the cameraman into court. Rodgers was fined $11.50. The film never sold. Rodgers told Clark, "Next time make it a gal in a bathing suit, and you'll sell it for real money."

Rogers helped finance the first airplane he ever built and flew, known as "Old Soggy No. 1," by making a deal with a local movie theater operator in Cleburne. He received $75 to display a model of the plane in front of the theater for a week. Another person from aviation produced motion pictures in Texas. In the 1920s Harold D. Hahl, who in 1909 flew the first airplane over Houston, opened a movie studio in that city making comedies and advertising films. Hahl also covered the southwest for Pathè newsreels.[10]

Wings

1926 was a significant year for filmmaking in Texas, especially San Antonio. Paramount Studios sent two production companies to San Antonio to film *Wings* and *The Rough Riders.* Victor Fleming directed *Riders,* which concerned Teddy Roosevelt's cavalry during the Spanish-American War of 1898. The movie was shot at the exact locations where years before Roosevelt had assembled the real Rough Riders. Paramount built "a replica of the old Exposition Building that had stood on the Fair Grounds during the time of the original Rough Riders." Mary Astor starred with Charles Farrell and Charles Emmitt Mack.[11]

Director William Wellman started filming the first scene of the $2 million feature *Wings* on September 7, 1926, at the Quadrangle of Fort Sam Houston. The

Figure 36. The filming of Wings *in 1926 at Kelly Field in San Antonio. Director William Wellman is in the white hat just behind the camera. Courtesy San Antonio Air Logistics Center Office of History*

Figure 37. The armed service pilots and crew who flew the airplanes for Wings. *Front row (only last names available): unknown, Beery, Elgin, Gre, unknown, Cornelius, Partridge, Wriston, unknown, Parson, Weddington, Booth, Moore, Kuntz, and Stanley. Sitting on the airplane: Taylor, Jamison, Gregg, Taylor, Johnson, Irving, unknown, Rice, Morehouse, and Nendell. Courtesy the San Antonio Air Logistics Center Office of History*

entire movie was shot there, at Kelly Field, and at Camp Stanley. Actors Buddy Rogers, Richard Arlen, and May McAvoy starred with Clara Bow.[12]

Wellman permitted no "faked" scenes of flying. Cinematographer Harry Perry acquired a gun-ring and secured it to the cockpit. A camera mount was made and attached, allowing Perry to film the first motion picture footage shot from an airplane. Faces of stars who were supposed to be piloting aircraft were actually shot in the air. "We had cameras shooting both forward and backward," recalled Lucien Hubbard, supervisor. "There were many scenes where we shot over Arlen's head as he dived to earth." These cameras situated in the rear cockpit were attached to

Figure 38. Wings' *head cameraman Harry Perry. Courtesy the San Antonio Air Logistics Center Office of History*

Figure 39. Family of Kelly Field officers portrayed French peasants in Wings. *Left to right: Mrs. Hal George, wife of Captain (later General) George, pursuit instructor, who later commanded Douglas MacArthur's air force on Bataan; Mrs. Burdette Wright, wife of Captain Wright, director of flying at Kelly Field; unknown; Connie Wash, daughter of Major Wash; and Mrs. Carlisle Wash, wife of Major Wash, director of training at Kelly Field. Courtesy the San Antonio Air Logistics Center Office of History*

the aircraft on mounts made in the shape of saddles secured with two straps around the body of the plane. Cameras shot over the head of the real pilot, sitting in the rear seat, to show the actor in the front seat apparently alone, flying a single-seater airplane. In shots from the front looking backward, the real pilot in the back seat would fly the aircraft to a designated position, turn on the camera by remote control, and duck in his cockpit, making it appear that the actor was piloting the airplane alone.[13]

One of the most spectacular parts of the movie was filmed on October 19 at Camp Stanley. An entire French village was built in a five-mile area surrounded by trenches and battlefield settings. The Battle of St. Mihiel used forty-five airplanes from Kelly Field and five thousand troops from the Second Infantry Division. A one-hundred-foot tower was erected to give directions by semaphore to the widely scattered troops. There were seventeen cameramen and crews located around the perimeter, plus twenty-eight electrically controlled Eyemo cameras located at other strategic points. One was in a captive balloon five hundred feet above the ground.

Wings premiered at the Texas in San Antonio on May 19, 1927. The fourteen-reel feature, which was cut to twelve reels for general distribution, added rudimentary blues and reds to various flying scenes. Sound effects and music recordings were made available for specially equipped theaters. *Wings* was the first large-scale drama of military aviation; it marked the first time movie cameras were mounted on airplanes for the filming of aerial shots; it used sound effects; and it won the 1928 Academy Award for "best production," the only silent film ever so honored.[14]

De Luxe Theaters

The de luxe theater trend that started in McGregor in 1912 continued into the 1920s. Odessa's first de luxe was built in 1926 by Joe Rice. It was located at Fourth and Grant with a second theater built a year later on West Fourth. "Mr. Rice, being an enterprising businessman, was ready to meet the demands of an expanding population before the demand was ever made.... He established the town's first picture show when there was still no electricity. The machine was cranked by hand and carbide lamps provided the illumination."[15]

Similar de luxe theaters established themselves across the state. By the 1920s, patrons were going to the picture show at the Mission in Abilene, Midget in Austin, Imperial in Beaumont, Elite in Bonham, Alhambra in Breckenridge, Majestic in Commerce, Gem in Cooper, Liberty in Corpus Christi, High School and Old Mill in Dallas, Grand in Electra, Pershing in Galveston, Bon-Ton in Honey Grove, Prince and Travis in Houston, Le Roy in Lampasas, Park in Longview, New Lindsey in Lubbock, Strand in Marlin, Grand in Paris, Princess in San Angelo, Orpheum and Zaragoza in San Antonio, Queen in Sherman, Paramount in Texarkana, Rapeeds in Tyler, Victoria in Wichita Falls, and dozens and dozens of others.

Minority Theaters

As the number of permanent theaters expanded, so did a similar but smaller number of minority theaters. In many communities minorities had their own theaters. In others they attended white theaters but could sit only in specified areas. Usually that was a "special" balcony like the one at the Texas in McGregor.

In the 1920s, some of the theaters serving the minority community were the Grand Central, Airdome, Century, Ella B. Moore, Othello, Palace (there were two Palace Theaters in Dallas, one for white patrons and one for black) renamed the Harlem, Star, Jungle Land, Lincoln, Mammoth, and State in Dallas; El Rey and Teatro Colon in El Paso; Pastime in Greenville plus another theater with no name; Teatro Union, Teatro Obrero, Teatro Nacional, Teatro Progreso, and Teatro Zaragoza in San Antonio; Lincoln in Honey Grove; Teatro Hidalgo and Harlem in Corpus Christi; American, Lincoln, Ideal, Jones, and Pastime in Houston; Ritz in Longview; Jungle Land Air Dome and Andrews in Sherman; Lincoln, Palace, Rapeeds, and White Star in Tyler; Gayety in Waco; St. Elmo in Wichita Falls; and many others.[16]

In 1921 the Mammoth in Dallas, managed by Joe Trammell, advertised itself as "The Amusement Home of the Colored Folk." John Harris owned and operated the Grand Central. The Palace promoted itself as the "South's Finest Colored Show." These theaters generally showed the same features as regular theaters: Westerns with Buck Jones and Hoot Gibson and Tarzan adventures.[17]

The Pastime in Houston was fifteen feet wide with room for only eight seats across. The Lincoln in that city originated in 1903 as the Olympia Opera House. In 1905 it was renamed the Standard but closed until 1916 when it was remodeled into a black theater. O. P. DeWalt operated it until the 1920s. R. A. DeWalt assisted his uncle in booking films and acts. "We always were a movie theater. Whenever we had a live act, we always threw it in extra, at no increase in prices." The theater played "all-colored" silent films from the Foster and Lincoln Studios, and occasionally a film from a major studio about blacks or one that featured a black actor. When sound was added, the theater ran melodramas from producer-director-promoter Oscar Michaeux who made movies for black audiences until the late 1940s. When Houston theaters were desegregated in the late 1950s, the Lincoln was renamed the Texan.[18]

The Lincoln, the black theater in Honey Grove, showed the same movies as the white theater situated a block away. "Bub" Nails, operator of the Lincoln, physically relayed reels of film back and forth between the two theaters. He would run to the Strand, and, as soon as they finished a reel of film, he would run it to the Lincoln and show it. When that reel finished, he would run it back to the Strand, get another reel, and run back to the Lincoln.[19]

The Ritz in Longview—a former feed store—was constructed of tin. A theater in Greenville with no name

Figure 40. The Harlem on Elm Street in Dallas was one of the first black movie theaters in the state. Courtesy Texas/Dallas History and Archives Division, Dallas Public Library

was also in a small tin structure that looked like a building in a lumber yard. "In Dallas, the black Palace became the Harlem," recalled Lawrence Birdsong of Longview. "The Central was two doors west of the Harlem. It had been a garage, and they just gutted it and put some seats in it. In my book, it was never the Grand Central, just Central. The State was on Hall Street. In Waco, there was one on the river. I think it was the Palace, and it was in derelict condition,

Figure 41. The tiny, twenty-foot-wide Pastime in Houston was among the state's first black motion picture theaters. Courtesy The Institute of Texan Cultures, San Antonio

Figure 42. The Teatro Zaragoza in San Antonio in the 1920s. Courtesy Zintgraff Collection, The Institute of Texan Cultures, San Antonio

Figure 43. The Teatro Obrero in San Antonio in the 1920s was operated by Paul Garza.
Courtesy Zintgraff Collection, The Institute of Texan Cultures, San Antonio

because I would see it from the interurban as I passed. I think the Gaiety (in Waco) was black."[20]

Texas theaters were partially desegregated in the 1920s. The Majestic in Dallas opened a "special balcony" in March of 1925. The theater's management made this adjustment because "This was the only opportunity for African-American citizens of Dallas to see a first run motion picture. Tickets were thirty-five cents for adults and fifteen cents for children."[21] For the next thirty years, selected theaters in the state reserved "special balconies" for their black patrons.

Frederico Trevino, who owned a bicycle shop in Corpus Christi, started renting Spanish-language movies in 1915 and showing them in a canvas enclosure on a vacant lot on Waco Street. The films were produced in Spain and obtained from an agent in Matamoros, Mexico. Soon, Trevino moved his business to a vacant building at 613 Waco and installed a big sign with red letters proclaiming its name: Teatro Hidalgo.[22]

San Antonio had at least five Spanish-language theaters in the 1920s. The Teatro–Salon de la Union, originally built for live performance, started showing movies in 1915 when live acts were not available. In February of 1918, Teatro Nacional started booking movies with live performances in between. Teatro Zaragoza started showing movies during the 1920s, then added live acts between film features.[23]

Theater Row

Just as the booming nickelodeons had clustered in one area of a town, the majority of new de luxe theaters were situated along one street in a city's downtown business district. "Theater rows" evolved. In the 1920s, Elm Street was the address of Dallas's picture

Figure 44. The box office of the Teatro Progreso in San Antonio, operated by Juan Garza. Admission prices were 10 cents for adults, 5 cents for children, and 2 cents for all at the daily matinee. Courtesy Zintgraff Collection, The Institute of Texan Cultures, San Antonio

shows. There was the Loew's; Hippodrome, later renamed Strand; Fox; Queen; behind the Queen the Lyric; Garrick; Rex; Telenews; Mirror, later renamed Pantages, later renamed Ritz, later renamed Jefferson; Capitol; Old Mill, later renamed Rialto; Washington; Crystal; behind the Crystal on Main Street the Embassy; Palace; Tower; Hope, later renamed Melba, later renamed Capri; Majestic; around the corner from the Majestic on Harwood the Circle; Grand Central; and (black) Palace, later renamed Harlem. Even with name changes and periodic "openings" and "closings," Elm Street in Dallas remained "theater row" through the 1950s.[24]

Walking past certain theaters on Elm could leave a person with impressions sometimes not to the theater's benefit. Lawrence Birdsong of Tyler vividly remembered that "the Queen stunk. It was cheap and . . .

Figure 45. Theater row in Dallas was Elm Street. Visible are the Queen, Jefferson, Old Mill, Palace, Rex, and Garrick. The Majestic and Harlem were beyond the Palace. Courtesy Texas/Dallas History and Archives Division, Dallas Public Library

smelled. . . . You would never forget the smell of the Queen or the Hippodrome. . . . They had dirt in there that had never been swept out. If you went into the Palace, you did not have your feet stick to the floor." Walking past the Palace on a hot summer day could be a wonderful experience. "You could always tell that that breeze was cool," remembered Birdsong, "and you just wanted to go inside and get out of that summer heat." The Palace was the first theater in Dallas to be air conditioned by the Freon method. The Old Mill, Queen, and Strand had wooden, attic fans; they were never air conditioned.[25]

By the 1920s downtown Houston had twenty-five theaters on or near its "row," six blocks of Main Street. It was a mixture of "hold-over" nickelodeons, new de luxe theaters, and three grand movie palaces. Houston boasted the Queen, Isis, Liberty (later renamed Pierce), Zoe, Dixie, Prince, Star, Travis, Vaudette, Gem, Rex, Best, Crescent, Cozy (later renamed Royal), Pastime, Olympia, Key, Crown, and Rialto, among others.[26]

In Galveston theaters were on or near Market Street. In different decades there were the Martini, New Martini, State, Lyric, Vaudette, Queen, Globe, Dixie One, Dixie Two, Dixie Three, Palace, Majestic, Isle, Casino, Best, Strand, Key, Leader, People, Galvez, Colonial, Theatorium, Tremont, Fortuna, Orpheum, Marvel, Royal, Lincoln, Liberty, Rialto, Ruby, Cozy, O'Donnell Jacob, Hippodrome, and Princess, among others.[27]

Jackrabbit Theaters

Even while de luxe theaters were dominating the downtown movie business, traveling exhibitors still showed films wherever an audience could be found. This type of business, which brought many communities their first moving images, was referred to as a "jackrabbit theater."

One such business worked the Cleburne area. The operator would go to a small community, set up a screen, sell popcorn, and show movies—silent, of course. It used downtown streets and had a projector sitting on a truck or trailer.[28]

Even after grand movie palaces became a reality, Dorothy Phillips of Sulphur Springs attended a "jackrabbit theater," in Dallas. "This is the Trinity Heights School grounds—1928 . . . all the kids from the Oak Cliff area . . . knew about it by word of mouth. . . . They got a . . . little metal projection booth that they brought in and set in the middle of the playground . . . just big enough for a person to get in and have a few films stored around. I'm sure that they had some kind of portable screen. Seems like it went on all through the summer vacation."[29]

There were also free movies in Dallas's Oak Lawn Park every Saturday night during the summers of the 1920s.[30] The merchants of Wolfe City sponsored movies in downtown once a week during that decade. Main Street would be filled with people sitting on the ground, or just anywhere. The projector was mounted on a truck and a screen was on the front of a building. There was no admission; the promoter made his money selling popcorn.

Grand Movie Palaces or "Supers"

As the number of de luxe theaters increased, the era of the grand movie palaces came into fruition. The most spectacular theaters of this classification were referred to as "supers." The grand movie palaces in Texas were in Austin, the Paramount; Beaumont, the Jefferson; Dallas, the Majestic and the Palace; and in El Paso, the Plaza. Texarkana's Perot; Houston's Majestic, Metropolitan, and Loew's State; and Fort Worth's Hollywood, Worth, and Palace also all qualified as supers. Others included the Texas in San Angelo; Paramount in Abilene; and the Texas, Aztec, Empire, and Majestic in San Antonio. Some of the largest and most spectacular were part of Interstate Circuit, Incorporated, the creation of Karl St. John Hoblitzelle.

Born in St. Louis in 1878, Hoblitzelle worked his way up from office boy at the St. Louis World's Fair.

Figures 46, 47, and 48. The Queen in Galveston. Courtesy Paul E. Adair

After it closed, he was asked by concessionaires to do a feasibility study about bringing vaudeville to the Southwest. With $2,500, he and his brother organized the Interstate Amusement Company in 1905. His theaters started presenting live vaudeville shows, but, as the population's taste changed, they started showing silent, then talking, motion pictures. On June 13, 1920, Interstate announced that an "elaborate and costly motion picture policy will go into effect." The first motion picture shown at Interstate Theaters was *Four*

Horsemen of the Apocalypse. Hoblitzelle believed that his theaters were not meant to be devoted solely to motion pictures or stage performances, rather, they were to be places of entertainment suitable for any type of show seen by any type of audience. He and Interstate pledged that each theater would be "a place where a man could bring his family without question."[31]

He initiated the Interstate Circuit in Houston by buying the Empire at 1309 Congress and renaming it Majestic. In 1910 he opened the second Majestic. If possible, Hoblitzelle always named his newest theater the "Majestic" and gave the older Majestic a different name.[32]

Bill Mitchell of Dallas personally knew Hoblitzelle and worked with Interstate Theaters:

> He was one of the most generous men I have ever known. He was very considerate, very charitable, and extremely intelligent with investments. He was very public-relations minded both from an employee standpoint and from an operations standpoint.
>
> Cleanliness counted. Each day, ushers had to stand at attention for inspection of hands and fingernails. I don't think you could get away with that today. I recall when we first put in the confection counters in the theaters, Mr. Hoblitzelle didn't want them. He said it would dirty the house.[33]

Hoblitzelle first collaborated with architect John Eberson for the Austin Majestic. Eberson's philosophy of theatrical design was "Prepare Practical Plans for Pretty Playhouses—Please Patrons—Pay Profits." Later renamed the Paramount, the Majestic was a preview of future Eberson designs. Construction started in 1915 and the theater opened the next year. It was the most luxurious vaudeville and silent motion movie palace in "rural" Texas.

Eberson—who would built over five hundred theaters throughout the world—for Hoblitzelle designed the predecessor of his nationally famous "atmospheric" theaters in Dallas in 1921. (Supers were classified as "hardtops" (or "standard"), or "atmospheric"). At the cornerstone-laying ceremony Rabbi Lefkowitz stated, "Stores do not make a city. Man needs churches for worship. He needs art galleries for beauty. He needs theaters for joy and laughter and recreation. What would a great city be without its theaters?" The cornerstone proclaimed, "Dedicated to art, music and wholesome entertainment in grateful recognition of the support always given me by the people of Dallas." The Majestic opened on April 11, 1921:[34]

> The great electric sign, reputed the largest in the

Figure 49. The Majestic in Dallas on opening night April 11, 1921. The marquee, the largest in the South, topped by the Majestic bird, proclaimed the opening week's special act: Olga Petrova. Courtesy Paul E. Adair

South, blazed the headliners of the opening $12,500 bill from a height that could be seen for the entire length of Elm Street. The big animated flashing sign was proudly topped by the famous Majestic bird that suavely maintained his precarious poise upon a whirling ball that flashed all the colors of the rainbow in its revolution.

Through the mirrored doors that lead to the foyer could be seen the waters of the Vatican fountain playing softly over the dolphins and cupids that are prominent in the decorative scheme. Ferns and cut flowers had been banked so thickly about these figures that they were all but obscured . . . great baskets of roses and lilies and carnations flashed their brilliance in colorful contrast to the Ivory and gold of the walls and ceilings. . . . One of the most beautiful things about the foyer is the wonderful lighting effects. Chandeliers of the Louis XIV pattern depend [*sic*] from the ceiling, their cut-glass pendants reflecting the glory of the high-powered lamps. . . .

The auditorium of the new house offers several distinctive features. The pitch of the floor is such that every seat in the long sweep of rows gives an excellent view of the stage. . . . There are no posts, there are none anywhere in the house. . . . The perimeter of the ceiling is marked by artistic lattice work draped and intertwined with colored vines and flowers to give the effect of a garden wall, which it does wonderfully. . . . A lighting system is so arranged that effects of the afternoon or the deepest night can be most realistically portrayed by merely playing the light switches. . . .[35]

Figure 50. The tuxedo-clad, opening-night crowd at the Majestic in Dallas on April 11, 1921. Note the special section in the upper balcony, theater right, for black patrons. Courtesy Paul E. Adair

The trellis work, which was a small part of the Austin Majestic, was given full use in Dallas. The interior was a Roman Garden scheme. The illusion of out-of-doors came from vines and trees that graced the upper-story decoration. The exterior was a French mansard roof from the Chateau style of the French Renaissance. That the exterior and interiors were completely different styles did not seem to bother Eberson.[36]

A staff of seventy greeted opening-night patrons. They included doormen welcoming guests at the entrance, floor directors assisting patrons into the inner foyer; twenty-three ushers outfitted in military uniforms greeting guests at the four aisles leading to the auditorium and escorting them to their seats; and uniformed elevator operators taking patrons to the upper levels. There was also an employee seated in the

Figure 51. Olga Petrova, the opening week's star performer at the Majestic in Dallas, posing with young patrons.
Courtesy Paul E. Adair

Figure 52. The ticket office at the Majestic in Dallas.
Courtesy Paul E. Adair

back at every performance whose job it was to check the screen for lint on the projector lens, to adjust the sound level if it were not correct, or to correct anything that might distract the audiences during the performance. The opening-night program featured:

> Colonel J. T. Trezevant of Dallas as Master of Ceremonies; the invocation was given by Bishop Henry T. Moore. . . . Dallas Mayor Frank Wozencraft provided the opening address. . . . He was followed by William Atwell who spoke on Civic Pride. Entertainment for the night be-

Figure 53. The stage proscenium at the Majestic in Dallas. Courtesy Paul E. Adair

gan with a special song "Hello, Dallas!" Written for the occasion by Dallas playwright John T. Rogers of the Majestic Music Publishing Company, and sung by Wells K. Egner. The vaudeville program featured the standard seven acts, with the addition of Petrova. [Olga Petrova, the famous actor/dancer, was brought in for the opening week for $3,500.] The lead performer was Paul George, and the Wilhat Trio wound up the show. Also on the billing were Carleton & Ballew, Gibson & Connelli, Lloyd & Goods, the Tilton Revue, and Keegan & O'Rourke.[37]

The top balcony had a "special" section for black audiences. They had their own separate entrance and box office at the foyer level. The Majestic provided for children with a sixty by forty-eight-foot playground in the basement called "Majesticland." A newspaper article stated,[38] "Inside there will be a merry-go-round with the horses all ready to leap forward at the starter's signal.... In another part of the playground there is a miniature Robert Louis Stevenson's Treasure Island. ... There will be an aviary, alive with singing birds ... there will be animal cages with the most attractive of animals that children love, Br'er Rabbit the cotton tail, the squirrels and a dozen others.... There are many toys, walking dolls, dancing dolls, squeaking animals and bears and toads and spiders stuffed so that nobody can get hurt....[39]

Next to Majesticland was the Land of Nod. It featured a complete nursery, free milk and crackers, and trained nurses. Parents would leave their names and seat number in case they had to be summoned. A few years after it opened the Majestic installed a radio receiver in the basement so patrons could attend the movie but not miss their favorite radio program, *Amos 'n Andy*. (Because of the difficulty theaters were having competing with radio's increasing popularity in the 1920s, some theaters would actually stop their feature films at the appropriate time so the audience could listen to *Amos 'n Andy* in the lobby broadcast on a radio receiver with a "loud talker," as it was first called. After the program, the audience went back into the theater, and the movie resumed. After equipment for sound movies was installed, theaters might stop and play the radio program over that sound system so the patrons did not have to leave their seats. In the 1930s, the Uptown in Sulphur Springs, like other theaters around the state, would time its features around those radio programs like *Amos 'n' Andy* and *Doctor I. Q.*, so no person coming to the movie would miss that show.)[40]

A few blocks down Elm Street in Dallas was the Palace. Its cornerstone was laid March 26, 1921. Originally named the National, it was built for the Earl Hulsey interest, controllers of Southern Enterprises, and managed by Raymond Willie. The Palace was intended for the exclusive showing of Paramount motion pictures. From the beginning it was the aim of the theater's staff to mix live musical numbers with motion pictures. Ten years later, the depression helped change the program to exclusive motion pictures.

The architectural style was Georgian, using various types of marble, intricate chandeliers, leather-upholstered seats, heavy drapes, among other features. The color motif was "cafe au lait." It seated 2,800, boasted a $50,000 Hope-Jones pipe organ, and had a thirty-piece symphony orchestra lead by Don Albert. A registering machine made it possible for persons in the box office and elsewhere in the building to know what part of the picture was being shown and how much of it remained. There was a private projection room for the staff.

The opening night movie was *Sentimental Tommy,* starring Garrett Hughes, Mabel Teliaferro, and May McAvoy. Packards and Pierce Arrows lined Elm Street on June 11, 1921, for the opening of the "Million Dollar Theater." Patrons were greeted by two white-gloved doormen who escorted them across a plush red carpet and turned them over to one of thirty-four ushers splendidly attired in uniforms that included top hats and swagger sticks. Although the seat-

Figure 54. The Majestic in Houston. Courtesy Paul E. Adair

Figure 55. The Majestic in Houston, the first "atmospheric" theater, was proclaimed as "the most beautiful theater in the South." Courtesy Paul E. Adair

ing at the Majestic was reserved, seating at the Palace was on a "first come, first served basis." Guests received a booklet specially prepared for the occasion with headings announcing: "'I Am a New Theater' ('Courtesy will ever be my creed; hospitality my religion'); 'There is No Plutocracy of the Theater' ('It is the sincere wish of the builders of the Palace that you may regard it as belonging to you'); 'The Motive' ('To make money was not the primary consideration'); and 'Don't try to tip a Palace usher—you'll only be offending a little gentleman.'" If patrons became thirsty, ushers regularly "came around" the auditorium with glasses of ice water.

"I don't think I shall ever forget the opening night," stated Willie. "I'm not sure I have ever again experienced the same kind of thrill I had that night. . . . We had almost a hundred people on the Palace payroll then, and I'm sure they were all on duty that night." Orchestra leader Albert spent hours "cueing" music to the screen action of *Sentimental Tommy*. The orchestra played the movie score for the first thirty minutes of the film, then Carl Weisemann, featured organist, played the score for the middle portion. The orchestra returned for the final half hour. In addition to the overture and musical score, there was an organ solo; selected "Topics of the Day" news film; "Palace Tour," a musical prelude with Peggy Gates; Leighton Edelon Cook singing "Hiawatha's Melody of Love" in front of a "setting of mountain scenery;" "The Guide," a film comedy with Clyde Cook; and the "Exit March" played by the orchestra. The theater and staff received a standing ovation at the close of the program.[41]

Hoblitzelle and Eberson continued their collaboration for a new Majestic in Houston. It opened on January 29, 1923, the nation's first "atmospheric" theater, a trademark of Eberson. He was to design and build approximately one hundred "atmospheric" theaters after Houston's, which the press hailed as "the most beautiful theater in the South." One reporter claimed, "It is a playhouse the duplicate of which cannot be found in America." On opening night Dr. Stockton Axson, head of the English department at Rice Institute, outlined the history of drama from Shakespeare to the Roaring Twenties. With Axson acting as master of ceremonies, the Reverend Peter Gray Sears spoke, followed by Mrs. H. B. Fall and Mayor Oscar Holcombe. The main attraction was Henry B. Walthall starring in *The Unknown*.[42]

Houston's Majestic was the first air-conditioned theater in the state. Reportedly, many patrons almost

Figure 56. One of the entrance halls at the Majestic in Houston. Courtesy Paul E. Adair

fainted when they exited the cool theater into Houston's heat and humidity. It was primarily a vaudeville house until Hoblitzelle introduced one-reel movie features to supplement live acts. A typical bill included a short movie, an hour or more of vaudeville acts, and music from the orchestra and organ. Headliners were Jack Benny, W. C. Fields, Milton Berle, or a magician, animal act, singer, dancer, or comedian. The bill changed each week.[43] Eddie J. Miller operated a spotlight at the Majestic, "Lloyd Finlay had an orchestra at the Majestic that was great—just great. You'd go to New York and hear vaudevillians say, 'Man, Houston, Texas is the town to play, they got Lloyd Finlay's orchestra there." He kept getting offers to go to Broadway, but never would. Eddie Bremer was the house manager then, and he'd get a new bunch of acts in every week. Friends would ask me if the shows were any good and I'd tell them 'They stink.' To my wife that meant it was a good show, and she'd tell everyone to go see it."[44]

In the early years, Monday was "society night" and many prominent Houstonians wanting to "see and be seen" held permanent season tickets for that evening. It became fashionable to drive downtown to the Majestic, park in front of the theater, and watch the audience enter and exit.[45]

Guests were met by a variety of staff members whose sole purpose was to make their visit pleasurable. A footman opened a patron's car door and held an umbrella if needed. A doorman checked for drunks, Pekinese dogs, and gate crashers. A streetman supervised crowds and could relay a ticket request to the lady in the box office with mysterious hand signals. That cashier was always blonde and good-looking. Inside there were two ushers per aisle to show patrons an empty seat with a flashlight, page boys to deliver messages or direct visitors, and elevator operators.[46]

As patrons entered they were transported into a fantasy land of an "Italian Renaissance garden sheltered by vine-covered travertine walls topped with cupolas, classic temples and preening peacocks." Rows of Roman maidens looked down on patrons. The garden walls were different on each side of the stage proscenium. On the right was a colonnade roofed with a conical dome with intricately carved pillars that resembled a small temple. An Italian palace façade with grilled roof was on the left side. Above the boxes were "reproductions of The Winged Victory; Polhymnia, the goddess of serious poetry; Euterpe, goddess of melody; the Venus of Aries and the Venus of Capua, the bust of Minerva, the Apollo Citharoedos and the statue of Diana robing herself." Eberson enhanced the outdoor motif in the auditorium with a ceiling where clouds drifted between tiny sparkling stars. The Brenograph Jr., the "magic lantern" that projected endless cumulus and nimbus clouds became the trademark of "atmospheric" theaters around the country, especially those designed by Eberson.[47]

Houston had two other grand movie palaces. The Metropolitan opened in December of 1926. It was admired by many; it was described by others as "an Egyptian nightmare." Loew's State, a $1 million theater situated at Main and McKinney, opened on Oc-

Figure 57. The Metropolitan in Houston was admired by some and described by others as "an Egyptian nightmare."
Courtesy Houston Metropolitan Research Center, Houston Public Library

tober 15, 1927. "We ran a good theater," stated Homer McCallon, manager. "We specialized in cleanliness and beauty. We had wonderful air conditioning. We put that in our ads a lot of times. . . . It was a lovely, beautiful theater. Inside we had marble floors, beautiful carpets and a second-floor lobby."[48]

The State's outside entrance gave patrons no hint of what was waiting inside, although they might suspect something when they came to the circular ticket booth in the vestibule. It was a combination of Italian marbles and black walnut, enriched with hand-carved ornaments and bronze grilles. The entrance vestibule exhibited Vermont Imperial and Italian Tavernelle marble. Rows of bronze doors separated it from a lobby that was vaulted and richly ornamented with beautifully modeled figures.[49] The mezzanine showcased French furniture, bronze statues, Meissen urns and vases and gilt mirrors. Many of these furnishings had come from the Fifth Avenue Vanderbilt mansion in New York City.

The main auditorium had elaborately carved alternating panels. Chandeliers hung from the ceiling. The stage was surrounded by a giant gilt frame inset with Wedgwood blue and white plaques. The central figure was a dome thirty-three feet in diameter embellished with panels of dancing figures with a large rosette in the center. Concealed around the base of the dome were thousands of electric lights affording an indirect flood of illumination. The color scheme was turquoise blue, gold, ivory, and cafe au lait. The proscenium and organ pillars had elaborate drapes of blue and gold. The lighting scheme could produce any color and intensity desired. The men's smoking room had a floor and base of fireflashed tile and walls of stained walnut. The ladies' parlor was carpeted and framed with marble.[50]

The play bill proclaimed five acts of vaudeville and a feature picture, running continuously from 1 to 11 P.M. The vaudeville portion of the bill lasted until the middle 1930s.[51]

The Worth in Fort Worth was designed in part by Eberson. Financier Jessie H. Jones of Houston hired local architect Wyatt E. Hedrick to join Alfred C. Finn and Eberson. Moviegoers found themselves in a pseudo-Egyptian temple closely modeled after the exotic artifacts discovered in the tomb of King Tutankhamen, which had been opened in 1923. Huge papyrus columns, mysterious gilded Egyptian relief sculptures, and figural friezes dominated the inside of the auditorium. Dramatic lighting and expensive tapestries combined with ornate ceilings and brilliantly painted moldings. An effect machine projected water, smoke, fire, and floating clouds on the ceiling or stage. Two orchestras, one classical and one popular, alternated between the live acts and the movie. A Wurlitzer pipe organ accompanied the stage and motion picture performances.[52]

Figure 58. The lobby of the Metropolitan in Houston. Courtesy Paul E. Adair

Eberson and Hoblitzelle designed and constructed the Majestic in San Antonio. The $3 million project seated 3,743 patrons—the largest theater in the South, the second largest in the nation. A separate balcony for blacks was located above the projection booth. The opening of the Majestic centered a city-wide celebration attended by 500,000. Special trains with reduced ticket prices brought people into the city for the celebration.

Figure 59. Loew's State in Houston. Courtesy Houston Metropolitan Research Center, Houston Public Library

Figures 60 and 61. The stage proscenium at Loew's State in Houston. Courtesy Houston Metropolitan Research Center, Houston Public Library

The Majestic opened on June 14, 1929, with a special stage and movie presentation. The next day, the regular program for the general public was Lola Lane and Dixie Lee in *The Fox Movietone Follies;* Jimmy Rodgers, the "Blues and Yodeling Star"; Don Galvan, "The Banjo Boy"; Paul Morton and Billy Scout in a sketch called "Hey, Taxi"; a comedy skit called "Crossed Wires"; the Shaw and Carroll Revue of dancers; and Eddie Sauer and his orchestra.[53] Ushers uniforms were "dark blue, with gold against light blue for stripes."

A canopy over the entrance gave protection from the sun and provided an upper-level balcony for an outdoor cafe. The vertical marquee was higher than any in the South. It had 2,400 lamps and rose seven floor levels: seventy-six feet. The Majestic's lobby encouraged the audience's escape from the outside world with a cave-like, one-story enclosure embellished with inlaid tiles, copper lanterns, vaulted ceilings with painted murals and lattice work. There was a huge aquarium at the end of the lobby, which opened into an encircling balcony decorated with twisted wooden Churrigueresque columns and Spanish Baroque features. A fountain, statuary, and tapestries graced the lobby along with red brocatelle royal armchairs, a seventeenth-century walnut table, wood, silver and bronze candlesticks, and torches. The lobbies displayed stuffed birds of all description. Real birds flew around the lobby and perched precariously on balconies. Specially treated Spanish cypress trees grew in the upper levels along with azaleas, oleanders, magnolias, blooming cactus, rose bushes, and South American palm trees.[54]

To complete the illusion of being seated in a castle's outdoor courtyard in Spain, the auditorium had a three-dimensional village scene forming the side walls. The ceiling had an immense domed skyscape complete with floating clouds, and the blue of the night sky was punctuated by small twinkling bulbs simulating stars and constellations. Experts at *National Geographic* were consulted about the position of the real stars on the night the theater opened, and the twinkling lights were arranged accordingly.[55]

Eric Brendler of San Antonio was employed at the old Majestic before the new one opened in 1929:

> There was a time when they were hiring ushers at the old Majestic Theater. I read it in the newspaper. . . . The qualifications were that you would be a straightforward person, you would be a likable person, and that you would dress according to the theater that you were going to. I put on my Sunday-go-to-meeting clothes and went down there. . . .
>
> They had a training manual to train the ushers. . . . We had about forty-six or forty-seven ushers. We had three shifts. . . . There was twenty-two on during a shift. We went on at nine in the morning and got off at nine at night. We had a fifteen-minute break at twelve. . . .
>
> Yes, I was there opening night [of the new Majestic]—it was very elaborate. I was an usher on the mezzanine floor. . . . You would take a survey of the aisle—the seats that you were working and remember where the seats were. You would take the people down and put them in those seats. . . .

Figure 62. The Majestic in San Antonio was the second-largest motion picture theater in the country. Courtesy Zintgraff Collection, The Institute of Texan Cultures, San Antonio

Figure 63. The ticket office at the Majestic in San Antonio. Courtesy Las Casas Foundation, San Antonio

Figure 64. The stage proscenium at the Majestic in San Antonio. Courtesy Las Casas Foundation, San Antonio

> We had hand signals that told the people [ushers] in the back of the theater who were directing that we had doubles or singles. If you had three you would hold up three fingers. If you had a double you would put your hands on you hips. Usually we didn't have too many singles. It was fine work as far as work was concerned. . . . I was making six dollars a week. We were making twelve and a half cents an hour. You felt like you were on cloud nine.[56]

The Aztec in San Antonio was designed by Robert B. Kelly in the style of authentic Mayan Revival architecture. Every surface and feature from the bas-relief panels to the water fountain idol rising from the floor were based on the Pyramid of the Sun in Teotihuacan, the Temple of the Cross at Palenque, and the Atlantean columns from the Toltec Temple of the Warriors at Chichen Itza in the Yucatan. Designers traveled to Central America to study the authentic temples before designing the theater. The ticket office, inlaid with green, black, and yellow ceramic tiles, resembled a pyramid. The foyer was modeled after the Hall of Columns at Mitla and exhibited a six-ton chandelier. Over the proscenium arch was Quetzalcoatl, the fair-haired god of the Aztec, and his emblem, the plumed serpent. The stage curtain depicted the meeting of Cortez, the Conquistador, and Montezuma, the emperor of all Mexico. The premiere performance had a chorus line, a seventy-five–piece orchestra, an organist, a stage spectacular concerning "the Court of Montezuma," and a feature film: all for fifty cents.[57]

Pianos, Player Pianos, and Organs

Silent motion pictures were anything but. Since the establishment of the nickelodeon, there was always a piano, organ, or automatic player piano accompanying the film and filling the auditorium with music (too often, very loud music). Some nickelodeons or theaters had small orchestras or live piano players. It was their job to match what was on the screen. In theaters with only an automatic player piano—playing constantly at full volume—the music hardly ever matched the on-screen mood.

When grand movie palaces were established, the orchestra, organ, or unit orchestra usually had music that complemented the show. There were services that arranged specific music for a movie, scene by scene. The musical scores contained visual cues for the organist or orchestra conductor. The coming of synchronized sound in the late 1920s lowered the level of noise that patrons had to endure in small theaters equipped with only loud, automatic player pianos.

Lawrence Birdsong of Tyler, an enthusiast of theater organs, remembered attending movies during the silent era:

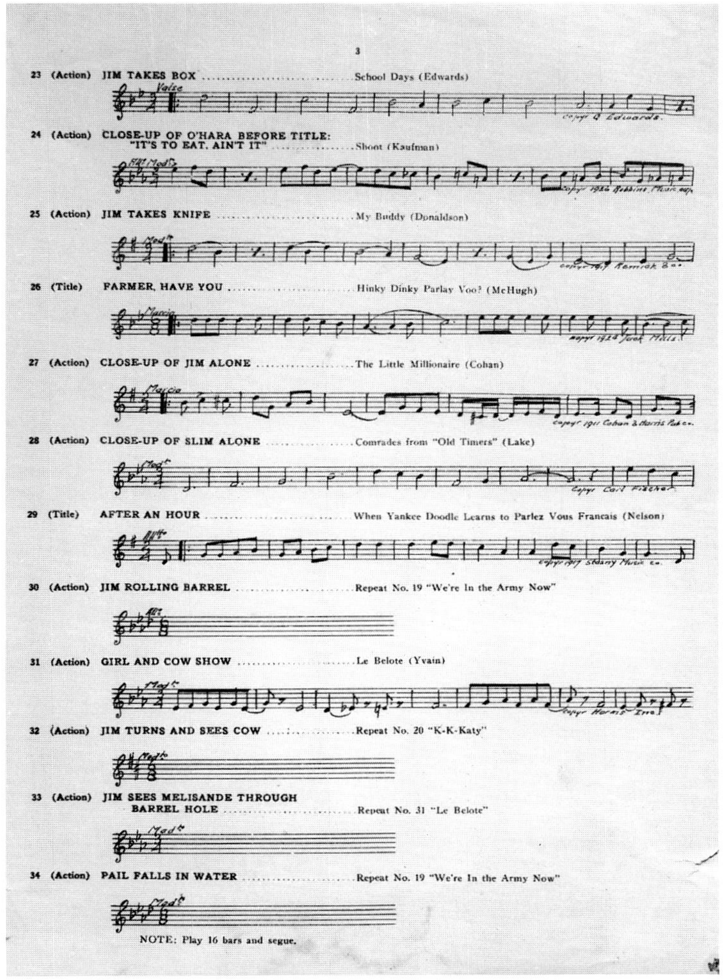

Figure 65. Sheet music especially arranged for an orchestra or organ to accompany a silent motion picture. Courtesy Lawrence Birdsong, Jr.

> [My] first movie was silent. I don't remember the picture—roll [piano] player, and the tune was *Blue Room.* They just turned it on and let it play. It had no meaning or sense with the picture. . . . The rolls were lined across the piano.
>
> At the Rembert, the rolls were down in the orchestra pit and the blower was also there, and it made a lot of racket. It was a pit organ . . . a combination piano and one keyboard organ. Two to four ranks of pipes.
>
> . . . The roll would get stuck. . . . Everybody would yell, "Stuck again!" . . . You would see him coming down the aisle. . . . It was very primitive.
>
> My mother took lessons . . . 1916—Washington Theater [Dallas]—a Hill-Green Lane organ. She had a good ear; she could fake like crazy. If it was a big picture, they would send a score. . . . A big theater, you would go down there after the evening show [preceding feature] was over and go through it and see what's there. If it was a big house and it was serious, you'd better rehearse. After you got to playing it once, you did not worry . . . you know the picture and you can play it blind. You can't sit here and look at the music, you'd go nuts. You can't look up at the screen and try to find the place; it's too big an angle. Most of the consoles were on the far left—for some reason nobody knows. . . .[58]

Figure 66. The auditorium and organ at Robb & Rowley's Palace in Corpus Christi. Courtesy the Dr. Fred'k McGregor Photo Collection of the Corpus Christi Museum

Figure 67. Mr. Havasa, organist at the Plaza in El Paso. Courtesy William C. Rast

Carl Wiseman, a concert organist from New York, came to Dallas to open the Palace in 1921. That theater was built with a three-manual, ten-rank organ. A few years later, the Palace installed a four-manual, twenty-rank Publix #1. The Majestic opened with a two-manual, fourteen-rank Kilgan Organ. (In comparison, the organ at Radio City Music Hall in New York City was a twin-consoled Wurlitzer with fifty-eight ranks of pipes.) Shortly after it opened, the Palace had nationally known organist Jesse Crawford come to Dallas to perform. Although there were dozens of pipe organ virtuosi, Crawford was considered the very best. He was billed as the "The Poet of the Organ."[59]

The orchestras in movie palaces could not accompany every showing of a film all day long; orchestra personnel did not have the physical stamina, and the theaters could not afford it. Consequently, there was usually an organ playing the music at the early and late showings. The first organs in theaters, as in the nickelodeon days, were no more than church organs and were terribly inadequate to accompany a motion picture. A silent photoplay with its changes of mood demanded special and unusual sound effects.

Organs capable of enhancing a silent movie became available during World War I with the Hope-Jones Unit Orchestra built by the Rudolph Wurlitzer Company. Wurlitzer was one of many manufacturers of theater organs. Others were Kimball, Robert Morton, Möller, Marr & Colton, Page, and Barton. The Unit Orchestra, especially those made by Wurlitzer, was considered "one of the most versatile instruments ever devised by man." It was basically a pipe organ that could imitate all the instruments of an orchestra plus many other sounds needed for movies such as bass drums, snare drums, xylophones, glockenspiels, marimbas, grand pianos, banjos, mandolins, sleigh bells, chimes, triangles, cymbals, castanets, Chinese blocks, tambourines, tom-toms, gongs, saucer bells, and any instrument of an orchestra. Additionally, that Unit Orchestra could add to a movie the sound of nightingales, canaries, galloping horses, steamboat whistles, train whistles, auto horns, fire-engine sirens, airplanes, hurricanes, swishing surf, rain on the roof, telephone bells, door bells, trolley bells, and smashing crockery. It could be specially ordered to produce most any sound.[60]

Earl McDonald has a fascination with theater organs and until recently owned the one installed at the Lakewood Theater in Dallas:

> I would get on the streetcar and go down to Elm Street and see Dwight Brown play the organ at the Palace. The story goes that he was some[what] of a "booze head." I guess this was back in the silent [period], they would have to get stage hands to go down there to hold him up on the organ bench or he would fall off. If someone would hold him up, he could play the movie. That was really early because they quit using the organ.
>
> They had had a smaller organ in there during the silent movies days, and so they let a contract with Wurlitzer to put in a bigger one. In the interim . . . when the contract was signed . . . talkies came along. That pretty well shot that, but the organ went in anyway—about 1931. . . . Publix #1 420 Wurlitzer. . . . The one that was in there before was moved to the Melba. . . .[61]

Motion Picture Operators and Employees

Boyd Milligan started working at the Majestic in Fort Worth in 1926. He started going to silent movies in 1913. His family lived on a farm near Palestine and his father would take Boyd along when he went to town for supplies and drop him off at the local nickelodeon. "That was the name of the theater," remembered Milligan. "He would not come back for two or three hours. I got acquainted with the projectionist and the cashier. I hung around there so much." He started working at the Majestic after his family moved to Fort Worth:

> I would pass in front of the Majestic here. . . . Finally I got enough nerve to go in there and ask them for a job. . . . They put me up in the balcony of the Majestic as usher. They would come up there and I would take them to a seat. You took them down the aisle . . . with a flashlight. I worked up there for about three weeks, and they moved me downstairs at a door taking tickets.
>
> I must of been doing a real good job so they gave me floor manager. I was over the ushers. I worked out a system of signals . . . if they had seats . . . how many seats they had on this side. Al Reynolds wrote a book on ushers and Interstate published this book, and it went out to all circuits. . . .
>
> I quit and went over on Main Street and went to work at the Odem Theater. I was the manager. . . . It was a small theater like the Liberty Theater. . . . I didn't like it; it was a cheap little theater. . . .[62]

Winston O. Sparks of Fort Worth first went to the movies as a child in 1925:

> Main Street at that time was the main highway to Amarillo. The streetcar came to within seven feet of our front gate. It must have been a summer afternoon because I was in my summer clothes; my mother dressed me up real nice; I wore knickerbockers. We walked out and stood at our front gate. The streetcar came around the curb and I vividly remember the "squalling." . . . He knew everybody from the stock yards to the end of North Elm Street. You did not have to go to the corner—he stopped right at the front door. We rode the streetcar to the stock yards and got off.
>
> We walked up to the old Isis Theater. . . . No charge because my uncle was the projectionist. The owner knew us—the ticket girl knew us—so we just walked right on in . . . and it was dark,

and we found a seat. . . . This was the first showing of *The Ten Commandments.* It had shown at the other theaters because the Isis always got the movies much later. I remember a guy playing the organ and piano. I remember the bouncing ball; that was before the movie. I remember the advertising they would flash on a picture, and it was just a lot of color. . . . I don't remember much of the movie except this scene with this big round rock rolling down the hill, the stone rolling away from the tomb—from Jesus's tomb. Immediately in my childish mind, I knew that that rock had to go somewhere so I jumped up out of my seat and ran out in the aisle to watch it come through the curtain on the other side—to see where it was going. I remember my mother getting up and coming out to the aisle and taking me by the hand. . . . She said something like, "Winston, that's not real, that's just a movie."

. . . The theater was named for the Greek God Isis. . . . Before that building burned, I used to sit in the alley and talk to my uncle, right behind the Isis. . . . When they built that they did not build a projection room . . . . The screen was on the front part of the building. . . . There was a room built onto the back of the building almost as an afterthought—that was the projection booth outside the building. He had to climb up a ladder to get to the projection booth and turn everything on. I remember many summer afternoons sitting out there on a sandbag talking to him after he got everything going. He had on his undershirt. He had his trousers cut off to the knees because with that big arc light burning in there—it was hot.

There was a little balcony on either side of the Isis. As best as I can tell, that was an afterthought. I think that there were three seats on each row. You had to . . . go up some rickety stairs.

I remember being up there when a film would break and he would put a slide on—let the audience know that we've got a little problem and the movie will continue in just a minute. . . . It would take him a moment to splice [the film] while he was showing advertising. Golly, he had boxes and boxes of glass slides; all those beautiful slides.[63]

Paul Humphries learned to be an operator at the Dixie in Paris. After moving to Dallas, he started working at the Cliff Queen on Jefferson. Then he worked thirteen years at the Lakewood and twelve years climbing into the "chicken roost" at the Palace. His early years were during the era of silent motion pictures where hand-cranked projectors were supposed to run at sixty feet a minute. Because there was no sound to become distorted if the projector did not run at the exact speed, projectionists hand-cranking a film had some flexibility. On occasions "there were no seats in the house and a noisy crowd was waiting to get in," remembered Humphries. "Operators often speeded up the film to 120 feet per minute. It made action on the screen a little more hectic, but who could tell in the days of the Keystone Cops or the Perils of Pauline?"[64]

The Motion Picture Operator's Union

Starting in the second decade of the twentieth century, projectionists could join the operator's union. Scotty Davidson left Tyler in 1921 and went to:

> Dallas to join " . . . Bill Estes, Harvey Hill, Billy Coleman, and Clarence Nix at the Majestic Theater. At the Palace they had Paul Humphries, Jimmy Schaffer, Earl Holt . . . the Palace Theater was right new and it was a honey: million-dollar theater and back then a million dollars was a million dollars.
>
> I walk up to the box office and I ask this lady if I might see the operator. She said, "You will have to talk to the doorman. I'll send you back

to the doorman but it is up to him if he lets you go up to the operator."

I told him my story. I told him that I was trying to get into the movies. He said, "Well, we're not supposed to let you up there. . . ."

I said, "How do I get up there?" This you're not going to believe unless you've been where I've been.

He said, "After you come through the lobby and all, you turn and down yonder is the screen . . . . You go down yonder to that door on the left; left side of the aisles. . . . You have to feel around in the dark for the door and you just open it and step inside." There's a ladder that goes up into the attic of the Palace Theater. . . . Now, can you image this. You walk this gang plank in the attic of the Palace Theater; a million-dollar theater. There's a big gang plank there and a rope that is used like a banister or rail. You walk straight across in that attic over to the projection room . . . . Then there's a door and you open it and go into the projection room.

I'm "dumb-founded." . . . I went in and I told the square-shouldered . . . fellow I'm so-and-so from Tyler, Texas. I'm trying to find out how to become an operator.

He gave me a little talk and he said, "Sonny boy, you haven't got a chance to be an operator in Dallas."

I said, "Why not?"

He said, "Papas, brothers, uncles, nephews, and the like. They've all got it sewn up ahead of you: home guard."

I said to myself, . . . I'm trying to break into show business. I'm getting a deaf ear from people telling me what not to do.

He said, "Where you from?"

I said, "Tyler, Texas."

He said, "Is there a local union there?"

I said, "Yes, there is."

He said, "You go back there and make application for a projector operator and you serve

Figure 68. The Cliff Queen was in the Oak Cliff section of Dallas. Courtesy Texas/Dallas History and Archives Division, Dallas Public Library

your time and whatever is necessary. You take your examination and then you come back here and maybe there might be somebody who dies in the meanwhile."

That's the advice I got from Penguila. He worked at the Palace for seven years and then got fired. He and his wife went out on East Grand and opened a little theater out there east of the Ford plant.[65]

Davidson worked as an apprentice in Tyler, and then, on July 12, 1925, he took the test for entrance into the union:

Apprenticeship—you're supposed to be schooled in optics. You're supposed to be schooled in electrical principle, film maintenance—preparation, any number of things.

I was moved from one theater to another. I started at the old Broadway in Tyler, Texas, in 1921. I went to the old Queen on the south side of the square where the Arcadia is now. You have to serve wherever they send you. I worked in every house in town.

You had an examining board consisting of two members that rode herd over you—even schooled you in things that you needed to know. . . . Always you're subject to the whims of the examining board.

I had seventy-five questions. I made eighty-three on the exam. . . .

In 1929 I went to Amarillo. I was part of the union. Mr. Wilson was the agent. He said, "I'll tell you what. We can use you if you can pass that full exam."

I said, "I passed one examination."

He said, "That was the union examination. The city requires you to pass a local examination. Anyone who works in the projector room in Amarillo, Texas, you've got to pass the qualifying examination."

I said, "I'd like to try it."

He said, "OK."

So I took the examination. It had about seventy-five to one hundred questions. The man who gave me the exam was W. E. Hawkins. . . . I took the examination at the Central Fire Station. . . . I went to see a man after the exam. He asked me about several question on the exam. He said, "How did you answer the question about what would you do in case of a film fire?"

I said, "I was real honest about it . . . I would do the best I could."

. . . He started laughing, "You probably passed . . . I was thinking about a fellow from Oklahoma City. . . . He came to that question about what he would do in case of a film fire . . . the gentleman wrote on his paper, 'Get my hat if I have time and run like hell!' "[66]

Davidson had had a nitrate film fire in a theater in Tyler in January of 1927 after he first became a licensed union operator:

I had my first film fire; it was a bugger—using nitrate film; very explosive. The man I relieved that afternoon, [E. L. "Britt"] Britton, he told me when I came to work . . . , "Scotty, watch that damn comedy; it's all to pieces." An old Our Gang comedy; nitrate film.

The first show that night, the seven o'clock show, I was on this comedy. Almost finished with it and I heard the film strip out—sprocket holes strip out . . . the film stopped. The electric arc set it on fire. The fire goes down on the rewind. All the comedy except a few feet was on this reel. The little fire trap rollers didn't stop it, it jumped right between those rollers; whole reel of film caught fire. That magazine was red hot.

I was trained not to jerk the magazine door open, keep the fire under control. The first thing I did, I jerked the master cord that controlled the port shutters. That master cord runs around to all the machines with the fusible links. You jerk that cord, and it will drop every one of your shutters like that so the audience knows nothing about what's going on. All that stuff in there was like white steam, and I was trying to breathe. First thing I tried to do, I grabbed a pyrene extinguisher and tried to shoot that stuff down between the rollers. It was too far gone for that. . . .

I finally got down on my knees—couldn't breathe. I crawled out to the washroom joining the projector room and I fumbled around for and found an old pair of coveralls . . . and I wrapped them around my face. By that time, they were pounding on the door. In my confusion I had kicked the Yale latch "on" and locked myself in. Mr. Shields . . . kept hollering and kicking on the door . . . "Scotty! Scotty! Scotty!" He hauled off and kicked the door in . . . . I was on my knees and he fell over me. He had a brand new Stetson hat on. I never will forget what he said, "It ruined my damn hat." This was on a Friday night and we were open at two fifteen Monday.[67]

Figure 69. The Hippodrome became the Waco Theater in Waco. Courtesy The Texas Collection, Baylor University, Waco

When Margaret Smith of McGregor was eight years old, she witnessed a projection booth fire at the Hippodrome in Waco:

> 1928—It was in that period between the matinee and evening. We were there with about fifty kids. . . . We had seen it [the movie] back to where we had seen it all and we were looking back to see where it came from. It was under the balcony—the projection booth—and you could see the little dust flakes and things.
>
> While we were looking flames shot out and licked up over the balcony . . . out the port holes. One of the ushers ran over and opened up the whole wall what I'm sure was the stage door. The projectionist tried to put it out, and when

Figure 70. The auditorium at the Hippodrome in Waco. Courtesy The Texas Collection, Baylor University, Waco

Figure 71. The Hippodrome in Waco with a special display for the 1930 movie Feet First *with Harold Lloyd. Courtesy The Texas Collection, Baylor University, Waco*

> they brought him down, he had blood from his elbows to his wrists: both arms. . . .[68]

In a short span of years, the crude, uncomfortable storefront theaters and nickelodeons had been replaced by de luxe theaters and grand movie palaces. Movies of everyday scenes such as fire trucks leaving the station or people washing clothes had been replaced by features with stories, plots, points of view, as exemplified by *Birth of a Nation* in 1915 and the Texas-produced *Wings.* Going to the movies had been upgraded from sitting in a rickety, old, hard chair on a dirty floor in a stuffy room watching a badly scratched, flickering image on a bedsheet, to the unbelievable experience of escaping to another world by the simple act of buying a ticket and entering one of the luxurious, grand movie palaces of the state.

"Talkies"—Motion Pictures Learn to Speak

1928 TO 1941

In 1927 a major advance in technology was destined to change the motion picture industry. "Talkies" revolutionized and in some ways reinvented the movies. Knowledgeable insiders had known for years that sound was imminent. Insightful ones knew it would change the business—forever.

Not long after sound's introduction to movies, the Great Depression "hit." Attendance declined, employees were laid off, and hundreds of theaters closed. Somehow, "talkies" would have to find means to establish themselves during one of the most difficult economic periods in the nation's history. After that short period of decline, attendance reversed its trend and started to increase, or at least hold steady at those theaters that were still open. During these desolate years, "going to the picture show" was one of the few affordable forms of entertainment. Although theaters had earlier used many and varied methods to attract people, it was during the depression that promotion took on a special imperative—to hold the audience it had. The years immediately after "black Tuesday" were a struggle.

The addition of sound would rapidly perpetuate the decline of one of the major reasons for the construction of grand movie palaces: the bill of vaudevillian entertainment performed live on stage. Sound movies introduced musicals, the one type of film not feasible during the silent era. Ironically, movie musicals were the one format that could most closely imitate and replace vaudeville. Whether expected or not, with the introduction of sound motion pictures, the singing and dancing projected on the screen expeditiously replaced the singing and dancing performed live on the stage.

Adding Sound to Picture

On March 27, 1927, Joe S. Phillips was showing the first "Vitaphone" movie in Texas at the Rialto in Fort Worth. A woman who had come to the screening brought her drunken husband with her to sober up. The man awoke from his alcoholic stupor just as George Jessel's image walked onto the screen and started singing. The drunk instantly sobered up, jumped up, and ran out yelling, "Let's get out of here! Them pictures is talking!"

The addition of sound to the projected image was met with widely diverse reactions and some hysteria. W. Hope Tilley, early Texas film producer, stated, "Slapstick comedy is dead. Once sound was added to motion pictures, dialogue took the coconut right out of those sailing pies."[1] Movie producers were standoffish. It was expensive to install needed equipment, and they would, in some cases, have to pay royalties for its use. Many producers had a backlog of completed or partially completed silent movies and were afraid that sound would kill their distribution.

Many actors were worried. They knew they might not record well on movie sound. Many silent stars did in fact lose their popularity and disappear from the public eye because of it. Until certain technical problems were overcome, actors were terribly inhibited by having their on-screen movements restricted to a very small area centered around the microphone. They could not move freely about the set or even turn their heads slightly away from the microphone. Directors and cinematographers were equally hampered by having their cameras confined to immovable, soundproof booths so that microphones would not pick up the sounds of the cameras as they filmed.

Theater owners had mixed opinions. Installing sound equipment would cost thousands of dollars. For those who waited, their reluctance was reinforced when hard times struck with the onset of the depression. It convinced many that they could not now afford this advance in technology. Others who had already spent the money hoped that sound might be a draw and help increase or hold the numbers entering their theaters during what was foreseen as very lean years in movie attendance. Theater managers soon discovered that installing sound was of benefit in the area of staffing. It allowed them to trim the payroll of the piano or organ player and in some theaters the whole orchestra. An Amarillo newspaper advertisement stated, "No longer is the organist or pit orchestra needed with this startling entertainment innovation." Many employees, such as nurses, ushers, musicians, and restroom attendants, lost their jobs because of the depression and sound. Male ushers were replaced by women who worked for lower pay.

Patrons did not agree on synchronized sound movies. ("Synchronized" means that the sound of the movie matches the picture, like the spoken dialogue coming from the speaker in the theater perfectly matches the lip movement of the image on the screen.) Some loved it. Others had little use for this advance in moviemaking and dismissed it as "just a passing fad." In 1929, two years after sound had been introduced, *The Dallas News, The Dallas Journal,* and the Palace Theater took a survey, which found that out of 700 people polled, 505 preferred not to attend all-talking motion pictures.[2]

Nevertheless, sound eventually won over movie patrons. It proved it was not "just a gimmick" like the crude forms of synchronized sound that had been tried for decades. Sound was a legitimate advancement in motion picture technology.

The Beginnings of Sound

Almost from the first moment a moving image was projected, someone tried to synchronize sound with it. In the late 1800s, Thomas Edison attempted to link his cylinder voice recorder to his early motion picture projector. While nickelodeons were increasing in popularity, numerous systems were marketed that claimed to bring sound to the projected image. The Gaumont Company of New York City suggested that owners building nickelodeons should have a system called "'The Chronophone' . . . the only machine which gives perfect synchronism between the voice and the lips which any operator can work. Without perfect synchronism you simply have a moving picture machine and a phonograph. . . . You buy a Chronophone complete, including Chrono Moving Picture Machine, lamp house, rheostat, synchronizing apparatus, talking machine, and connecting cable for $600."[3]

Other sound systems were the Photophone, Edison's Kinetophone, the Cameraphone, the Cinephone, Webb's Electrical Pictures, the Viviphone, Lee De Forest's Phonofilm, the Actophone, the Unaphone, D. W. Griffith's Phonokinema, and Humanuva Talking Pictures.[4] The Humanuva process attempted to produce sound for movies by having people stand behind the screen, read a script, and recite lines that corresponded to what the images were saying on the screen. Theaters in Greenville, where Walworth Harrison attended movies, tried several approaches:

> The films began going in for printed titles scattered through the film explaining the plot. Some exhibitors felt it necessary to stand in the projection booth and read the titles aloud to the audience, speaking through the opening near the projector. No one knew why they thought this necessary, and sometimes the exhibitor's pronunciation of words new to him was more amusing than the picture. Once we recall hearing the title *Charlie Goes into the Cafe* read as *Charlie goes into the calf*. . . .
>
> Something really fancy came along when sound was added back of the screen by a skillful man rubbing sandpaper together to imitate trains and clopping half shells of a coconut on a marble slab to suggest horses' hooves on pavement. Other props were train whistles, a bag of broken crockery which was banged on the floor to illustrate crashes, and many other sounds; but the coconut halves and the sandpaper became the standard in every theatre.
>
> . . . At one time we recall a troupe of actors played the Lyric with a film in which they spoke the dialogue standing behind the screen. They did a surprisingly good job of it too, everything considered, but this was not the answer for, "Why have a picture at all if you can afford actors in the flesh?" . . . Pantomime is much funnier than the spoken word, and the greatest comedies ever made in motion pictures were silent films. Charlie Chaplin never needed to speak to panic an audience, and the same was true of Harold Lloyd. . . .[5]

The Humanuva system was used at a theater in Paris. The movie was accompanied by half a dozen people. They stood behind the screen and spoke words to fit the action on the screen. The consensus in Paris was that it was not very successful, because sometimes they talked too fast or too slow.[6]

In 1907 the Grand in Corpus Christi advertised, "See and hear the marvelous synchroscope moving pictures that TALK and SING." Harold and Yuill Robb, part owners of Robb & Rowley Theater circuit, made an attempt that year at adding sound to motion pictures at their Lyric Nickelodeon in Big Spring. Yuill stood behind the movie screen and created sounds for obviously noisy occurrences like bugles, horses' hoofs, and gunshots, accomplished by slapping two boards together at the appropriate moment. One night he stampeded the customers when he tried to be more realistic by firing a real gun to match the screen action.[7]

J. K. Jorgensen used a system of motion pictures sound in one of his nickelodeons in Galveston:

> Back in about 1912 the movie-going public was flabbergasted by announcements that the quivering images on the screen had been endowed with voices. . . . The only thing wrong with the scheme was that it wouldn't work.
>
> Here's how it was done. A large phonograph was set up on the stage. The records were to be synchronized with the action on the screen. But, here was the rub . . . the phonograph moved ever so much faster than the screen figures. Projectionists tried to "synchronize" voice and action by speeding up the film. The result was that the actors leaped about on the screen with amazing and ludicrous agility . . . and even with the film going at terrific speed, the shot which ended the dastardly career of Dirty Dan was

usually heard about the time he first laid eyes upon Golden Haired Fanny, fifteen minutes before the arrival of the hero and his pistol.[8]

This phonograph/film system was called "Movie-Tone." That was the name eventually used by one of the two processes that brought sound to film in 1927—the actual system adopted as the standard sound-on-film process in the 1930s.

Frederico Trevino operated the Teatro Hidalgo in Corpus Christi in the 1910s. On occasions phonographs were synchronized with the silent motion picture providing music and speech in Spanish.[9] The first attempt at a sound motion picture in New Braunfels was at the Opera House. Frederic Oheim attended as a child:

> The sound came from a phonograph on the stage behind the screen, with a huge horn projecting from it under the lower edge of the screen, which had been raised a few feet for the occasion. A belt from the projector in the booth stretched over the auditorium to drive the phonograph; it was, probably, a fish line of the sort we called trotline then, and ran the entire distance in the cone of light from the projection lens. There were two knots in this loop of driving belt and I was fascinated watching them slowly traveling down to the stage and back to the projector, particularly since there were a couple of "snake doctors" in the auditorium which regularly attacked the knots.
>
> I do not remember anything about the pictures shown except that the talking, singing, pistol shots and whatever else that was phonographed out from under the picture was always out of synchronism, sometimes too soon, and sometimes too late. It was quite sometime before sound pictures became a regular thing in New Braunfels, after Emil Heinen put in one of the first sound on synchronized disk machines. This, too, suffered from faulty synchronization and was soon replaced by sound on film shows.[10]

On April 17, 1913, the Electric Palace in Tyler ran an ad in the local newspaper stating, "We take pleasure in presenting to you the latest novelty in talking motion pictures. They sing and dance; they talk and act. . . ." In Austin, Earl Walker, manager of the Midget, demonstrated "talking motion pictures" on April 24, 1915. The feature was the best scenes and choruses from Gilbert & Sullivan's comic opera, *The Mikado.* "There isn't anything too good for patrons of the Midget Theater," stated Walker. "I know that my friends and the public in general will get what they want in the offering at the Midget. This innovation in the motion picture business has been expensive but I wanted to put Austin at the head of the live amusement city list in Texas and I believe I have succeeded. It's a good show. . . ."[11]

In early 1926 the Liberty in Houston exhibited the first talking picture in that city. The system used a phonograph record and a huge horn. Showings were not well received because of the lack of sound volume and the fact that the synchronization wasn't perfect. Characters would be heard talking after their images had left the screen.[12]

Sound motion pictures actually began on August 6, 1926, when Warner Brothers Studio premiered its Vitaphone sound-on-disc process, showing a number of shorts at the Warner Theater at Fifty-second and Broadway in New York City. On January 21, 1927, Fox Studios introduced its Movietone sound-on-film. This process had its sound on a strip down the edge of the film, while the Vitaphone had its sound on a sixteen-inch record that was played on a turntable in synchronization with the projector. Dallas's first sound movie was shown three weeks later on February 12. *Don Juan* with John Barrymore was featured at the Circle, the first theater in the city equipped for sound. Prices for a night performance were ninety cents on the lower floor and fifty cents in the balcony. After this initial "road show" engagement, E. H.

Figure 72. Will Horwitz's Iris in Houston advertising that it was equipped for showing both "Vitaphone" and "Movietone" sound motion pictures. Courtesy Houston Metropolitan Research Center, Houston Public Library

Figure 73. The Ritz in Houston proclaiming it showed "TALKING—SINGING—PICTURES." Courtesy Houston Metropolitan Research Center, Houston Public Library

Hulsey, manager, offered to move the Vitaphone equipment to a downtown theater. Even though the film had shown good strength at the box office, no other theater showed interest, and the Circle discontinued sound features. The large downtown theaters did not become interested until December. Then, the Majestic ran a short feature using the Movietone process.

The first sound feature shown in Wichita Falls was *King of Kings.* "That was our first movietone," remembered E. T. Pool, projectionist. "I really didn't appreciate that picture until I'd seen it again and again. On the seventh day we showed it, I got more out of it than I did the first day." The first feature in Amarillo was *Ham and Eggs,* described as a doughboy comedy featuring Elsie Janis. Vitaphone equipment had been installed at the Mission weeks before, and the movie played on March 17, 1927. This was the third Vitaphone installation in the state.[13]

The Jazz Singer with Al Jolson opened in New York City on October 6, 1927, and in Waco in March of 1928. The Orpheum, managed by Abe Levy, ran the feature, which had music on records synchronized with the film but no talking except for one song, "Mammy," sung by Jolson. Repeat patrons stated that they came back just to hear that one song. It played several weeks, a record in Waco movies. "*The Jazz Singer*—there was so much hype on that picture," remembered John Rowley, "the next two or three sound pictures, you were going just for the sound." H. F. Dunn, a projectionist in Waco since 1910, discovered that sound added new headaches for him. One night when the film broke, Dunn had to splice in 135 frames of blank film "so Jolson's lips would synchronize with the record when the picture began again."[14]

Real enthusiasm in Dallas for sound did not occur until *The Jazz Singer* ran at the Arcadia early in 1928. That equipment was moved to the Melba and the film started another run on April 7. *The Jazz Singer* stayed for three weeks, a new record in Dallas for a continuous run at popular prices. The previous record for any movie had been two weeks. Movie managers predicted that by July "every first-run Elm Street theater will have equipment for showing either Movietone or Vitaphone synchronized films and sometimes both."[15]

Scurry "Scotty" Davidson of Tyler went to Dallas to see *The Jazz Singer* and determine just what sound movies were:

> Long before it ever came, he [Davidson's former projectionist partner] said, "Son, I want to tell you something. One of these days, what we see on that sheet, they're going to be walking and talking—singing and dancing."
>
> I said, "Oh, what the hell are you talking about?"
>
> He said, "Wait and see." He told me that sound would be coming from that sheet. . . .

My partner and I were working at the Rialto. . . . We heard about sound but didn't pay much attention to it. . . . I went to Dallas to see what it was all about. I saw *The Jazz Singer*—Al Jolson. . . . I also saw a film with Lionel Barrymore. I was so impressed. . . . I came back and I told [E. L. "Britt"] Britton, "Man, . . . I saw the revelation of a lifetime."

He said, "What are you talking about?"

I said, "Britt, I saw Al Jolson in *The Jazz Singer.*"

He said, "You know what, that's a passing fad . . . you see that screen down yonder. It's going to be just like its been all these years. That screen's not going to talk, Scotty."

I said, "That screen is going to talk, you wait and see."

The Jazz Singer came and he [Britt] said, "In five years, there wouldn't be anything such as sound movies. . . . In five years, you can forget about it."

We opened with sound in 1929 at the Arcadia. They had to install everything we never heard of before: sound equipment and the machines. . . . It took them less than a week. They called it "eurpy installation." Owned by Western Electric, "eurpy" was Electrical Research Products.

When we opened with sound, it was on a disc. . . . We opened with *The Lights of New York.* House was packed; [people] standing outside. Britton was one of the operators; I was one of the operators. We had two engineers: one from Shreveport and one from Dallas. We had Grady Patterson from Oklahoma City; we had Bob Foster from Waco. We had seven men in that limited space in that projection room. . . . We were all set. We had an 8 o'clock showing. . . .

We opened, and—*no sound!* Packed house—people standing out in front and—*no sound!* I wish you could see that picture. Engineers running over each other trying to find out what was wrong. They checked this and they checked this. This all checked; this all checked. It was a mad house. Me and the other operator, we were trying to keep out of the way. . . . These engineers, they would take the blueprint and they would run down here and look, and look, and look, and, "That's all right!"

I'd say [it was] about ten minutes. People were starting to raise all sorts of hell downstairs. . . . Anyway, Britton, my partner, he was snickering about the whole thing. He didn't know why we didn't have sound [any more] than anybody else.

"I told you it wouldn't work, I told you. . . ."

There's a red machine and a white machine. This is the white machine . . . left machine. The red machine is the right machine. . . . With sound on record there had to be two men on a shift. I was running the right machine, he was running the left machine. They started on the left machine. We're running along, *no sound! no sound! no sound!* We didn't stop. . . .

We had what we call a fader between the machines; it's a volume control thing. The fader box had a big dial on it. . . . He [Britton] never said a thing to anybody. He pushed by me; I didn't even see it. He reached around here, and he got hold of that fader—the fader is sitting on the dead machine. He . . . brought that fader up, and he almost knocked the ceiling out of the theater. You talk about bedlam. "What did you do? What did you do?" That was a sight to see.

Britt said, "Told you it wouldn't work."

. . . On your leader of your film you've got the word in print "start." On your record over here on your turntable is an arrow pointing "start." You set your stylus right here . . . at your starting groove. . . . Everything is fine until you lose some frames of your film; they strip out. Three or four frames are just a flash on the screen but you still have the same number of grooves on the record. If you don't replace what you lost here, you are going to be out of syn-

Figure 74. Turntables that played and recorded electrical transcriptions at radio station WOAI in San Antonio were earlier used to play sound records for the first Vitaphone sound-on-disc motion pictures in that city. Courtesy Hoxie Mundine

chronization down here. You put in blank film. . . . If someone cut out some frames and did not replace them, you got it back in sync by pure damn luck.

One night, I don't remember the name of the picture, we had a packed house. Everything is fine, and I'm at my machine and the record is playing, and his machine is dead. . . . He's sitting over there doing nothing, and he takes a notion he wants to mop the booth. What's that got to do with my sound, it's got plenty to do with it. He got up and he went out in the washroom. . . . I got the idea that he's crazy as the dickens; he's fixing to pull something. I went out there and looked out the door and I said, "Mac, what are you fixing to do?"

He said, "I'm about to mop this filthy booth."

I said, "What!" He gets a mop and mop bucket under the wash basin; he brings it in the booth. "Mac, for heaven sakes don't." This record playing round and around she goes. He starts mopping . . . and all of a sudden out of sync I went. . . . There's a woman singing and Ted Lewis is playing the clarinet. Now . . . more hell started. The audience started whistling and stomping. I said, "Mac, you really played the dickens now!"

He said, "How far out am I?"

I said, "Ted Lewis is playing and the woman is singing and one is in one place and one in the other."

He said, "Da, da, da, da. Wait just a minute."

I said, "Mac, Mac, Mac, you can't do it."

He said, "Just a minute. You watch that screen and let's see how far I'm ahead or behind the action."

He moved it, and I said, "You're out of sync, still out." He would pick up the stylus and jump a groove. Would you believe, the third time he dropped that stylus in that groove I yelled, "We're in!" You couldn't do that again in a thousand years. . . . That broke him from mopping the booth.[16]

Bill Keeler, a projectionist at the San Antonio Majestic, for forty years remembered early sound. "Yes, but it was a headache!" Keeler was in the projection booth the first night a sound movie was run:

> We had six guys in the projection booth. The sound wasn't on the film—like today—it was on a phonograph disc. You had to synchronize the record with the action on the screen. You cued the film frame with the record and "let 'er rip." Often, the needle would skip a groove and then lips would move but not say anything for a split-second later. Once, we had a big exterior scene and a cow started singing! In cases like that, you just stopped the film and tried to get it and the sound together. It usually didn't work and everybody would raise hell—scream and shout. Just like now. That hasn't changed. . . .
>
> Another time the picture was in the middle of a big dramatic scene when Cab Calloway started singing. It filled the theater. We discovered that by some crazy deal a radio broadcast from Chicago had been tuned in on our sound system and we had to work all night to ground the system to prevent that from happening again.[17]

Charlie Donnell of Canyon started working at the Olympic rewinding films "so I could see the pictures free." By the time sound came to the movies, Donnell was the projectionist. "We waited for the sound to be recorded on the film itself because sound on phonograph discs had just too many synchronization problems. That was obvious from reports we got from the larger cities."[18]

In May of 1929, the Teatro Nacional in San Antonio started showing Spanish-language talking motion pictures on Wednesday and Thursday nights. S. T. Donnell, who owned the LeRoy and the Rio in Lampasas, built his own sound projector and showed the first feature with sound in that area on June 17, 1929. Talkies came to the Majestic in Wills Point on December 9, 1929. The movie, *The Girl from Woolworth's,* staring Alice White, played for two nights.[19]

Some of the other early sound features played in Texas were *Lights of New York,* starring Helene Costello and Cullen Landis; *Abie's Irish Rose,* starring Nancy Carroll, Buddy Rogers, and Jean Hersholt; *Alias Jimmy Valentine,* starring William Haines and Lionel Barrymore; *My Man,* starring Fannie Brice; and *The Broadway Melody,* starring Bessie Love, advertised as a spectacular all-talking, all-singing, all-dancing feature.[20]

Lawrence Birdsong visited a Dallas theater after the introduction of sound and remembers that the organ there was still an important, integral part of the evening's performance:

> They [organists] would play into the news, right up to the place in the news where the action started, and they would stop and turn the [film] sound on. Then, when the [news] sound finished and they had another title, the organist would play again. . . . He would play the introduction to the comedy. The comedy would run for ten minutes and then he would play a chaser for the end of the comedy. . . . They played throughout the titles of the feature pic-

Figure 75. The Teatro Nacional in San Antonio in the 1920s. Courtesy Zintgraff Collection, The Institute of Texan Cultures, San Antonio

ture. That was very well synchronized with what the picture was about. . . . It was quite a production . . . and live organ music surely beat that darn loud speaker, just "tinny" like it was. They would do tricks with the light . . . then everything would quit and the organ would go down. Then we would have this "itsy bitsy" picture screen after all this beautiful stuff. . . . Then the house would exit [after the feature] and he would play when the house lights came up.

. . . Bernie Cohen—he used to syndicate rhyming music to organists for them to use in their solos. He would take the news of the day and put it in a rhyming format; put a tune to it. . . . 1932—They used these for solo organists when they would come up out of the pit. The screen would have the song. . . . They would come up with a slide that would say, "All the ladies, now really yell it out." Then he would work into the song that everybody was supposed to sing . . . they would start singing, "Daisy, Daisy,

Figure 76. Publicity at the Isis in Houston. Courtesy Houston Metropolitan Research Center, Houston Public Library

tell me your answer true." . . . It was a service. He did these all his life.

There were slide companies. You could type them [titles] up on a typewriter, send them in . . . and have them developed . . . and colored by hand with special designs. Then they [theater personnel] would take the area around the screen in the bigger theaters [which] was heavily masked, and they would put a border around this screen and use what they called a border matching to change this four-foot area. . . . As the words change, they would change the colors on the border. Then they would have what was called an effects machine, and the effect machine would finish out all that was past the proscenium arch, and would have a scene of football games or anything that would tie in to the piece of music.

It took three projectors [and three projectionists] to run all this stuff. They were slide projectors with arc lights—glass slides. . . . It was bright; you could read this thing. The organist . . . watched as he played, and when it was time to change the slide, he would press a button and the projectionist would hear . . . and he would change the slide. . . . That was part of every de luxe theater operation. Here [Longview] they mostly played straight songs. It was up to the organist to make his part—ten minutes—interesting.

After talkies came in, organists would go around the country like vaudeville acts. They would stay two and three months in a theater, and then move on to another place. . . . They might get familiar with the organ and build up a following, and some of them never left.[21]

Even after sound features started being shown on a regular basis, silent motion pictures were still in distribution. Because the audience had probably seen a sound movie, some local theaters made an effort to make these silent features seem like sound features. Kenneth Ragsdale of Austin worked at a theater in the early 1930s that tried:

I was born in 1917. My mother and father took me to this church . . . near Jacksonville, Texas. It seems we went on horseback. Either my mother or my father carried me; I was very small. I have no recollection of what the images were, but, I remember it was moving images. . . . I remember that the house was dark and the pictures moved. That was the first projected image that I ever saw.

This was in a small theater in Troup, Texas, in East Texas near Tyler. I had wanted to be a projectionist, and this was one of the chores. At that time they did indeed have sound-on-disc, a very large platter, and there was always a problem with the synchronization there. I recall that sometime someone would take a clip out of the film and if they did not put back the exact amount of leader in the film, you would be off sync. It was kind of embarrassing when the sound would get off; people would scream or whistle.

At the same time we had sound-on-disc, we still ran silent Westerns on Saturday. It was my assignment to run what was called the "non-sync," which consisted of a double turntable in the balcony adjacent to the colored people. This was just outside the projection booth where I could see the screen, of course. For the silent films, they had a series of what you might call "mood records." There was one for "storm at sea," and I remember one called "cyclone." Another was called the "chase." There were several different discs. This was music, I assumed, that was recorded specifically for this purpose. There was a mood for a love scene. This was a standard set.

I just watched the screen and was supposed to pick the proper music for the scene. For the two-reel comedy they specified "fox-trots."

Well, I liked the "fox-trots" better than I liked the "storm at sea." I remember during a "storm at sea," I was playing "Five Foot Two, Eyes of Blue." The manager brought it to my attention that I had picked up the wrong disc. I guess it added some interest to the film with the proper background music.[22]

Ragsdale remembered that in the 1930s in the middle of the depression when theaters were running sound features, grand movie palaces were thrilling audiences, and many theaters were closing, itinerant motion picture businesses were still roaming the countryside of the state:

We lived near Troup, and we always went to my grandmother's on the weekend.... We drove up in front of her home and there was a tent stretched out in front of the house.... It was one of the itinerant movies.... I know that he didn't have any electricity.... I remember seeing the block of carbide. The thing that I remember about this—it was a hand-cranked projector. Instead of having a take-up reel, the film just dropped down in a sack. I guess he rewound it later.... I went to the movie and it was a Western; Denver Dixon was the star. I assume that people paid or gave him produce or something. I guess we got to see the show free. That was in the depth of the depression....[23]

Movies During the Depression

During the difficult times following "black Tuesday," the number of operating movie theaters in the United States dropped from 22,000 to 14,000. Those that survived did so in part with the assistance of gimmicks and special promotions like "bank night," "glass night," "dish night," and "bingo night," and by cutting back on their schedules. The Dixie in Huntsville reduced its operational schedule to two nights a week. Many theaters were open just on weekends. The Majestic in San Antonio, the second-largest theater in the nation and considered one of the most beautiful grand movie palaces in the nation, was devastated by the depression, which started just after it opened. In 1930 it closed for a couple of months.

During this period Texan Howard Hughes, who had recently purchased the Robb & Rowley circuit of theaters, designed an "automatic theatre." Billed as the "World's Most Unique Theatre," Hughes had streamlined the design so it could operate with a staff of two: a cashier and a projectionist. In the lobby, coin-operated machines would sell cigarettes, candy, "soda fountain" drinks, and even photographs.[24]

One of the most depressed areas of entertainment in this period was vaudeville. Many theaters that had been running bills of live acts stopped booking performers and converted to motion pictures. Transporting a movie from town to town was considerably less expensive than transporting a troupe of performers. The Majestic in Dallas abandoned its full vaudeville season in 1932, thereafter running only complete programs of motion pictures.[25]

After the effects of the depression in the theaters started to lessen in the early 1930s, that decade became a period of strong growth, especially for "neighborhood" or "suburban" theaters. The Delman, the first in Houston, was quickly followed by the North Main. By the end of the 1930s, Houston had more than a dozen. The Texas in Dallas was that city's first suburban theater. Howard Hughes was among the 7,000 guests at its opening in April of 1931. Hughes had started constructing the theater but had sold the R & R circuit back to Robb and Rowley before it was finished. In November, 1963, police would apprehend Lee Harvey Oswald at that theater.[26]

John Rowley, son of Ed Rowley, remembered Robb & Rowley Theaters' association with Howard Hughes and the Texas:

There was a fellow that lived in Oak Cliff, owned three or four theaters over there.... They [Robb and Rowley] bought a half interest from C. R. McHenry in the Roseland, the Midway, the Bison . . . they decided to build the Texas Theater.

Early on in 1931, Robb and Rowley were approached by Howard Hughes to sell the theaters to him. He had made the movie *The Outlaw* which was a very successful picture. . . . Like a lot of fellows in the movie . . . making business, especially at that time, they wanted to get theaters of their own, particularly showcases, to show their movies around the country if they could not get another customer to take them. So anyway, he [Hughes] had a little chain of theaters in California and his partner was a fellow named [Harold] Franklin. He sent Mr. Franklin down here and they negotiated a deal to buy Robb and Rowley out, and gave them a contract to operate these theaters for them. . . .

1931 was a terrible part of the depression and the theaters did not come up to Hughes' expectations. Toward the end of 1931, he called Franklin into his office and said, "Franklin, go to Texas and give those damn theaters back to Robb and Rowley, they're going to break us. . . ." There was a down payment of a million dollars that was part of the deal and the balance was going to be paid over a period of time. The million dollars that they paid . . . carried Robb and Rowley through the depression. So they got the theaters back.

The newspapers said that Howard Hughes built this theater [Texas in Dallas]. When he first

Figure 77. The Village in Dallas. Courtesy Paul E. Adair

Figure 78. The Knox in Dallas. Courtesy Paul E. Adair

> bought the company, the plans were to build it and [he] may have broken ground, but he was not there for any publicity pictures, or when it opened; he had backed out. 1939—they sold a half interest to United Artists, Inc., which was a circuit of theaters started by Mary Pickford and Douglas Fairbanks. . . .[27]

The Texas in Dallas was followed by the Knox, Lawn, Maple, Village, Wilshire, Cliff Queen, Casa Linda, Major, and Fair. These first neighborhood theaters, built on the premise of making "going to the movies" easy and pleasurable, introduced new and unique features. Some theaters installed "love seats" so couples could snuggle. The Bowie in Fort Worth had arrangements for the deaf. Special seats had an audio connection for earphones furnished by the theater. Numerous theaters, like the Texan in Hamilton, were constructed with smoking rooms and "cry rooms," sometimes called "monkey rooms," where a baby's fretting would not disturb the other customers. In 1937 the Community Amusement Company of Fort Worth began constructing a neighborhood theater for blacks. It was called "Texas' finest colored theater." The New Liberty was situated at Fabons and Verbena near the swimming pool on Rosedale. At that time black patrons in Fort Worth did not have their own theater. They could only use seats available in the upper balconies of the Majestic, State, New Isis, and Gaiety.[28]

A few grand movie palaces were constructed during the depression. Although the Paramount in Abilene, the Texas in San Angelo, and the Yucca in Midland were not as large as those in Dallas, Houston, or San

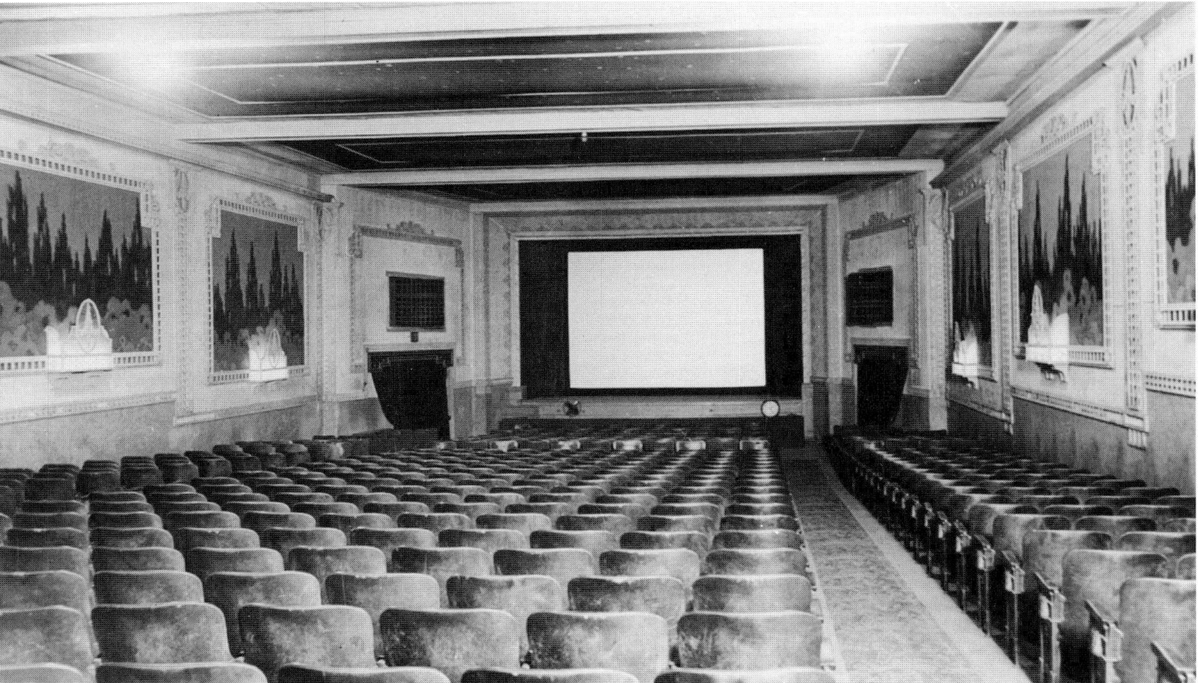

Figures 79 and 80. The Lawn in Dallas. Courtesy Paul E. Adair

Figure 81. The New Liberty, built in 1937, the first theater in Fort Worth catering especially to black patrons, was hailed as "Texas' finest colored theater." Courtesy the family of John Henry Sparks III

Figure 82. The Gayety was one of a few theaters in Fort Worth that made a special balcony available to black patrons. Courtesy the family of John Henry Sparks III

Antonio, they were beautiful and comfortable places to view a movie. The Paramount was part of the Wooten Hotel project owned by Horace O. Wooten and designed by David S. Castle. Opened May 19, 1930, the Paramount was an "atmospheric" theater with slowly drifting, fluffy clouds and twinkling stars in its Spanish-Moorish design. The Texas also had clouds floating across a ceiling amongst hundreds of tiny twinkling stars. The side walls were a Spanish courtyard. The Yucca was owned by oil businessman T. S. Hogan.[29]

Theater Promotion and Ballyhoo

Starting with storefront theaters in the first decade of the century, managers used every promotional idea, device, or gimmick they could think of or create to get patrons into the theater. Early ballyhoo could be a parade, a band, or just loud music in front of the theater. Nickelodeons—due to the large number usually located in a small area along one street—employed many forms of ballyhoo to help assure their survival. De luxe theaters, especially along "theater rows," used elaborately decorated façades, live acts, carnival people, automobiles, or just about anything.

The period of the depression was one of the most difficult times for some theaters to attract an audience. Many unusual promotional ideas originated in and because of that period. "Monday nights they gave away free sets of dishes—depression glass," stated Winston Sparks about the Isis in Fort Worth. "Some people got full sets of dishes. That probably cost Mr.

Figure 83. Movie promotion in Corpus Christi. Courtesy the Dr. Fred'k McGregor Photo Collection of the Corpus Christi Museum

Figure 84. Advertisement for the Ritz in Corpus Christi in July of 1933. Courtesy the Dr. Fred'k McGregor Photo Collection of the Corpus Christi Museum

Figure 85. The "kiddies" matinee on January 16, 1932, in Corpus Christi. Courtesy the Dr. Fred'k McGregor Photo Collection of the Corpus Christi Museum

Figure 86. Advertisement for the Ritz in Corpus Christi in September, 1932. Courtesy the Dr. Fred'k McGregor Photo Collection of the Corpus Christi Museum

Figure 87. The officers of the Mickey Mouse Club at Robb & Rowley's Palace in Corpus Christi on January 30, 1932. Courtesy the Dr. Fred'k McGregor Photo Collection of the Corpus Christi Museum

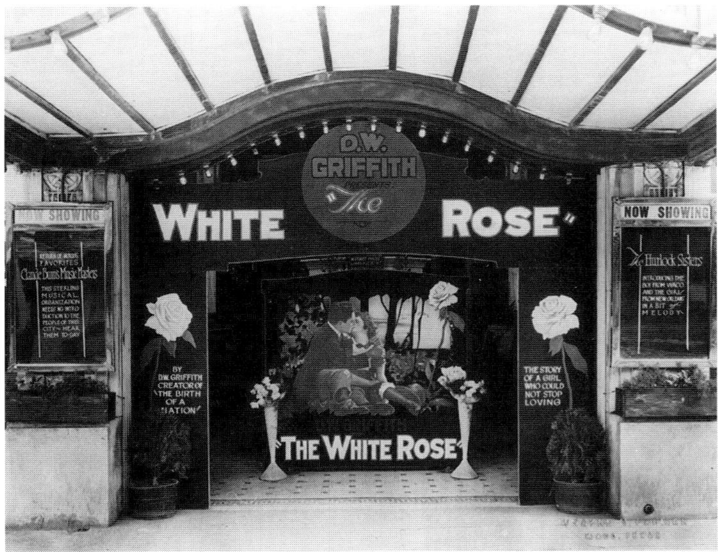

Figure 88. Promotion at the Waco Theater in Waco. Courtesy The Texas Collection, Baylor University, Waco

Tidball two dollars. . . . Sometimes they would give away ten-dollar bills." Wednesday night at the Trinity in Sulphur Springs was "depression glass night." Every patron received a piece of glassware. Homemakers collected cookie jars, salad bowls, plates, cups, and glasses. The Majestic in Dallas took cans of food in lieu of money at the ticket booth. During the period of the depression when banks were closed, "the Majestic took IOU's for up to four admissions per person. The only identification required was a listing in the local phone book."

The Fair Theater in Amarillo had "bank night" and gave away everything from groceries to live pigs to money. It tried to "interest" customers with elaborate fronts and lobby displays. For the movie *Strongheart and the Brawn of the North,* the marquee, box office and lobby were lined with split logs. Animal skins were stretched across them and two muzzle shotguns were hung over the box office window. Wolf dogs from Oklahoma were chained out front. A local hunter and his prize deer were on display. "Few people in Amarillo were willing to miss the picture showing inside."[30]

The front sidewalk of theaters had been one of the most consistently used areas for promotion. Along "theater rows," like Elm Street in Dallas, there were so many theaters competing for the attention of passersby that individual theaters tried to display something special to attract patrons, inform them what was showing, and entice them into that theater. The Majestic, like many major theaters during the depression, had a lobby man who stood out on the sidewalk and greeted passersby walking down Elm Street, encouraging them to come into the theater to see the current feature. Despite all such efforts, many theaters in Texas closed.

Just down the block from the Majestic, according to Lawrence Birdsong, the Palace's front featured elaborate displays:

> How much trouble was it to start a new picture at the Palace in Dallas. They had to get the art director to design what you wanted the front to look like; they had an art director—John Bounds. He designed all the stage setting; he designed all the fronts. . . . He was a painter; he was a carpenter; he was an artist.
>
> They would take all this beaver board down to the warehouse on Jackson Street and get a jigsaw and hand cut every bit of this front—spelling the name of the actor, spelling the name of the feature, put glitter and glue on everything they wanted to highlight. They would do this for a week and then throw it away. That was every theater on Elm Street. . . . I'm surprised that people today know that movie theaters are operating.[31]

Bill Mitchell remembered that Interstate Theaters either constructed special fronts or rented them from a national service:

> The Capitol [Dallas]—we built a special front there with every change of picture. . . . We built it in the basement of the theater. [The]

manager and his staff—had somebody on the staff who had a knack for doing that. . . .

National Screen Service furnished these big sheets; loaned these boards . . . for that picture. They would ship it to you automatically. You would get it whether you needed it or not. . . . That was their business; posters for the front.

In Tyler, Texas, we built many special fronts for the Liberty Theater down there. In Waco, we built many fronts for the Orpheum Theater. Special stuff—you would have to do that locally.[32]

Glen Carr worked at a theater in San Angelo that only used the national service's promotional materials, "The single sheet is a poster that you will find in front of the theater. . . . That's what they call a one-sheet. A two-sheet is a two sectional sheet that is twelve to eighteen inches—larger than a one-sheet to get your attention to the next coming attraction. . . . A twelve-sheet is . . . in front of the theater affixed to the sidewalk for people to walk over as they go in to the theater; it catches their eye as they look down to get their money. . . . I have seen people push other people aside to see what it is. You will find the same type of poster on a [highway] billboard."[33]

William Rast of El Paso started working for Interstate Theaters in Waco. His first job was to help build special displays:

> About 1929 my twin brother and I used to go to the show. He would go to one show and I would go to another, and then we would change places. We liked the Westerns. . . .
>
> Reggie Owens saw me on the street, and he was going to hang a sign at the Strand in Waco. 1931—the Strand was closed at that time. He asked me, "Would you like to help do it? I'll give you some passes." So I went with him and we got up on the marquee and we hung the sign. We got down and he gave me the passes.
>
> I walked with him back to the Waco Theater and we went in the alley where the art department was in the back. This artist, I guess he liked the way I looked. He said, "You want to

Figure 89. Promotion at the Waco Theater in Waco. Courtesy The Texas Collection, Baylor University, Waco

Figure 90. Display at the Waco Theater in Waco. Courtesy The Texas Collection, Baylor University, Waco

come down and help us? You won't get any money out of it, but you'll get some passes to see the show."

I told him, "Yes, I'll do that."

I started working in the art department. I was helping the artist . . . there, and he did all the painting of the signs and the movie story. . . . We would lay it out on the stage and cut beaver board out. . . . They had a machine called the "cut-all" to cut the beaver board. You could do anything you wanted, make circles out of it, cut in a straight line, or whatever. They showed me how to use it, and I started cutting out things for them. So, every week we built a new front for the theater. This artist also painted pictures of movie stars, and he put them on a one-sheet or something. Then we tore them up and started over. We did not throw them away; sometimes we painted over them, depending upon what them were. I built a million fronts while I worked for him.

I used to be a bill poster; I posted the twenty-four sheets. I put them on the front of the theater up on a sign. We put a big piece of cloth up there, Mr. Harrison had it made, and I would get up on top of it and post it. We put paste on it just like you do wallpaper, and hung it up there. . . . I put the twenty-four sheets on the sidewalk so people could see it to help advertise the picture. . . . People who were walking could always see it.

J. P. Harrison, who was city manager in

Waco, had the most unique ideas on promoting motion pictures that you have ever heard. We had a picture called *Manslaughter*. It had to do about a motorcycle cop run over by someone in a car. He [Harrison] parked a car in . . . the lobby and he had a model there . . . laying out on the floor and [it] looked just like a cop. . . . You'd be surprised how real it looked. . . . Mr. Harrison was in the wrong place. He should have been head of advertising for Interstate Theaters instead of being a city manager.

Then we had a sound car. The white truck was originally a funeral home ambulance for children. . . . We had a car [truck] that had two six-sheets on each side of it and you would go around the town, and up and down the streets. This white truck had a sound system in there. Mr. Harrison had a route for you to follow; you took every street. You would play music on it or you would play commercials. You would drive around town and broadcast commercial ads about pictures. You did that every day. Nobody ever objected to us broadcasting. . . .

We contracted with National Screen and we got the advertising from them. It was shipped in to us automatically. They got our bookings, and they shipped it into us about ten days ahead. We used some of their material and some of our material. . . .

We put these [paintings] on the sidewalk if the city allowed us to. . . . We had the city's permission therefore we didn't have to go back and clean them up. We did this often. It's cheaper than having "harrows"; that's the circulars. We would take a piece of twenty-eight by forty-four cardboard and cut it out with the cut-all. Then

Figure 91. Display at the Waco Theater in Waco. Courtesy The Texas Collection, Baylor University, Waco

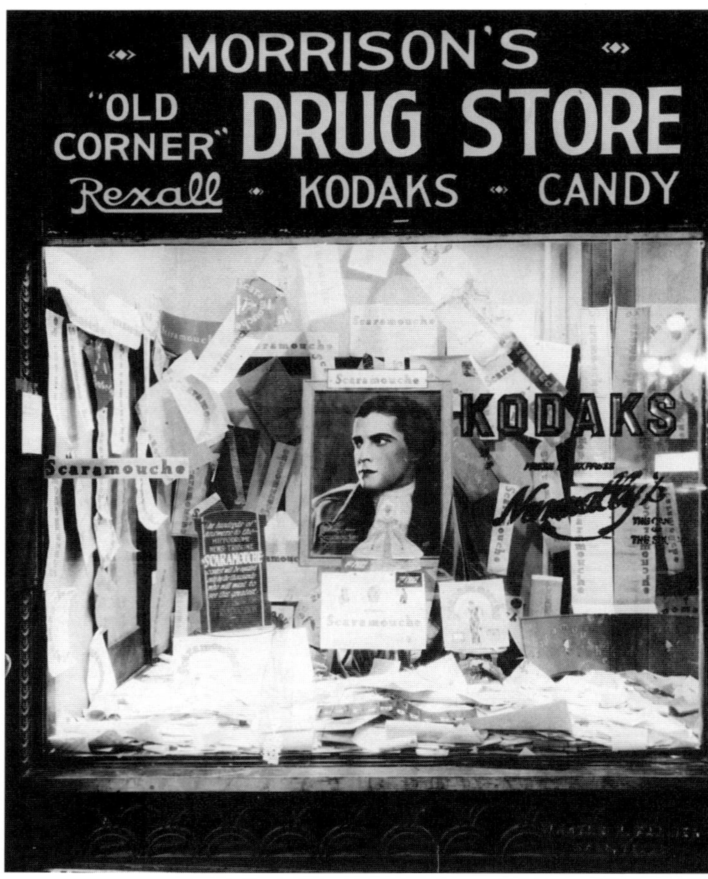

Figure 92. Sidewalk window display in Waco for Ramon Navarro in the 1922 version of Scaramouche *at the drugstore where Dr Pepper was created and first served. Courtesy The Texas Collection, Baylor University, Waco*

Figure 93. Bill Rast drove this movie display, sound truck around downtown Waco in 1935 to publicize the Waco Theater. Courtesy William C. Rast

all you had to do was spray it or use watercolor paint on it . . . and then pressed it on the concrete. . . . It wore off with people walking over it. We didn't do it every week; it was only on special occasions.[34]

James Dear's first job working at a Mineola theater was to spread handbills throughout the city announcing the movie being shown or movies which were coming in the future, "They needed someone to put out their pretty program, circulars, handbills; so I did that. . . . In the cars . . . you put them in the windshield wipers, but a lot of the cars in those days were open so you just put them in the cars. In a business you would just lay them on the counter and they would say, 'Oh boy! We got so-and-so showing.' At homes you put them in the door handles."[35]

Birdsong remembers an unusual device used in Longview to call attention to the current movie, "The theater was down the center of the block. . . . They had a sign on the corner . . . 'Today' in an oval of three and half by five and a half [feet]. . . . They had some stenciled silhouettes of some stars that they would place in this oval. . . . They had a stenciled silhouette of Tom Mix. . . . They would remove the 'Today' and put this stylized photograph of the star in the sign. . . . It would be just the bare outline, but you knew if it had a black hat on it, it was Tom Mix. The title of the feature was under that."[36]

Corpus Christi theaters used various transportation vehicles for promotion. The Ritz had trucks and/or trailers behind trucks drive around downtown with large painted sides promoting the current movie. Attractive girls rode bicycles painted with movie information along the sea wall. M. W. "Pic" (short for "Picture Show") Larmour used many different promotional devices at the National in Graham. "He even made his own wooden signs to promote the films," stated Pam Scott, owner in 1998. "He had a small print shop upstairs to print *The National News,* a hand bill that advertised new features. He sponsored giveaways and bingo every Friday and made it a real event to come to the National."[37] Many theaters, like the Majestic in Waco and Wills Point, used decorated automobiles. In Weatherford a "sandwich" man walked around downtown on stilts. In Dallas decorated elephants paraded through the downtown business sector.

Sulphur Springs theaters had horse and automobile parades. As a teenager, Wilber Myres helped publicize a theater there:

> I worked for the newspaper at the time and I delivered all the theater notices at the time, and all the funeral notices. . . . They had a little red wagon that had a sign printed on the side of it showing what was at the Mission Theater. . . . I pulled that thing around the square all day Saturday in order to go to the theater free all week long. Old man John Lilly was the owner. He had Steve the sign painter. . . . Each week he would tear that off and put a new one on. The man from the theater did not want to be out any money to run the ads in the newspaper so he told Mr. Bagwell, "You run our ads in the newspaper and all your employees can come in free."[38]

Around Sulphur Springs, what was showing spread by word of mouth. Myres's father was a Watkins salesman. He would leave town on Monday morning and return Friday. He spent the night in the country with his customers. Many asked, "What's on at the air dome this weekend? . . . It must have been the only one at that time," recalled Myres, "because it was the only one they asked him about."[39]

Wally Akin, nicknamed "Mr. Showman" or "Peanuts," became famous for his promotions after he was transferred to Abilene during the depression. He staged dances, various competitions, and anything to promote the Paramount. He held Saturday morning movie clubs for kids where admission was only a milk-bottle cap. He started cow-milking contests. Eight cows from a local dairy were lined up across the stage, and the contest was on. "It was a riot," remembered

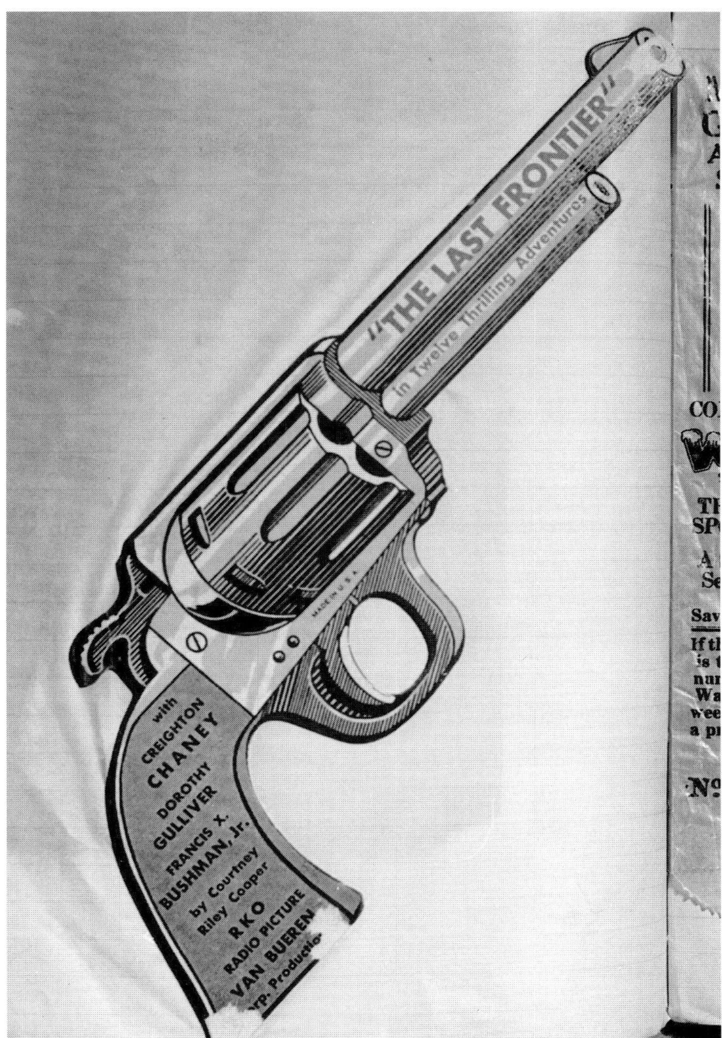

Figure 94. A handout given to kids promoting a chaptered movie coming to the Waco Theater in Waco. Courtesy William C. Rast

Akin. "Word had gotten out what we were going to do, and we packed the theater." On Saturday evenings a tuxedo-clad Akin was out front greeting patrons. "I can show you where the end of the sidewalk is two inches lower than the rest," remembered Akin. "[That's] where I [walked back and forth and] tried to talk a few people in."[40]

One of the best-known theater owners and promoters in Texas was Will Horwitz of Houston. He had a reputation for doing anything to keep prices down and increase attendance, especially during the depression. When Horwitz first came to Houston about 1910, he had $13 "to his name." He borrowed $150 and bought the Travis, an old burlesque house. He wanted a new marquee and name for a new image, but money was "tight," and he was forced to "make due." As a solution, he removed the top of the "T" in the old marquee's name "Travis," and made it into an "I." Then he removed the "a" and "v" and condensed the remaining letters to spell "Iris," his theater's new name. Later Horwitz built the Ritz and Uptown, which was later renamed Ravioli. He claimed the Texan was the first air-conditioned theater in Texas.

The Iris had the distinction of being the first movie theater in Texas to house a radio station. WEAY began broadcasting on June 9, 1922, Gerald R. Chinski was the operator. Just after the station started, Horwitz held free "taking it apart and seeing what makes it go" radio telephony and telegraphy demonstrations on Saturday mornings for school-age boys and girls. They were shown all stages of radio operations and how to construct a crystal receiver for $10 to $15. WEAY's tower was on the *Houston Post's* building with the antenna running across the street to the theater. During the 1930s, Horwitz was owner/operator of XED, "The Voice of Two Republics," one of the Mexican border radio stations. It had studios in Reynosa and its transmitter just south of the Rio Grande, and it broadcast to English-speaking audiences in the United States.[41]

Almost immediately after purchasing his first theater, Horwitz started special promotions. Each summer on the first day after school was dismissed he offered a "vacation party" for his "kids." With a coupon from a local newspaper, each child received a free bus ride, free admission to the movie, and free peanuts. Newspapers mysteriously disappeared from front lawns all over Houston. During the depression, Horwitz gave Christmas parties for the "poor little people." Thousands of youngsters received bags filled with toys, fruits, and candies. Each year the party grew larger until it finally had to be held at the city auditorium. The Iris held "Tin Can Matinees." A can of food got anyone into the movie. The theater distributed the collected items to the needy. Horwitz's theaters had "old clothes" matinees, "grub stake" soup kitchens, and free employment bureaus.

During the bad economic times of the 1930s, Horwitz fought other theaters over admission prices. While many theaters charged as much as fifty cents, Horwitz's continued to charge fifteen cents for adults and five cents for children. This instigated a war with movie producers who threatened to stop booking movies into his theaters if he did not raise his prices. Horwitz dramatized this conflict by placing live hogs in the lobbies of his theaters and staging parades with trucks loaded with hogs. The swine were accompanied by large signs identifying them as "movie hog trust."[42]

Theaters in some cities devised ways to promote themselves and circumvent state blue laws. "Some towns had an ordinance against operating a theater on Sunday," remembered John Rowley, whose father was Ed Rowley of Robb & Rowley Theaters. "My dad . . . worked out a deal with churches to sell "Church Checks" . . . for fifty cents. . . . The theater got thirty-five cents." "Church checks" allowed theaters to be open on the Sabbath.[43]

The marquee was extremely important as a promotional device to Horwitz and every other theater owner. From 1910–20, a theater's marquee was a flat, dark, unattractive display on the front of the building. In McGregor, the Texas wrote titles of movies on a store-type plate glass window at the front of the theater. By the late 1920s and 1930s, marquees in most theaters had become a bold, bright landmark, with moving lights known as "flashers" and "chasers" and big letters that stood out physically and aesthetically from all other signs and displays on that street. Marquees visually proclaimed to anyone in sight, "This is a movie theatre, this is the Tower Theatre; and we are currently showing 'Woman Wanted' and 'The 39 Steps.' We're also giving away $1,100." Marquees were supposed to be seen the entire length of the street and, equally important, as the automobile grew in importance, a marquee had to be clearly legible from a moving, passing car.[44]

Thomas Jefferson "Stout" Jackson and His Teatros Carpas

After the worst of the depression was over, the 1930s were years of considerable growth and expansion for motion pictures in Texas, including minority theaters. One individual who contributed as much as any to the establishment of Spanish-language theaters in Texas, especially in South Texas, was Thomas Jefferson "Stout" Jackson, born in 1889 on a ranch near Perrin. At the age of twelve Jackson saw a strong man in a circus. He was amazed to realize that he could match the feats of this carnival performer. So, at seventeen he joined a circus and traveled over the country achieving the title of "The Strongest Man in the World." Jackson's all-time weight-lifting record was proclaimed the world's record and got him listed in Ripley's "Believe It or Not." At Bob Holmes's gin in Lubbock on March 19, 1924, Jackson "back lifted" a platform loaded with twelve bales of cotton: 6,472 pounds.[45]

Jackson was associated with a group in North Texans who toured small towns and showed some of the first talking motion pictures. "Stout came to Corpus Christi in the winter of 1935," remembered his widow. "He went to Robstown to visit some friends. . . . Spanish-speaking people were not allowed in the local theaters then. It was really a sad thing. Mr. Jackson felt real bad after that, so he decided to do something." With the help of an old friend, Tom Mix, Jackson obtained three large circus tents. He erected one in Robstown, one in Falfurrias, and one in Kingsville.[46]

Jackson purchased portable projection machines and established three "Teatro Carpas," later renamed "Jackson Theaters." Stout got his first movies from Ramiro Cortes who worked for Mr. Jimenez of the Latin American Film Agency, the first distribution office for Mexican and Spanish-language motion pictures in the United States. Cortes worked out of San Antonio. His job was to open places that would show Spanish movies. Jimenez ran the branch office in San Antonio; the main office in El Paso was run by the Calderon brothers. The brothers produced motion pictures and bought films from independent producers in Mexico. These pictures were distributed to California, Arizona, and Texas. Cortes helped Jackson start in the theater business when he met him in Corpus Christi and told him, "Why don't you set your tent over here in Robstown, buy a couple of projectors, and have somebody show movies in them. . . . I'll send you the motion pictures on a percentage basis." Cortes charged twenty-five percent of ticket sales. The first film Cortes sent Jackson was *Chucho el Roto.* On opening night in Robstown, Jackson's box office collected $1,000. Jackson understood why his Teatro Carpas were successful. "The people like to go to a tent. They like to go to the circus. The people . . . the cotton pickers and all those kind of people, they don't like to be in a nice theater. They like to go where they can spit and eat and everything."

"Teatro Carpas was a place where the boys and girls would meet," stated Rudy Mendez, projectionist. "People of all ages would attend, and we always had a full crowd. I remember that people would line up for blocks to get inside the teatro. We used to charge ten cents a person and popcorn sold for five cents a bag."

At times Jackson drove to Mexico City to book movies and "movie stars." Celebrities like Tin Tan, Cantinflas, Dolores Del Rio, Lupe Velez, Gene Autry, Kathryn Grant, and many others performed live at Teatro Carpas. Bullfighter Jose Gonzalez brought his complete show. "I remembered," stated Mrs. Jackson, "that even the news in English was dubbed in Spanish so that people could understand [it]." Later, with additional tents, Jackson added Carrizo Springs, Alice, and other cities so that at one period there were fourteen Teatros Carpas in South Texas. As the audiences increased, the tents got larger and larger. Consequently, in 1946 Jackson built a more spacious "miracle" theater in Kingsville constructed entirely of pipe and canvas. The permanent structure, which still looked like the tent, seated three thousand. This structure still stands today.[47]

Jackson operated the largest circuit of Spanish-language theaters in Texas. (Refer to Appendix 4 for a list of early 1930 theater circuits in Texas.) Most towns and cities in Texas, especially South Texas, had Spanish theaters. Glen Carr recalled a Spanish-language theater in San Angelo:

> This man . . . called me at home. He said, "Glen, can you meet me at the Parkway?"
>
> I said, "Sure I can."
>
> He said, "I have something I want you to see."
>
> We got in his old pickup and we went over in the Spanish part of town. We went in this little place that looked like a hardware store . . . but it was closed. He went in and he said, "This was a theater."
>
> I looked, and my curiosity just opened up. I said, "What do you mean, theater?"
>
> He said, "This was the first Spanish motion picture theater that was in San Angelo, Texas, in 1931."
>
> I could not believe what he showed me. . . . We went to a place called a box office. It was a little square, cubical type thing that the ticket seller sat in. Behind the ticket box was this big flat wall that [had] two little doors, one on each side of the wall. We walked in there and there was forty seats—wooden-backed seats. I looked at the back part of this building; the projection room was there off to one side.
>
> I said, "Felix?"
>
> In the meantime I had turned around and there was a little white area, a white-painted screen. I said, "Why is it this way?"
>
> He said, "It's this way for one reason." The people would come into the theater, buy a ticket, and in the back of the theater, where the restrooms were, was a big square room.
>
> I said, "I still don't get the topic of this visit."
>
> He said, "This was the first Spanish theater, as I said. The room in the back was for chicken fights—cock fights. The people . . . that would come in, they would pay the admission to the movie and would go down the aisles, and they would go back and they would have the cock fights. That is what they would be doing early in the morning and late when the movie wasn't showing; they would have cock fights. The purpose of the reverse screen was that the chickens were put in through the fire escapes in the back, and the projectionist's job was to watch for the sheriff."[48]

Gone With the Wind

One of the most anticipated motion picture events in Texas in the 1930s happened just before the Second World War. "The greatest amount of business I would reckon we had at the Orpheum Theater was when we ran *Gone With the Wind,*" remembered Herschel F. Dunn, Waco projectionist. The four-and-one-half-hour movie consisted of thirteen reels and came with a cue sheet for changeovers. The Orpheum had three shows daily beginning at 9:30 in the morning. "When I got to work," Dunn continued, "the people were plumb around the block." When the show would start, the streets would empty. As the time approached for the next showing, the streets would fill again. Some crowds were so large and excited that their surge to get to the box office broke the lobby doors off the hinges. Dunn remembered one particular older woman who was at the box office every morning for the first show for the entire two-week run.

"I learned more history in *Gone With the Wind* than in school," stated Scotty Davidson of Tyler. "No telling how many times I've run *Gone With the Wind.*" It opened at the Liberty in Tyler on February 13, 1940. Seats were reserved and cost $1.25. At many theaters the management, knowing that the crowds would be extremely large—making it difficult for employees and

Figure 95. Mr. and Mrs. Karl St. John Hoblitzelle in Civil War attire attending the opening of Gone With The Wind *at the Majestic in Dallas. Courtesy Hoblitzelle Foundation*

their families to see a regular showing—had a special screening just for them a day or two before the actual opening.

The lengthy feature exacerbated an existing problem for Interstate management. It was of such length that many people could not stay away from their jobs that long or just could not sit in a theater seat that long. Interstate created a "rain check" for *Gone With The Wind* audiences. A patron could leave the theater anytime during a screening and with the rain check return at a later date and watch the remainder of the movie.[49]

With one technological advancement the "flickers" became "talkies." Vaudeville was dead or dying. Some large theaters continued live stage performances until the Second World War but most dropped their bill of acts during the depression. As the worst of that period ended, the motion picture industry resumed growth. It would soon be called to assist in its nation's struggle against fascism, and television would challenge its dominance of visual mass communication.

War to Wide Screens
1941 TO 1960

As World War II erupted, motion pictures came under new and different influences and restraints. Although it was a good period for people attending movies, staffing a theater with fewer personnel was not easy. The upkeep of the physical theater was difficult because of war-related shortages. Spare parts did not exist, so repairs were a nightmare. Building a new theater—virtually unthinkable.

After cessation of hostilities, the industry resumed growing. Many new theaters were built in the late 1940s and early 1950s. Drive-in theaters, which had barely appeared in Texas before the war, rapidly gained in numbers and popularity. During the postwar period, a competitor emerged that would make the motion picture business fight for its survival. "If people spend two or three hours in front of the television," stated Bill Mitchell of the Interstate Circuit, Inc., of Dallas, "they don't spend that time in the theater."[1]

To help counter this, in the 1950s motion pictures introduced Three-Dimension, Cinerama, stereophonic and surrounding sound, VistaVision, Cinemascope, 70mm, and even Smell-A-Vision. Many were gimmicks and did not help the plight of the industry. Critics deemed this reverting to technical gimmickry as the sign of a desperate industry.

Wide screens and advancement in sound survived the gimmick label and became an integral part of the movies. 3-D and others died a rapid death. For the motion picture business, the postwar period was a time of rapid improvements, great losses, self-imposed "belt tightening," technical innovations, rediscovery and refinement, gut-wrenching self-examination, and embarrassing failures.

Movies and the War

"The theater had its heyday during World War II," stated Ronda Wojtek of Bronte. "Back then, everything was rationed. You couldn't get gas or tires and people had to stay close to home, so they went to the show."[2]

Theater attendance during the war was excellent, especially if you were located near a military base. Audiences were seeking lighter entertainment and escapism: something to help them forget the events of the world. A public weary of war would watch just about any motion picture a theater ran. The industry helped

Figure 96. The Texas in San Angelo, an "atmospheric" theater, outfitted in the 1950s for Cinemascope.
Courtesy Glen and Charlene Carr

to boost morale, keep the public informed, sell war bonds, and spread government propaganda. It was not easy for the movie business to sustain this. Actors had joined the armed services and local theater personnel had "gone off to serve their country."

Boyd Milligan tried to open a theater in Fort Worth during the war. Assisted by his son Mike, he bought the Pix Theater from the person who had converted it from a jewelry store:

> It was during the war and materials were scarce. The first couple of rows [of seats] did not have cushions . . . they were hard-bottom seats. You had to shimmy up a ladder to get in the booth . . . through a hole in the ceiling. They were Powers Projectors, and the bulbs—what they were using were not even carbon arcs . . . they were Mazda. . . . It was like a glorified projector lamp—like in an 8mm projector. . . . Powers was a junkie projector.
>
> The booth had these red bulbs which looked like light bulbs hanging from the ceiling. . . . They were the fire extinguishers because they were using nitrate film. . . . They were all over the ceiling, and they had thermal fuses on them. . . . It was [a] Mom and Pop [operation].
>
> It was during World War II and people were starved for entertainment. You could put virtually anything on the screen and people would come out to see it. After the war, he [Boyd] sold it. The man went broke, and it turned back into a jewelry store. . . .[3]

Figure 97. The armed service theater at Fort Sam Houston in San Antonio. Courtesy The Institute of Texan Cultures, San Antonio

Boyd outfitted the Pix with used equipment purchased in Dallas from Johnny Harden, a used equipment dealer. It was the only equipment available. War shortages affected all aspects of theater operation. The screen at the Haltom was made of Celetex, a kind of ceiling tile. The River Oaks in Fort Worth was built in a Quonset hut. The front was like a regular theater, but the audience sat in the hut. Many theaters built after the war were constructed in Quonset. It was one of the few construction material types available, and it was inexpensive to build and operate and had excellent sound acoustics. Even the production of popcorn machines was limited.

"You had a tax, a war tax," remembered James Dear of Mineola. "At first it was called a 'Defense Tax,' then it became a 'War Tax.' Children were ten cents. From ten cents and above was taxed; under ten cents was not taxed. So we dropped the price to nine cents. That cut out all the book work. . . ."[4]

Bill Mitchell worked for Interstate Circuit, Inc., before, during, and after the war:

They had one hundred and seventy-five theaters in Texas. . . . He ran every number one run theater in Dallas, Houston, San Antonio, Austin, Fort Worth; all these were Hoblitzelle theaters. He operated in small towns too, Denton, Waco, El Paso, cities of that size as well.

. . . We had a tremendous operation in the Rio Grande Valley. They would come across from Mexico into Brownsville or McAllen or Harlingen where we operated. They would come over particularly on weekends and holidays. They would come across the bridge legitimately. We were doing more Mexican business than American business. Our deposit would be more in pesos than in American dollars. These were all American films. They loved pictures—they loved action pictures—Western pictures.

The war broke out, and we had a number of people who were in the military service so we started a little publication that we called *The Interstate* that we sent to all the men in service. We sent them gifts. We kept up with them all over the world; wherever they were. That was my job along with the personnel work I did.

You had a shortage of all types of equipment. We would manufacture or rebuild something we had, or do the best we could with it. Many times a smaller town like a Sulphur Springs or smaller city would . . . have a problem and could not buy something. Many a time we lent them something to keep them in business. . . . We may be a competitor in the town, we may not be. The man was in trouble, we tried to help him. That was Hoblitzelle's policy.

He was very public relations minded both from an employee standpoint and from an operations standpoint. I'll give you an example. We have had places where a person would die who was operating a [competitive] theater. . . . We would operate that theater in that town for that widow until she decided to sell them, dispose of them, or do whatever she wanted to. If she wanted to continue to operate those theaters, that's fine. If she decided she wanted to sell them, she would put a price on them and we would either buy them or not buy them. Arlington, Texas, was an example. We operated them for her [a widow] for many months. . . . We booked them and sent her the money at the end of the month—whatever the profits.

We had practically all women running our theaters during the war—no, not projectionist. In many towns, the city managers were women and the theater managers were women, and they did a good job. When the men came back, we would use them [women] as an assistant.

[During the war] You may not have as many prints as you might like. If we needed twelve [prints] to service twelve first-run theaters, we might not get twelve, we might get six or eight. Then we would have to book a week later on the others. We operated the Capitol, the Telenews, the Majestic, the Palace, the Melba [in Dallas]: we had all the first-run theaters. We operated the Queen. . . .

The Capitol Theater was an action theater, and we built a special front there with every change of picture. It would be Western or it would be detective; it wouldn't be a love story. Mostly action pictures ran at the Majestic—a Western [mysteries] and things like that—dog or animal pictures. Palace would run love stories—things of that sort. Melba—whatever didn't run at the Palace or the Majestic ran at the Melba. Queen—it ran just whatever was available. It was a grind house.

The Telenews didn't have a feature film. It was news; that was all that it was. It just existed during that time [the war] and then it went out. It did what television does today. It had pictures of different things happening, newsreels, special newsreels. All day long, that is all they ran. To see every thing—an hour. . . .

During the war and right after—we couldn't build a theater without government approval—called a Government Consensus Decree. We couldn't buy a theater; we couldn't build one. . . . There were areas that were building up that needed a new theater. We would go out and buy a piece of property and make application for a theater in that area, and the government would turn us down. . . . They said we were a monopoly. Where Foley's [Dallas] is operating, we bought that property and were going to build a theater there; they turned it down. Out where Sears Roebuck is, across the street from them on LBJ, we bought that property and they turned us down. For years we could not build a theater without government approval. I don't recall when it went off. During that time you had competitors coming into the area and building theaters. They didn't have to have government approval because they did not have any theaters in the area. They were scot-free to build whatever they wanted. We were pretty well hobbled.

. . . [After the war] We had to bid for every film. If a film was shown at the Majestic in Dallas, we bid for it. If it was shown in one of the suburban houses, we bid for it. Prior to that time, they sought us because we were the principal operator in that town. They wanted our theaters because we were the best showplace in town.[5]

The war changed the responsibilities of a theater manager, according to Lawrence Weldon of Fort Worth. "Before the war, the Interstate manager would be out in front of the theater meeting the people. He was supposed to be on the floor. They did not manage the theater like today. He was a member of the Kiwanis, or on the fund drive. That was part of his job. He was a public relations man. He had a treasurer, he had an assistant manager, he had a snack bar manager. All he did was sign these reports. After the war, they cut all this out. After the war, the manager did it all."[6]

Figure 98. Interstate's staff in Brownwood. Bill Rast, later city manager of Interstate in El Paso, then manager of the Lyric in Brownwood is standing on the curb at the far right. Next to him is Pat Hudgins, manager of the Bowie, then Oscar Dooley, city manager of Interstate Theaters in Brownwood. Courtesy William C. Rast

Figure 99. The Capitol in Dallas. Courtesy Paul E. Adair

During the war Margaret Smith sold tickets at the Texas in McGregor. She continued a tradition learned from her mother-in-law, who had been the cashier since the theater opened in 1912. Because most people and their children did not have much money, if a kid went to the movie on Friday, she would let him go back to that same movie again on Saturday or Sunday, for free. She would tell kids who had perhaps spent all their money going to the movie earlier and now were broke, "It won't cost any more to run it with you in there—go on in and sit down." Smith remembered a crippled boy who came to the Texas. When he got to the box office and put his money down on the counter, Smith refused to accept it. That was also a policy she learned from her mother-in-law. "It made that kid feel like the richest kid in the world."[7]

During the war, on October 23, 1944, Interstate Circuit, Inc., applied for a television construction permit for Channel 8 in Dallas. It was the first television application in Texas. In 1946 when shortages were no longer a factor and theaters could be constructed, Interstate built the Wilshire in Dallas. The grand opening was broadcast by closed-circuit television. Hoblitzelle purchased $30,000 worth of equipment and presented the first demonstration of all-electronic television in Texas, and possibly the South.[8] Bill Mitchell attended the opening and demonstration:

> We had a demonstration at our Wilshire Theater. We were able to show people coming into the theater on a screen on the inside in the lobby. . . . We had some dealings with KRLD about our joining them. . . . I knew that he [Hoblitzelle] had applied for a television license. . . . We had a management team and I was part of it. . . . We discussed applying for a license; we did.
>
> I remember that we went out to the demonstration to see what it looked like; I had no idea about television. . . . I don't think that he wanted a television station, but the public relations with the newspapers. That's my opinion, it was public relations.[9]

Figures 100 and 101. The Aggie in Arlington. Courtesy Paul E. Adair

Interstate's application proposed two studios in the Republic National Bank Building with offices situated in the Majestic Theater. Interstate never received a permit, and the equipment was sold to KRLD, which started Channel 4 in 1949.[10]

To counter the popularity of television after it started in the Dallas/Fort Worth area in 1948, Hoblitzelle experimented with theater television. He installed large-screen television receivers in viewing lounges in the basement of the Majestic to attract audiences with televised wrestling matches or so they could watch the baseball game before the main feature upstairs began. Some drive-ins offered television lounges adjoining the concession stand.[11]

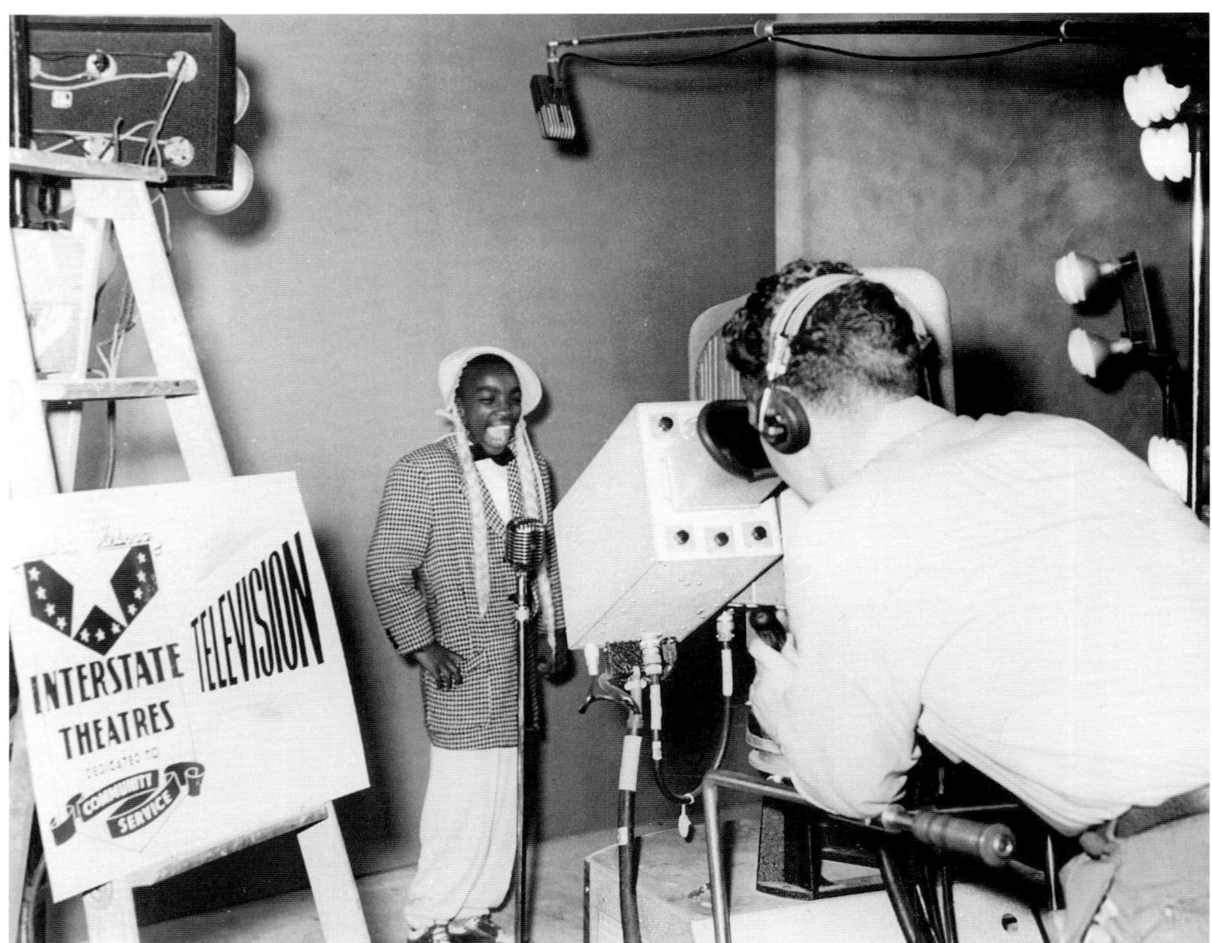

Figure 102. Little Willie, singer and dancer, and Bob Chambers, cameraman, in 1946 presented a closed-circuit demonstration of television at the grand opening of Interstate's Wilshire Theater in Dallas. Courtesy Paul E. Adair

According to Earl McDonald, the organ at the Palace in Dallas was forgotten until after the war:

> The organ was used up to the war and then it laid dormant for a while. Then this kid who lived over here on Peach Street . . . had been an organ nut, and he went down there and hornswoggled himself into looking at the thing. He said, "Can I get this thing going? Will you let me work on it and see if I can resurrect it and get it going?"
>
> Weldon Flanagan—this kid resurrected the thing and got it to playing again. They had stored paints and mops [in the organ works]. . . . There is a blower room in the basement and a relay room with the organ relays in it . . . and glass windows in front so you could see the internal workings. . . . So they had to fix all that stuff . . . but he got it up and going again. Then he went to playing the thing at intermissions; did this for quite a while. This was a big feature because this gave them a second candy break. . . . At the intermission, people would go out and get candy and then the organ would play and then the people would go out again. Gave them two candy breaks. He made a deal . . . that when the theater closed, that he would get the organ.[12]

After the war, giving the audience a "candy break" was important because the concession stand had become one of the main sources of income at theaters. In many it contributed more that fifty percent. Concession stands had originally been a horse-drawn peanut and popcorn wagon stopped in front of nickelodeons selling to people waiting in ticket lines. Then, candies, nuts, and tobacco products were sold by "butchers," people who roamed up and down theater aisles.

In the 1920s, a few large theaters introduced the sale of candy in coin-operated devices attached to the backs of the auditorium seats. In the 1930s, many managers started confection areas in the lobby to offset the cost of cleaning the debris and trash that people were bringing into the theater from the outside. Hoblitzelle resisted selling concession items in Interstate theaters for as long as possible because he thought "it would dirty the theater." The Majestic in Dallas did not have concessions until the depression. The management finally agreed to the idea to keep patrons from constantly running "in and out" of the theater during the movie. It was situated on the fourth-floor balcony and run as an independent operation by an usher. All Interstate Theaters installed full concessions after the war. Some theaters in the 1940s experimented with vending machines that sold frozen foods, sheet music, records, and even toys.[13]

After the war Boyd Milligan built the Seventh Street and Poly Theaters. His most famous patron was Amon G. Carter, publisher of *The Fort Worth Star-Telegram* and owner of WBAP radio and television. When Carter wanted to see a movie, he always saw it at the Poly. Knowing this, if Mrs. Carter wished to locate him, one of the first places she would call was that theater.

"Is Mr. Carter in the show?"

"Yes," replied the cashier, "and I can tell you just exactly where he is sitting." Carter sat in the exact same seat every time he attended.[14]

Bill Mitchell remembered one reason why Interstate's downtown theater operation declined in popularity after the war:

Figure 103. The Uptown in San Antonio. Courtesy Paul E. Adair

> Our business on Saturday was the biggest of the week. Our theaters downtown, like in Dallas as an example, they were big, tremendous matinees. . . . People would come downtown, eat at Dutton's Cafeteria, come to our show, and do their banking. . . . When the banks closed

Figure 104. The concession stand at the Tyler Theater in Tyler. Courtesy William C. Rast

downtown, our business immediately dropped. I'm sure that it affected the merchants the same way. When you think of all the theaters we operated in downtown at one time, and now your downtown theaters are gone.[15]

Figures 105 and 106. The Star in San Antonio. Courtesy Paul E. Adair

Booking Movies

Starting with the earliest movie enterprise, determining which features were available and booking them was one of the major jobs of the owner/manager. In the first decade operators purchased films outright, and then, after showing them a reasonable number of days, traded or sold them to another owner. Later, operators rented movies from exchanges or agencies. Then, exhibitors usually "bought" pictures from lobby posters exhibited at those exchanges. If the posters pleased the owners, they booked the films.[16]

Margaret Smith helped her husband book movies for the Texas in McGregor for decades:

> We went to Dallas to book pictures . . . once a month . . . all our married life. I did not go . . . during the war . . . the film salesmen would come here. . . . They all showed up every time they had new pictures. . . . We pretty well ran almost anything they had. . . .
>
> You had to figure out when you were going to run it. You had a Sunday, Monday, and Tuesday film; a Wednesday and Thursday; and a Friday and Saturday. We ran double features on Friday and Saturday. . . . You ran what the Saturday crowd wanted. They came in from the country everywhere, so we ran Westerns a lot.
>
> Your top shows ran on the Sunday, Monday, and Tuesday. Wednesday and Thursday were off days, so you just ran something—you ran anything. . . . You had the Ritz, so you had that many movies showing in McGregor every week.
>
> First they [prints] came in on Railway Express. . . . The projectionist would put it in the

Figures 107 and 108. The Harling in San Antonio. Courtesy Paul E. Adair

cans and put labels on it and sit it in front of the theater. They would pick that up and leave other films. In later years, when Joe Inix was in Clifton, he and Henry would take turns going to Dallas and picking up films. He would pick-up Henry's films and Henry would pick up his films.[17]

Liberty Film Line delivered motion pictures to theaters throughout Texas. They had special "Liberty" trucks with a "Statue of Liberty" on the side—a look like no other. The trucks were fireproof because they were transporting the highly flammable nitrate film. Other film delivery services included Merchants Fast Motor Lines and a company that worked out of Oklahoma called Mistletoe.[18] Bill Stanford, a native of Waco, drove a film delivery route for Film Forwarding Agency of Dallas. He drove the "Cleburne truck." Stanford's late-night circle had him drop off and pick up movies in Cleburne, Glen Rose, Walnut Springs, Meridian, Clifton, Valley Mills, Crawford, McGregor, Gatesville, Evant, Hamilton, and Hico—then he returned to Dallas.[19]

James Dear booked movies after the Second World War for a theater in Mineola:

We went to Dallas about every Monday. They were all located . . . on Young Street and Park Avenue. Usually we did not look at the movies. Occasionally they would send everyone a letter that they were going to screen a certain movie at the Palace or the Majestic, and you were invited to come up there.

In the thirties they formed the Liberty Freight Line, they had a big old truck—Studebaker truck—they came through all the towns. They came at night, and they had a key to the door. They would leave your film, and the movie you were finished with, they would pick it up—every night except Sunday.

Sunday and Monday were your top playing time. . . . You showed a picture Wednesday and Thursday. Then you showed one Friday night, Saturday afternoon, Saturday night. Then the times changed and you showed a show more nights.

There was a time when you had cheap admission. You could get a Western for $12.50. Then they went to $15 or $25. Then they wanted $50. Later they got greedy and they wanted sixty percent and a $100 guarantee.[20]

The operator of theaters in Canton and Mineola booked one print of a movie and "shuffled" it back and forth between the two towns by airplane so it could be seen at both locations on the same night. Lawrence Weldon booked movies for theaters in Longview:

> You buy a theater—you go into Dallas and you go to all the film exchanges: Universal, Fox, Metro. . . . They will assign a salesman to you, each place. You may have him for years. They will also assign you a booker. The salesman will notify you when a picture is going to become available. So you put it in your book. . . . You could see the salesman once a week and on the phone a lot.
>
> You arrive at the terms. . . . He'd say, "It will be 25 percent. If you want a second feature—$15." I bought them for years for 15 bucks and even 12.50 for a week, and 2.50 for a cartoon for a week. If it were a big John Wayne it might be $35 but that would be tops. The second feature was always a set fee. . . .
>
> You already have the available date down in your book. When that date comes up you call your booker or your booker may call you. He'd say, "Well, you want to book that in? Yeah, Yeah, still available at that date." So you book it in and you write the terms of it in the book by it. They send you a confirmation. You always wanted that confirmation.
>
> Sometimes with small companies, not big companies, they would try to push a picture that they could not get anybody to take—or very few.

Figure 109. The Arcadia in Ranger. Courtesy Paul E. Adair

They would sell it to you on a "TL" basis: Tell Later. For a show like *Earthquake;* they book it at ninety/ten. You have already determined what your overhead is. The ninety/ten means that they want ninety percent after you have made ten percent over your overhead. . . .

The Majestic, with Hoblitzelle, they were in Hollywood and they made their deals there, and they made good deals. So the Majestic would, say, pay thirty-five percent for *The Ten Commandments* for first run for a week. . . . You can book it for a week with hold time behind. That hold time gives you another week or two. Back then, they were striking so many prints, holding a film over was not a problem. You notified them you intended to hold over, and they did not expect this print to come back to Dallas.

At that time, the minute a print was finished [at a theater], it went back to Dallas, and it was fully inspected. Now, it is about every eighth or tenth run—which is terrible.[21]

Bill Mitchell helped make special booking arrangements for Interstate Theaters after the war:

We made many trips out to the West Coast to see a picture maybe before it had the music put to it, or it had the finishing touches. I remember seeing *Around the World in Eighty Days* before they wrote the music to it. You just don't have any idea what a difference it made when they put the music to it. They probably had a hundred people there; we were not the only people there. They would have special screenings and invited people out to see them. *Around the World,* you might pay fifty or sixty percent and have a guarantee . . . maybe $5,000 or $10,000; maybe $25,000 for a really big picture.[22]

Large theater circuits like Interstate that ran all the "A" rated, first-run movies benefited from the "rule of clearance." That guaranteed a certain cushion between the time a theater showed a film and the date that that movie would be made available to the next level of theater in the same city. After its initial showing, the "rule of clearance" could keep a movie out of a city for thirty to sixty days.

John Rowley booked movies for Robb & Rowley Theaters, the movie circuit co-founded by his father:

Technically we were film buyers. In a setup like that, we usually had one film buyer who was the person who buys the films from a particular film company to run in fifty or how many theaters we had. . . . We might book 150 prints. He set, by agreement with the film company, the film rental terms that we were to pay. Then there were four or five film bookers who booked the films into the theaters they were responsible for. . . .

There . . . was a film company . . . called Central Shipping here in Dallas. Most of the film companies stored their films there. . . . They would send them in there a week or two weeks before release, and their office would tell them to send these out to such and such a theater. There was Morgan Film Truck Lines; there were two or three of them. These film truck lines would take . . . them to the territory that they covered around the state. They [Central] had a contract to inspect them [prints] every run or every other run depending upon how important the film was. . . . They would run it first run, and it would go back to Central Shipping. They would inspect it and then it would go out to second run. It would come back and be inspected and then go out to the country runs.

Mistletoe might take it from one theater to another and it might be in a hell of a shape—all scratched up. Consequently, we all got in the habit of having the manager or operator inspect the film the minute it got to the theater. If it was a bad print, an emergency call came in and we

PALACE
WHERE THE BIG
PICTURES RETURN
Complete
CHANGE OF
PROGRAM
Every
TUESDAY
& FRIDAY
FLYNN
SMITH
San Antonio

RITZ
RITZ
NOW PLAYING
THE DALTONS
RIDE AGAIN
NO
PARKING
STATE LAW

Figure 110. The Palace in San Antonio. Courtesy Paul E. Adair

> tried to get another print . . . plus you did not want the blame of tearing up the print. . . .[23]

Theater "Checkers"

When a theater was showing a particular motion picture, the producing company had the right to check that the theater was reporting a correct admissions count. The individuals who came to see if the theater were being honest were called "checkers." There were "open" and "blind"—sometimes blind checkers were referred to as "closed." Although this was not really necessary for movies booked at a flat rate, sometimes the companies checked anyway. James Dear was always ready for a checker; they could show up anytime:

> There were two kind of checkers. One would come in with a letter from MGM. He came up and he presented the letter. We invited him in. We gave him our starting numbers and about every hour he would say, "Can I have the number now?"
>
> "Sure!" We gave him the ticket number and he put that in his report.
>
> Occasionally we would have what we called a "blind checker." He would come up and buy a ticket and go in. We could just about spot a blind checker. He was from out of town; he might dress different from the way the average person would come and see a movie. Sometimes we would see them come in after the movie started and stand there and count the house. We did have some local area people who were assigned to check our theater. We had one lady who would check us for one company.
>
> "Well, I'm here to check you today."
>
> "Well, come on in, get your numbers."

Figure 111. The Ritz in Weslaco. Courtesy Paul E. Adair

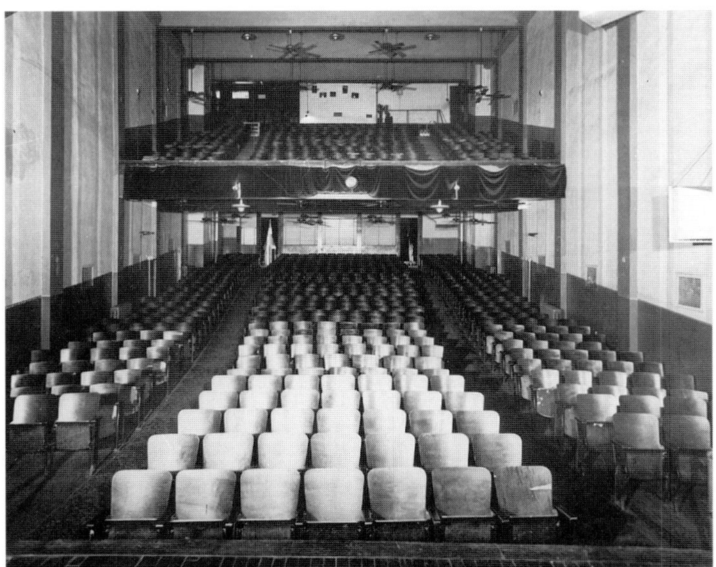

Figures 112 and 113. The Highland in San Antonio. Courtesy Paul E. Adair

> We would sit down and talk. We would do the numbers, and she would fill out a report. She would sign the report, and I would sign the report. We would send it in.
>
> We had a Mr. Hill who taught school—was the principal. He would call me and say, "Dan, I'm supposed to be up there and check, and I'm going to be late. Save the tickets for me."

Figures 114. The Texas in Austin. Courtesy Paul E. Adair

> I said, "OK."
>
> He would come in after he got out of school . . . and get out his report and fill it out and we would visit.[24]

Karl Lybrand, whose family owned and operated a theater in Wills Point since the nickelodeon period, was checked regularly:

> They can have an "open check" or they can have a "closed check." The open check—the man walks in and said, "I'm from Paramount Pictures and I'm going to be here for the movie tonight. I would like to see your count and see how it jibes with mine."
>
> "Enjoy the movie."
>
> "I won't get in your way and I'll see you when I leave."
>
> The "blind check" means that they come in, buy an admission, they fill out their report, they leave, and you never knew. They had a lot of clout. If you are abusing those box office reports, they can refuse to do business with you. If they want to, they can take you to court. When we had tickets, there would be two of them. They would make sure that they bought the very first ticket and then they would buy the very last ticket. Then they would simply do their own count.[25]

Lawrence Weldon of Fort Worth almost got in trouble because of a blind check at a drive-in:

> The branch manager called me one day and said, "Hey, Weldon, we got a problem. You reported Waco, and we figured it and my God, you really put it to us this time."
>
> "What's the matter with you? I'm coming down there."
>
> It was just a little ways to Universal. Walked in, "What's your problem?"

He laid it all out to me there. He had a checker there. "Man you talk about getting to us. We're going to make a settlement or bring suit."

I just let him rave. I said, "How did you figure this anyway?"

"The checker got a count on everything [every person] there." . . . The checker had counted every individual who came in the drive-in. . . . It was Saturday and that place was packed.

I said, "It's two dollars a car load." It said on the box office report, "Two dollars a car load."[26]

Motion Picture Operators and Employees

"When I was seven," stated Paul Adair of Dallas, "my father asked me what I wanted to be when I grew up. I told him, 'I want to be one of those guys that sits up in the little room in the theater and runs the projectors,' and here I am."[27] Adair got his first motion picture projector, an Excel, and some 16mm silent cartoons when he was nine years old:

I had always been fascinated by what came from the pinhole in the back of the theater that put out those beautiful radiated light beams. . . . A friend happened to know the operator at the Chapultepec Theater in Mexico City. We went up there, and there were these huge lamps and big red knobs. Later on I recognized they were Ashcraft Lamps. This guy had a big terrace outside. He would go sit out on the terrace and read the newspaper. When the reel end alarm went off, he made his changeover from one reel to the next, rewound, and went back and read the paper or sipped coffee or iced tea.

I was describing how I had gotten this Woody Woodpecker cartoon where he goes to this taxidermist that he's mistaken for a restaurant and

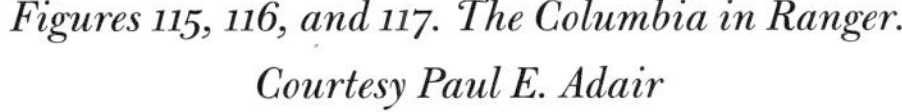

Figures 115, 116, and 117. The Columbia in Ranger. Courtesy Paul E. Adair

there's a big reward for a king-size woodpecker. I looked up there on the screen and there is *Woody Dines Out,* the same cartoon I had. . . . Dad bought it at a Goodyear Store in San Antonio for the whopping sum of $9. I remember sitting there running the same cartoon over and over and over at the Western Courts in San Antonio.

In the basement of a friend's home in Mexico City, we put in the Star Theater—16mm for the American community kids. It was a hobby; it was a fun thing. We shuffled up a few pennies and went downtown and rented *One Million B.C.—Return of the Vampire*—16mm films with beautiful Spanish subtitles. I would order posters from Duncan Posters for the whopping sum of seventeen cents each. . . .[28]

"I'd always been fascinated by that flickering light that came out of a little hole in the wall of Abe Levy's Strand Theater at Waco," stated Bill Stanford, projectionist and native Wacoan. During a 1939 Christmas shopping trip to Goldstein-Migel department store, Stanford noticed that same kind of flickering light from a movie and projector that that store was trying to sell. He bought the Excel 16mm movie projector and a reel of film for $17. He started the Park Street Theater at 1901 Park Street. It was located in the old servant's house behind the home of W. G. Dorris, Stanford's grandfather. Admission was a nickel.[29]

Glen Carr of San Angelo became interested in motion picture theater operations in 1946:

I was wondering what type of machinery made that image; what made those things tick. What type of machinery put that light out that tiny hole. . . . I became involved with two theaters, the Palace in Cisco and the Majestic in Eastland. I went to school with the kids whose parents worked in these theaters or owned them. I would go with one of their daughters or be friends with one of their offspring.

. . . My first job was to deliver circulars—age eleven. That was not good enough. I wanted to go up—up in that little square room above that balcony and see what came out of those little square holes up there . . . I had no idea. My curiosity was so great that I did not take up football, I did not take up baseball; it was my goal to find out what made those images on the screen. I wanted to go up there where that little "clicking" sound was coming from.

A friend's father was a projectionist at a theater; the Alice in Cisco. He took me upstairs, and I got to see the "Big Castle," this big projection room with carbon arc lamps. He put me on a big stool sitting over there by the reel rewind and he told me to "shut up," "behave," and I could watch what he was doing.

He said at that time, "Do not look at this light!"

My curiosity got the best of me and I said, "What are you talking about?" About that time he raised up one of the lids on the lamphouse, and I got a flash of my first carbon arc light. . . .

My uncle was a maintenance technician at R & R Theaters in Dallas. . . . I was promised a trip . . . to the Texas Theater where my uncle worked. I could stay for two weeks and follow him around as he did his job. . . . That was the highlight of my life. I spent a little more than two weeks; I spent two months.

On April Fools Day, 1953, I climbed into the projection room of the Joy Drive-In Theater in Cisco. A gentleman named Joe Gallos—I was his first student that he had ever trained to be a projectionist. My first job was his relief projectionist. I was paid $18 a week and worked seven days a week.[30]

Earl McDonald of Dallas wanted to be a projectionist in a motion picture theater since he was sixteen:

Santa Anna—The old projectionist bailed out and they hired a new one. So I wandered in one day . . . and said I would like to learn how to run this machine. He said, "Help me sweep out and I'll teach you how to run the machines."

I had about two or three lessons and barely knew how to thread up the machine; barely knew how to strike an arc; and came down one night and the place was dark; the lights were not on. The cashier was in there.

"What's going on? Where is Tim?"

She said, "Someone saw Tim getting on a bus this afternoon with his duffel bag, and he's not here. Can you run this thing tonight?"

I said, "Mmm, I don't know. I'll see." I went upstairs and got the lights on, got the thing threaded up and going, and I didn't know how to change the carbons or anything. The little motors that feed the arcs together were cranky, and I didn't know about that. Nobody ever loses an exciter light for sound, but we lost one that night. . . . I did not know where it was. So we were running along there for a while, and there was picture and no sound for a while and sound with no picture for a while.

. . . The thing that yanks [down] the film one frame at a time is called "the intermittent movement." It is a complete package in itself. When you take the machine apart you loosen four screws and you take that whole thing out; that whole assembly comes out. You clean it up carefully on the outside. . . . You don't take it apart . . . it's brain surgery inside there. . . . You never open up an intermittent movement. If something goes wrong, you have a spare and you put on the spare and the bad one goes back to Dallas.[31]

Even into the 1950s, projectionists and theaters had to contend with movies printed on nitrate-based film. "I had my nitrate film fire in the Texas Theater in Seguin," stated Paul Adair. "We got a print in from San Antonio and a splice broke on the second run." Adair's fire was in July, 1958, long after most people believed only safety film was in use and this type of fire hazard was no longer possible:

I was threading the other projector, and the intermittent movement . . . apparently jarred the splice loose in the light beam and heated up and "away she went." Nitrate film as it burns produces oxygen, so you don't put it out; it's just gunpowder. You pull your little rope or ring. You had a little rope that goes up over the windows and that lets the steel fire shutters close the windows off. Throw the switches off and try to do this all in one breath and get out and let it burn itself out.

I went racing downstairs, and we had a very elderly lady named Jane Hubbard. So "Mother Hubbard was in her cupboard" in the box office. I said, "Call the fire department!"

She turned around and as pretty as the sunrise in May and said, "What for?"

The old man who owned the theater got there before the fire department did, and then he started fussing at me. "Why didn't you try to fight it?"

I said, "I did but your extinguishers were last inspected in 1947."[32]

Earl McDonald worked at a theater that had a projection booth built to be as fireproof as fire laws recommended:

The projection booth was lined with sheet metal. Every wall, floor, and ceiling was sheet metal. Over the ports where you could look out and the machines projected out, there were metal shutters that would drop and there were fusible links with a rope that held it open. . . . If you had a fire this fuse would burn through and drop the fire shutters and contain the fire within the fire shelter. The instructions said, "When she goes, get the hell out of there and slam the door hard after you."

I remember a fire when I was a little kid—at the Queen. Luckily it all stayed within the machine. The machines were all built to contain it. Every door had a spring latch on it. A splice could break and peel a chunk of film off and shoot it back through the gate. Usually the aperture plate that was holding it in place would snuff it out. But if it got a bunch of film wadded up in the machine, then it would burn in there then go on up into the supply magazine. There were little things called "fire rollers" . . . gravity-loaded rollers that were in slots . . . and they would press against the film. Their purpose was to stop a fire from getting up into the film magazine. This was near the end of the nitrate stuff. . . .

In the early days it was all wide open. You were cranking raw film, and you could look at it. . . . There was nothing around it; you were looking at the film jumping. You did not have many fires in the later machines, but, in the open machines, that was when they were burning the place down.

I was in the theater one time when a fire started. . . . You could see the film go "crackle." . . . I looked around in the back and here was this guy closing the fire shutter. He closed them himself. He yanked a rope and . . . then kind of stood by the door until everything calmed itself down. The machine contained it.[33]

Lawrence Weldon, who managed theaters in Texas in the 1940s and 1950s, saw many projection booths that were equipped for fire prevention:

Back then, there was still nitrate film. . . . When I was manager at the Meadowbrook Drive-In in Fort Worth, I had an insurance man come in and inspect the theater. . . . He said, "Where are the things that go over the port holes in case you have a fire?"

I said, "We don't have anything over the port holes."

"Well, you're supposed to." He said, "Where is it?"

I said, "We don't have it—a drive-in theater: no way!" . . . I did go by a theater in Iowa Park that had burned because of nitrate film—1962.[34]

A projectionist in Sulphur Springs did not fare well from a projection booth fire. When it started, he tried to get out a window. He was badly burned from the waist down because he got stuck. He had rolled a cigarette and lit it, and started the fire. That was what he told people before he died.[35]

Mistakes by operators were not unusual. "I've put the film in the projector every way you could," stated W. C. Shaver of Wichita Falls. "Upside down, sideways, and once I even forgot it." A projectionist in Dallas mixed up the order of the reels. He accidentally threaded reel five instead of reel four for the Western he was showing. A few minutes later, at the end of reel three, he changed over from reel three to reel five. Realizing his mistake, he quickly threaded reel four, and a few minutes into reel five, changed to reel four. Then when reel four ended, he again changed to reel five. He remembered that, interestingly enough, no one seemed to notice. Bill Stanford, a projectionist in Waco, changed over to a reel for a color romantic feature in the middle of a black and white Western. The audience did notice.

Projectionists also liked little practical jokes. While showing a black and white movie with a color film coming next, one operator sent new, inexperienced employees running to all the other theaters in downtown trying to borrow a Technicolor light bulb because they had just burned out their last color bulb and only had black and white bulbs left. Another projectionist, claiming that the film he was running was too short and was not going to fill the published time, sent new employees around to theaters to borrow their "film stretcher."

Throughout the decades, there have been many

advances in projection booth equipment. Consequently, the only motion picture theater operator in Texas *known* still to be "doing it the old way": striking carbon arcs, watching for "cues" at the end of each twenty-minute reel of film, and performing changeovers from one projector to the other is Lambert Little at the Texan Theater in Hamilton.

Minority Movie Theaters and Film Production

The idea of a special balcony for minorities, or theaters specifically built for minority patrons continued until the 1950s when all theaters were integrated. In 1941 the Harlem, a movie house exclusively for blacks, was constructed at the corner of North Staples and Chipito in Corpus Christi. Bruce Collins was the manager. The Lincoln was "El Paso's first motion picture theater for negroes." F. J. Oviedo was owner. The first movie shown was *The Brown Bomber,* starring Joe Louis. The Texas in San Antonio was originally constructed with three box offices. One was for colored patrons and was located around the side of the theater. After purchasing a ticket, patrons went up six flights of stairs to a small third balcony. Blacks had their own restrooms and concession stand. The Lariat in Fort Worth and the Star-Lite in Dallas were drive-ins built for African-American moviegoers.[36]

Karl Lybrand remembered that the Majestic in Wills Point had a special area for blacks:

> There were two balconies, one for blacks and one for whites, separated by a projection booth. One had an internal exit and one had an external exit. There was an "admission taker" for the blacks. He sat in the balcony at the top of the stairway. Blacks were not allowed to enter the theater proper. They would come to the front of the theater . . . doors and stand there, someone would come out to them, take their order, bring them their popcorn, make the change . . . not inside the theater.[37]

Wilber T. Myers worked at a theater in Sulphur Springs that had a special ticket taker just for the black balcony:

> Old man Eugene Harrison . . . collected the money from the black people that had to go up to the mezzanine to watch the movie. He had Bull Durham sacks in each . . . of his pockets. He had a little vest-like thing that had two extra pockets. He kept the pennies in one pocket and the nickels in another pocket.
>
> It was just an ordeal for a black person to get into the theater. They had to go to the back of the theater . . . and you opened the back door and there were two steps . . . leading up to the mezzanine and that old man. He had these Bull Durham sacks with the strings hanging out and if you needed to make change, he would pull them out. Just an old man sitting in a chair. . . .[38]

The Plaza in El Paso had a "special balcony" when Bill Rast was city manager there for Interstate Theaters: "It had three balconies. It had a lower balcony, then a second balcony, and the colored balcony. The

Figure 118. The El Rey in El Paso was a Spanish-language theater. Courtesy William C. Rast

Figure 119. The Texas in San Antonio. Courtesy Paul E. Adair

colored balcony was way up there. There was one exit and one stairway that went to this colored balcony. We had a separate ticket booth for the blacks. Anybody who went to this colored balcony . . . there was only one way to get to it. . . . When it [the movie] ended, there was no way to get out of that balcony except one stairway."[39]

According to James Dear, the LeRoy in Mineola allowed blacks to watch movies from the balcony:

> When the LeRoy was opened, it had a balcony for blacks. It was called the "colored balcony." During the war, sometimes we would have a midnight show for colored only. They made movies back in those days with colored casts; singing cowboys with white hats.
>
> We got our black movies out of San Antonio. . . . We might have gotten some from Sack Amusement Company . . . Sack "Mark-of-Merit" Pictures [Dallas]. That's the top thing, "Mark-of-Merit" Pictures. We would run them and we would fill the house. . . . It was black on a Saturday midnight about once a month.
>
> . . . After we integrated they asked me, "Why don't you open up that balcony and let us go up there? That's where we grew up and that's where we like it."
>
> I said, "Well, the great white father in Washington said that if you are going to go to the movies, you're going to go down here and sit with the whites. I have to obey the law. I don't control it. I just have to abide by it."
>
> "Well," they said, "we wish we could go back up there."[40]

Midnight showings specifically for black audiences were often referred to as "midnight rambles." These were a common occurrence in the South before theaters were integrated. Lawrence Weldon remembered balconies in theaters for black viewers and theaters just for blacks, and was present when all that changed:

> In those days, if you were going to let blacks into the theater, you designed your box office so you could wait on the whites over here and then turn and wait on the blacks over here. The blacks had another entrance by the box office. Interstate built their places that way. Then they'd go up the stairs to the balcony. They had to go straight to the balcony. They could not step into the foyer and get anything at the concession stand. It was only five or six steps over to the concession stand, but they could not do that; that was restricted. The State in Denison was the only one that let blacks in.
>
> . . . I was working for Interstate in Denison when the order came through to let blacks in [downstairs]. I may be wrong but I think that it was *Strategic Air Command* that I was showing. They had a Color Guard ceremony on the stage from Perrin Air Base and there was one colored in the Color Guard. The manager was all upset. He called Dallas, which was the home office for Interstate, told them, "What am I going to do? There is a black color guard and his family wants to come to the show. Some other blacks who know him want to come to the show. What are we going to do?"
>
> They said, "We'll call you back." They had a big conference about it. They said, "We can't refuse it now," so they let them in. Then Interstate ordered all theaters in Texas to let them in. It was all caused by the theater in Denison.[41]

During the war, the Sack Amusement Enterprises of Dallas and Spencer Williams teamed up to produce motion pictures specifically for black audiences. Williams became a highly respected writer-director-actor of nine motion picture features during the 1940s. His first, *The Blood of Jesus* produced in 1941, was very successful. This was followed by *Brother Martin* in 1942; *Marchin' On* in 1943; *Of One Blood* and *Go Down, Death!* in 1944; *Dirty Gertie from Harlem, U.S.A., The Girl in Room 20,* and *Beale Street Mama* in 1946; and *Juke Joint* in 1947. *Juke Joint* was filmed in Dallas, *The Girl in Room 20* in San Antonio, and *Dirty Gertie* in Fort Worth, Dallas, and San Antonio. Williams produced these for $12,000 to $15,000 each. In the 1950s, Williams became famous as Andy Brown in the television series *Amos 'n' Andy.*[42]

Some of Williams's films were part of thirty motion

Figure 120. A newspaper ad for a "Mid-Nite Ramble," a special late-night showing for black patrons only. Note the feature was 42nd Street, *with Texas star Bebe Daniels. Courtesy William C. Rast*

pictures produced by black producers, directors, and screen writers found stored in a Roosth and Genecov Warehouse in Tyler in 1983. The films were identified and preserved by G. William Jones, Southern Methodist University's film specialist. Jones discovered them among one hundred features when the warehouse manager asked him to look at some items he planned to throw away. "My heart sank when I opened the first can," recalled Jones, "because a yellow-brown cloud of nitrate dust bellowed out at me, signifying that at least some of the films were on nitrate stock and were already in a state of decomposition." Fortunately all were not, and by 1985 sixteen had been restored.[43]

Figure 121. The State in Fort Worth advertising its "Colored Balcony—10 cents" and a "Mid-Nite Ramble," a special movie showing for black patrons only. Courtesy the family of John Henry Sparks III

Drive-In Theaters

One innovation in motion pictures introduced in Texas just before the Second World War was the drive-in theater or "outdoor." The idea of sitting in your automobile and watching a movie was new; the idea of watching a movie in an outdoor setting was not. As early as 1905 motion picture establishments were being established on vacant lots and empty land in Texas cities. Air domes were numerous and popular because they were cheap and easy to build and operate.

Richard Hollingshead of Camden, New Jersey, opened his Automobile Movie Theater, the first "drive-in," on June 6, 1933. Texas had its first the next year. It was situated on the beaches of Galveston. The Drive-In Short Reel Theater had automobiles facing the Gulf on ramps sculptured from sand. The theater ran cartoons, comedies, news reels, and short subjects. This enterprise ended after twenty days when the screen was blown down by a storm.

The first permanent drive-in, or "cow pasture theater" as some people called them, was the Texas in Corpus Christi, which opened in 1939. "The success of the theater was due mainly to the ease and comfort with which patrons can come, see and enjoy the current feature," stated Charles A. "Doc" Richter, man-

Figure 122. The Airline Drive-In in Houston. Courtesy Houston Metropolitan Research Center, Houston Public Library

ager. "The fact that the theatre-goer does not have to leave his automobile is a selling feature in itself." Richter quickly discovered one of the many drawbacks to operating a drive-in. Movie distributors were reluctant to have current features shown at what they considered an experiment. Also, owners had to drive and pick up prints themselves because motion picture transport companies would not deliver films to these remote locations. After the Texas started showing movies, the Texas in Houston opened on June 7, 1940, with *The Under Pup,* starring child actress Gloria Jean. Situated on an eighteen-acre tract on South Main, the theater cost $50,000 and accommodated 475 automobiles.[44]

Figures 123 and 124. The Cactus Drive-In in Pharr.
Courtesy William Rast

The operational characteristics of the drive-in theater were novel to moviegoers. Patrons purchased a ticket from their automobile while an attendant cleaned their windshield. If the movie had already begun, they drove up and down aisles with their headlights off, looking for an empty, tilt-back parking spot. Once parked, they had to find the speaker (after there were individual speakers) and get it situated in a window. Later, they "picked" their way through a parking lot of automobiles to get to the concession stand or restrooms. If they inadvertently passed a car on the wrong side, they might walk into the speaker cable. Returning from the concession stand with their hands full of snacks was even more arduous. After the movie, they joined the traffic jam of cars trying to leave.

"When drive-ins started they had just one speaker up near the screen," remembered Lawrence Weldon of Fort Worth, "then they put more speakers around the edge. Soon RCA introduced individual speakers." Some speakers were on top of the screen; others were under it. Then speakers were tried on poles along the side of the parking lot in addition to the ones on the screen. One of the main problems with this arrangement was that there was one level of volume for all cars no matter how close or how far they were. Cars in front and cars in the rear heard the sound at different times. At some locations, people had to contend with an echo. Some drive-in owners

Figure 125. The Mission Drive-In of San Antonio promoting its feature with a line of milk trucks. Courtesy Zintgraff Collection, The Institute of Texan Cultures, San Antonio

tried speakers on top of the concession stand or projection booth.

W. G. Underwood, owner of a chain of drive-ins, introduced "Sound in the Ground." A speaker was placed in the ground under a metal grate in each automobile parking space. The patron parked on top of the grate. The sound entered the car through the floorboard. The Waco Drive-In, owned by Doyle Garrett and Lone Star Theaters, used Underwood's "Sound in the Ground" system when it opened just after the war. Bill Stanford of Waco thought "it worked very well. I went to the movie there and I could hear fine." This system suffered from other problems and quickly disappeared. Individual car speakers with separate volume controls were introduced by RCA just after the war.[45]

In October, 1947, the state's largest drive-in opened in Fort Worth. The Pike, situated at 7500 East Lancaster, opened with *State Fair.* It featured two concession stands, the largest neon front in the state, and individual speakers for each of the 610 parking spots. The $225,000 Gulf Drive-In on South Port Avenue in Corpus Christi opened in January, 1949. The 750-parking-space capacity theater offered patrons individual speakers with adjustable volume control; a play beach with swings, seesaws, merry-go-rounds, and slides for children; and for mothers with infants, bottle warmers at the snack bar. Other services or attractions offered by various drive-ins at different times included miniature golf courses, swimming pools, miniature train rides, gasoline service stations, hand-held bug killers, in-car heaters, piped-in cool air, television lounges, horse stalls, and permanently parked cars for patrons who did not own an automobile and walked into the theater.[46]

After the war and throughout the 1950s, the number of drive-ins in Texas expanded rapidly. There were the Red Bluff, Trail, Shepherd, Airline, Epsom, Henstead, Irvington, King Center, Shepherd, South Main, Winkler, Sharpstown, Post Oak, and Hi-Nabor in Houston; Red Raider, Trail, and Westerner in Lubbock; Rocket, Atomic, and Jet in San Angelo; Hunt in Greenville; Key City and Park in Abilene; Riverside in Meridian; Circle, Pyramid, and South Park in Beaumont; Wagon Wheel in Amarillo; Airport and 271 in Paris; Lilly's in Commerce; Bel-Aire, Chalk Hill, Osage, Surf, Thunderbird, Boulevard, and Buccaneer in Corpus Christi; Big D, Bruton Road, Buckner Boulevard, Chalk Hill, Denton Road, Garland Road, Hampton Road, Hi-Vue, Kaufman Pike, Linda Kay, Lone Star, Northwest Highway, South Loop, and Twin in Dallas; Chief in Gainesville; Downs in Grand Prairie; Hill in Hillsboro; Mission in San Antonio; Texas in Seguin; S & S in Stamford; Hi-Vue in Sulphur Springs; Midway in Turkey; Sage in Van Horn; Circle, Joy, Lakeaire, Oak Lawn, Trefoil, Westview, and Waco in Waco; Falls in Wichita Falls; Cactus in Pharr; and Belknap, Boulevard, Bowie, Cowtown, Jacksboro, Mansfield, Parkaire, Riverside, Meadowbrook, Southside, Twin, and Westerner in Fort Worth. In the 1950s Texas had the largest number of theaters of any state: 475. The Dallas/Fort Worth area had 43. As of the year 2000, this area does not have one single drive-in.[47]

The Sky-Vue in Lamesa opened in 1948. From the earliest days Sam Kirkland, present owner of one of the eight or nine drive-ins still operating in the state, started attending and working there. Kirkland purchased the theater from the man who built it:

Mr. [Skeet] Noret built this theater. This is the only drive-in he built.... This was his original theater. He lived in Lamesa. He went and looked at one in Lubbock ... and one in Plainview up north. There wasn't many to look at to get any idea of what you wanted to do.... I think that when Skeet built it; he would have been happy if he could have gotten ten years out of it. ... It was a lark.

I had never gone to the outdoor theater; I had only got to go to the indoor theater. My dad was building the building [an indoor theater] for Mr. Noret. My dad was a building contractor, a carpenter. I was helping him; I was holding the string. ... I was a pretty good worker. ... He made the comment that it looked like I worked pretty hard for somebody my size—I was little. He said he had a [drive-in] theater, and I said I'd like to have a job. Ten years old. ... I was hired for the snack bar; I did cokes.

When they first opened it, people would sit on the ground. They didn't have places for cars to park like we have now. You sat outside your car or on your car. You could bring your car, but you didn't have speakers to put in the cars. They just had a big speaker.... Under the tower was the original big speakers. Eventually they came out and put big speakers on the building [snack bar] here.... We got to the point where we had speaker poles.... There were a lot of drawbacks to open speakers. You get an echo sound. The people up here can hear it long before the people can in the back....

The trouble with drive-in speakers is that all the wiring is underground. In the original days, when the theater was wired, all the speakers were wired together. If any one pole in your theater had a short, you shorted out the whole theater. So, if you got a theater with three or four hundred speakers, where do you go to look for the short? It could be in any one of those speakers....

This theater's got stuff that no other theater's got. ... This was the first [drive-in] theater to put in a ramp house ... where people could sit down and watch the movie; had chairs like theater seats. About two hundred people could sit in the ramp house.... Where we are sitting now used to be the colored ramp house. ... They could drive in or walk in. They could sit in their cars....

It had a playground. ... Most of the equipment on the playground was hand built. They put it out here in the early fifties.... We rented a Ferris wheel one time and put that on the playground.... In the early days ... before the show would start ... we had little carts that would go around with a horse pulling.... The kids could get on this little hay wagon, and it would go up and down the ramps, and when you got back to your car you could get off. We had a little train that looked like a regular little train; it was motorized. This little train would go around all the ramps. Kids could get on and off; go all over the theater. ... It was just to entertain people before the show started.

In the old days you would give gum to every kid who came in; you would give balloons to everybody.... At that [entrance] drive—the kids would come up—you didn't pay them—they washed windows.... They would come out on their own, voluntarily, and wash windows. People would tip them, give them what they wanted to. You never came to the movie and didn't get your windshield washed, if you wanted it washed.

We got robbed one time. ... I was twelve years old, so it was in 1958. I was working here in the snack bar. . . . I was the "coke jerk. . . ." The box office up front had a buzzer so he could buzz us if he had a problem. . . . He buzzed . . . and said, "We got robbed . . . and he's going across the field to the flats." He [the robber] took off across that field—it's a little farm field. That's the "flats" on the other side of that field, colored town. The older boy . . . took off after him running and he hollered at me and said, "Someone has robbed the front. Let's go try to catch him." We took off running . . . across that field. . . . It was dark but . . . you could see him running and you could hear him too. . . . We got about half way across the field, and he turned around and fired a shot at us. . . . When he fired a shot I fell in the furrow out there. The older boy, he kept chasing him. . . . They ended up finding him; it took a couple of hours. The older boy dawned that I wasn't with him. He knew that I was running across the field with him so he thought I had got shot. . . . When he came back, I was still laying in the furrows.

The building . . . where the projector shoots out . . . every Saturday we put a piano on top of that building and we had live entertainment at intermission. In the fifties, this is where big entertainment came. This is where Buddy Holly started; right on top of that building next door. . . . Roy Rogers was here at one time—early fifties. . . . My understanding was that he was in Lubbock. . . . They got him to come to Lamesa somehow or another. I think that he sang some for them; it was not a charged performance. . . . All the [live] entertainment was on top of the building in the old days.

At intermission we played games. We played bingo in the old days. This theater had a game . . . called "Quiz-Bank." You would get these little cards when you came in the theater: "Quiz-Bank" cards. It had twelve numbers on it, and it had little holes that you could mash "in" and "out." They would ask you twelve questions at intermission time, "true" or "false." . . . Boy, people really came out on Saturday night to play "Quiz-Bank." They would add $50 a week, and I can remember at one time it got up to $1,250. . . .

There's been 2,000 people in this theater on a Saturday night. It [offering the games] was never because we didn't have any business; we had tons of business. . . .[48]

In the 1950s the Wagon Wheel Drive-In, situated three miles from Spearman, solicited a different kind of patron. Half the Wagon Wheel's parking lot was the usual layout for drive-ins, but half was the leveled end of a runway for the convenience of fly-in moviegoers. "Lots of folks around here used private planes to get about in," stated J. D. Wilbanks, owner. "Why shouldn't they fly over for a movie?" There were seven parking spaces for light aircraft. Pilot patrons watched the movie from their aircraft and listened using a speaker on an extra-long, flexible cable. There were other drive-ins with hitching posts in the parking lot for patrons who rode their horses to the theater. Houston had an experimental drive-in in the 1950s. The Autoscope had two hundred automobiles parked in a circle like a wagon wheel. Each car had its own individual speaker and its own individual rear-projection screen situated ten feet in front of that car. The projection booth, with its "fly's eye lens" was at the center of the circle. The full and complete image of the movie was projected on each individual screen in front of each individual automobile. The drive-in was billed as the "world's first private screen theater."[49]

Lawrence Weldon managed the Meadowbrook Drive-In in Fort Worth. At times he affectionately refers to it as:

The Drive-In from Hell!

It was the meanest drive-in in Texas. I kept three cops at that drive-in. . . . I had two policemen who came in early and another one who came in a little later. The fourth one, who was on Friday and Saturday nights, was a deputy sheriff. On top of my cops, I had three guys around the theater . . . I could use for bouncers.

We kept a set of police mug shots in the office. . . . We had murders, we had shootings—everything, you name it. The main problem was sniffing glue; they would get so wild. It would take three people to subdue one of them. They were going to get me. "I'll find you—I know where you live!" Nearly every night we were sending someone to jail.

Back then you could arrest them for trespassing. We would catch them coming over the fence. When we caught one who was a regular, I would have them bring him to my office and I would say, "OK, empty your pockets." They would have three or four dollars. I would say, "The only way you're going to get out of this is go to the snack bar and spend all of that. I'd make them spend every penny of that." We had [motorcycle] gang wars. . . . They would get in there and run around there and spin out and cut donuts.

Christmas Eve night . . . I had set it up so we would break early and go home. My policeman on duty called me and said, "Mr. Weldon, come up here right quick." I went up to the snack bar, and out on the patio . . . was a Marine in uniform laying there. There was a puddle of blood; he was dead. So I called the police, and I started to ask what happened.

The cashier said, "Well, these two hippie-type guys, long dirty hair, they were the only three in the bar—getting ready to close up."

The hippie looked at the marine and said, "What did you say about my hair?"

The marine said, "I did not say anything." Of course he was clean cut.

"Well, my buddy said that you said something about my hair."

"No, fellow, I did not say anything about your hair."

"Well, I think that you did."

The guys went out the south, and the Marine went out the north door. . . . They had a coke bottle out there, broke it, and they walked around to the patio, and they got him right in the jugular vein. He died right there. . . .[50]

Weldon experienced other crimes at the Meadowbrook. One evening a man attempted to rob the box office with a pair of ice tongs. Another evening a man approached the cashier in the box office and declared he was robbing the place. The quick-thinking cashier told him that he would have to go to the snack bar, that's where they had the money. The man started walking across the parking lot toward it. By the time he arrived, the cashier had security guards waiting for him.

Another night the Meadowbrook was showing the movie *With Six You Get Egg Roll.* The snack bar manager phoned Weldon saying that he had better come because there was a serious problem. When Weldon arrived, he found a tall, stout lady raising hell and yelling at snack bar employees. After discovering the problem, Weldon tried to explain that it was just the title of the motion picture. She kept yelling, "Well, it says that in the newspaper. I have seven children, and I wants my egg roll!"

Like all theaters, the Meadowbrook advertised titles of its movies in newspapers. In parentheses underneath the titles it gave the times the movies were shown. In the 1950s, since there were still more black and white movies than color, Weldon specified "color" or "black and white" below the movie's title. He received numerous phone calls from African-American patrons wanting to know, "Is this 8:55 time that says "color," is that when we can come to the show?"[51]

One of Weldon's biggest problems at the Meadowbrook was people stealing everything from soft drink cups to car speakers:

We tried many things over the years like . . . running this cable along the speaker wire. That made them mad because it took a pretty good pair of cutters. So they would wrap the speaker . . . wire around their bumper and pull off, and jerk the speaker out. They may jerk the post clear out of the ground. We had some who drug the post clear out of the drive-in and we found some up on Riverside. People had tried many things for years. One method was to wire it so if the wire was cut, it would show on a board. . . . I solved this by putting the speaker on a four-inch diameter pipe . . . welding the speaker to the pipe. I never lost a speaker like that.

Once a week you had an inventory. . . . That's an old carryover from Interstate days. You counted every cup—all your merchandise. That cup—we did not care what was in it, but that cup was worth a dollar or dollar and a half. You counted popcorn sacks or tubs. . . . You were allowed a half of a percent shortage. More than that, the manager was in trouble. The trick was to tear a box and turn it in as damaged and give it to a friend. The only thing we did not count were straws.

We had heaters. The Cowtown [Drive-In] had electric heaters, but we had butane heaters. We charged twenty-five cents. It would hang on your window; the butane tank is on the outside. It was a pretty good heater. To comply with the state regulation concerning butane, we had to install a little butane filling station. The manager, in the winter, would spend his morning filling these tanks. We had racks of them hanging there in the snack bar. Some people wanted two. It did not make any money, it was just a draw. They . . . had to leave their driver's license. We had some . . . hoodlums who had two or three driver's licenses. . . .

We would open early in the summertime, let people in the snack bar. . . . You could not get on the screen until nine o'clock. We began with a cartoon. I still started with a cartoon when everyone else was dropping them.

We had a huge marquee all lit up, and the box office was right under it. So many times people would drive up right under the marquee and ask, "What's showing?" They didn't pay any attention, they were just going to the show.

One of the rules in a theater was you had a real attractive cashier. If you drive in or walk in, the first person you had the public see is an attractive woman. This lady is still living, she is a good friend of mine. She was in the box office at the Meadowbrook Drive-In the first time I came here. I parked out there and walked up to the box office . . . and the closer I got to it, I thought, "My god!" "Surely not." She reminded me of a witch. I thought, "Jesus Christ." She fit this *"Theater from Hell";* she fit it. It was not long that I found out that she was just made for the job. I never did change her until I made her a manager. She was good as gold and a heart of gold; would do anything for you. She knew all these patrons that were coming in and were regulars. She knew them; she could shoot the breeze with them.

We had people who were working for us who would break in the theater. . . . There were these guys who committed a series of robbing drive-ins—Sanders Brothers. . . . They knew that my wife and I were at the drive-in working, and they tried to rob our house. Jimmy Sanders, who broke into the drive-in and came back the next day to almost gloat about it, sent me a Christmas card this year.[52]

Another problem was people driving in the exit ramp to avoid paying. The Kaufman Pike in Dallas had a solution to people sneaking into the theater. When the theater opened for the night, the management hid a boy with a supply of rocks in a bush near the exit. If a car tried to enter, the boy would throw a rock and break the car's windshield.[53]

The drive-in theaters in Texas still operating today are the Sky-Vue in Lamesa, Graham in Graham,

S & S in Gatesville, Valley in McAllen, Wes-Mer in Weslaco, Mission in San Antonio, Brazos in Granbury, and Tower in Rule. The S & S is the only drive-in known to still be running movies seven nights a week.

Three-Dimensional Movies

"3-D—it was a flash-in-the-pan," remembered John Rowley of the Robb & Rowley Theaters. Three-Dimensional motion pictures "hit" the industry as quickly and as powerfully as sound had twenty-five years earlier. *Bwana Devil,* starring Barbara Britton and Robert Stack, opened on November 26, 1952, in New York City and Los Angeles and in Fort Worth on January 16, 1953, the first of fifty-six such features. The Hollywood Theater installed a new screen and special projection equipment. In April, 1953, the Worth Theater in Fort Worth premiered *The House of Wax,* starring Vincent Price. Producer Bryan Foy decades earlier had produced the first full-length "talkie," *The Lights of New York,* in the 1920s.[54]

3-D movies had been experimented with almost as early as movies had. C. Grivolas projected a stereoscopic motion picture in 1897, the year moving images first came to Texas. Grivolas's process used two cameras, two projectors, and two films shown through red and blue filters. Audiences had to wear red and blue glasses. Henry H. Fairall introduced a process on September 9, 1922, at the Ambassador Hotel Theater in Los Angeles. *The Power of Love* had red and green colored stereoscopic images printed on opposite sides of double-coated film.

The "Teleview" stereoscopic process was used to

Figure 126. Promotion for the first 3-D motion picture, which opened in January, 1953, at the Melba in Dallas. Courtesy Paul E. Adair

Figure 127. Promotion for the second 3-D motion picture released in Texas. Courtesy William C. Rast

show *M.A.R.S.* at the Solwyn Theater in New York City during Christmas of 1922. This process had a mechanical shutter mounted on the back of each seat that was synchronized with the projector. The shutter covered each eye so the right one only saw the right projected image and the left eye only saw the left. A German company produced *Zum Greifen Nah* (You Can Nearly Touch It), which premiered at Berlin's Palast Theatre on May 27, 1937.[55]

Paul Adair is a 3-D enthusiast. He owns a full-format print of *Bwana Devil* and has 35mm projection equipment in his home to show it in 3-D:

> There was "Audioscopiks" around 1936. . . . MGM made—*Third Dimension Murder,* a Pete Smith special—not very good. They released them all together as a featurette three-dimensional program. I saw it in Havana [Cuba]. . . .
>
> Apparently in 1941—they had not done all the experimenting they could have because if you toe the cameras in . . . you can create depth. That is what the Natural Vision [camera] did. It shot into mirrors, and you could adjust the mirrors. . . . The Natural Vision filmed from a distance of 3 1/2 inches not 2 1/2 inches, which exaggerated depth but does not hurt your vision any. The Natural Vision camera was designed by a guy named Fran Baker. His patent was bought up by the Gunsburgs: Milton and Julian. Julian was an optometrist, and he was able to work all the bugs out of the Natural Vision. *Bwana Devil* was filmed with Natural Vision. They had tried and tried for years to get the studios interested in using it. They said, "It's going to use the two projectors that are already in the theater. All you have to do is synchronize them." The best device was a selsyn motor; self-synchronize as they called them. . . . The selsyn motor had the added advantage of if you had a missing frame, you could adjust them while you were running.
>
> They [3-D features] showed everything, flame throwers, baseballs, anything that they could throw out of the screen at you. There was a fire truck down here, and you looked at it while the ladder came closer and closer and finally out of the screen. The audience howled and laughed. . . .
>
> The Germans and the Italians made 3-D movies that were run by a single film. There were red and green glasses. I remember when we went to see *The House of Wax,* and they did not give us red and green glasses. When that title came on, the audience was just going bananas; full color. . . . My fascination was looking back at the projection room and both projectors were running. Then I would close one eye and one light beam would disappear, and I would switch eyes and the other light beam would disappear.
>
> Then Herb Copeland invited us to a late-night running of *It Came From Outer Space.* That is when I got to go up in the projection booth and see all the rigging, polarizing filters, air blowers to keep the filter cool, projection

lights, and of course, it ran on over-size reels. Your average theater reel was twenty-eight minutes or less, and so they had three reels spliced together. One carbon would run about forty-five minutes before it had to be changed, and one reel would run about forty-five minutes. After forty-five minutes you had an intermission.[56]

Glen Carr of San Angelo worked as a projectionist in a theater when it was converted to 3-D operation:

> This new 3-D—I had seen it in *Box Office.* I had no idea what it was. . . . The first thing they did—the screen came down. . . . The next thing, the machines that I had trained on all these years, they took them and made scrap out of them. They installed these big Simplex projectors; the top of the line Century; RCA sound system. I looked down and saw that these two synchronous motors were tied together with one switch. This shaft that tied all this together was going to this control panel. "Well, what is going on here?"
>
> . . . The gear-lash in your projector head would sometimes throw the synchronization out of motion. You're looking at a three-dimension screen . . . like something is going to run at you like a car. The left side may be coming a little faster at you than the other. If you look right in the center, you can see a dividing line because the two projectors are running at the same time but the images on the screen were about a half inch overlay. The image of one projector would override the other. It had to be exactly the same or you would have a headache. . . .
>
> At the end of the movie they had to shut that down and separate one projector to run your cartoons, preview, [or] short subjects. Then you had to shut down again and put that back in operation. . . . *The Robe* was the first color we got in 3-D. . . . It was a very short-lived film. A bunch of religious people got that pulled. That was the first time that a complete movie was spliced together and put on one reel. The reels were twenty-thousand-foot reels; one great big reel. It was three to three and a half feet in diameter. You could put an hour and a half show on one reel. I lifted them up and put them on myself. The projectors that we had were the new type . . . that would hold the whole movie.
>
> There was a company that made carbons especially for them. We got them out of New Orleans, Louisiana. They were a two-hour carbon. They were extra long and extra big. You could get one hour and fifty minutes out of one set of carbons.[57]

In 1953 Metro-Goldwyn-Mayer used two cities in Texas to determine if audiences preferred 2-D or 3-D. The movie *Kiss Me, Kate* was shown in 3-D in Dallas and "flat" in Houston. The results were to help determine if the studio would concentrate on 3-D or continue with its conventional format movies.[58]

James Dear and the theater he worked at in Mineola resisted the move to 3-D:

> They came out to sell the equipment [for the polarized 3-D] to the exhibitor. You had to run it on two machines. You had to have an electrical interlock so they both started at the same time. If this one had a break, then you had to splice in so many feet of blank film to make it coincide with the other one. Big sale, "You're going to have to put all this equipment in; so many thousands of dollars worth of equipment."
>
> We said, "No, we don't have to."
>
> "Oh, you've got to run one. The public demands it."
>
> "We're in business now, and when that business is gone, you're going to have a lot of junk that will be thrown away because it won't last. We're going to stay with conventional films." It wasn't more than a year that they stopped making those for two machines.[59]

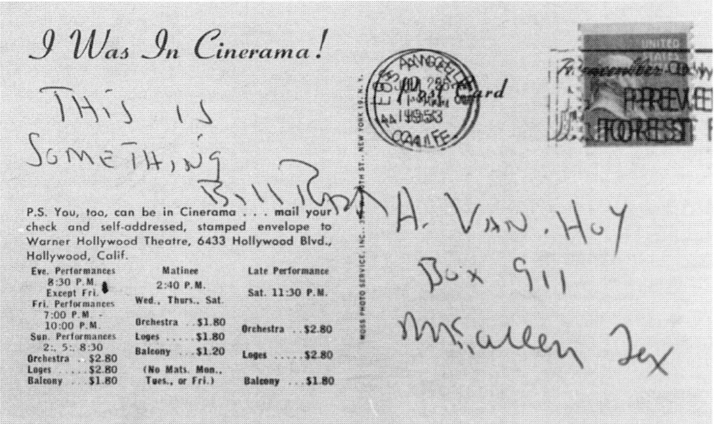

Figure 128 and 129. This postcard from Hollywood, California, sent by Bill Rast, general manager of Interstate in El Paso, promoted This is Cinerama. *The reverse side depicts the opening scene of the movie, a wild ride on a roller coaster. Courtesy William C. Rast*

During the short life of 3-D films (by the end of 1954 sixty feature films had been produced and forty more were in production), customers continually complained of eye strain and fatigue. Others complained that early movies like *Bwana Devil* had little or no plot or story. Too many 3-D features depended upon the over-used gimmick of having objects thrown at, poked at, or stuck at the audience through the imaginary "hole" in the screen. By the time the industry started developing better story lines, the public and the industry had lost interest and one of the "miracles" that was going to save motion pictures from television disappeared as quickly as it had arrived.

Cinerama

Approximately one year after 3-D started making audiences "duck," a second technical advancement, which proponents believed would also save the industry, opened in Dallas. *This Is Cinerama* premiered September 30, 1952, at the Broadway Theater in New York City, and opened July 1, 1954, at the Melba in Dallas. The process, invented by Fred Waller, had high-fidelity, surrounding sound, and a screen that filled the entire front of the auditorium.

The first wide-screen process was demonstrated in 1922 by John D. Elms. "Widescope" recorded and projected two 35mm pictures side by side on a screen that filled the theater. Three early wide-screen processes appeared in 1929: the Spoor-Berggren "Natural Vision," Fox's "Grandeur," and Paramount's "Magnafilm." Metro-Goldwyn-Mayer's "Realife" debuted in 1930.[60]

Like many other technical advancements, *This Is Cinerama* had serious drawbacks. First, the image on that screen was projected by three separate projectors in three separate locations. This caused two fuzzy lines of intersection between adjoining images about one third of the way in from each side. Second, in the process of filming with three cameras and showing it with three projectors, the image could become distorted. A horizontal line running across the screen could bend at the point where the image moved from one projector to the other. It took special equipment to load and run the projectors. A small crane was needed to lift a single reel of film containing half the *Cinerama* feature onto each of the three projectors.[61]

As a projectionist, Paul Adair worked *This is Cinerama*. He remembers that the introduction, which was black and white and on a regular-size screen announced that this movie feature was different:

As Lowell Thomas said in the beginning, "This is not a musical, this is not a drama, this is not a theatrical [production]. What you are about to see could change the whole theory of motion picture story telling. Ladies and gentlemen, *This is Cinerama!*"

They changed from the single screen to all three projectors, "Able," "Baker," and "Charlie," onto the roller coaster ride.... We were in three different projection rooms isolated from each other. *Cinerama* was . . . three projectors running 35mm film. A frame and a half with no sound track on it; so all that area was used. The sound ran separately on a sound deck. You had four selsyn motors going at once.

We would get on the introductory reel and get a call on the intercom, "Check your carbons." This was not, "I've done it." It was a, go to the projector, open the lamphouse, check positive, check negative; do it. Don't say, "Oh, yeah, I've taken care of it." Then, suddenly, halfway through a reel . . . you are low on carbon and are about to run out, and you have to go off screen for a few minutes. So, "Able," "Baker," and "Charlie" would check carbons....

In certain installations of Cinerama, you could see where the picture came together. The blending lines—they had what looked like a jigsaw on the inside gate of the projectors that vibrated up and down. Because of that vibration . . . they called it the "gigolo." This was supposed to fuse the three pictures together.

These were Century projectors. Instead of focus knobs and framing knobs, we ran a rod through the hole of the framing knob and the focus knob. We would sit there and watch the screen and raise or lower this . . . frame. "Baker" had nothing to do. He did not have to frame "up" or "down." "Able" and "Charlie" had to frame "up" and "down" to match "Baker."

There was something the public seldom saw—the emergency reel. If something went wrong, that projector had an introduction to the process; small screen black and white.... It was just a thousand feet. If something went wrong, then they [the film] explained, "The Cinerama camera works this way. Here's the projector here," so you would understand that every once in a while we would have a little technical problem and for ten minutes they would sit there and charm the audience with the explanation of the whole thing while we were upstairs patching up film.... The film was edge marked so you had "A1000," "B1000," "C1000"; so we would very quickly get threaded . . . so we could restart....[62]

This is Cinerama suffered from one of the same criticism that plagued 3-D. The movie was basically a travelogue presenting spectacular and exciting scenes from around the world but had little or no plot. Most importantly, any effort to get *Cinerama* into standard theaters was stymied because the Melba was one of very few theaters in Texas that was physically wide enough to hold the screen. The other theater that showed *Cinerama* was the Capri in El Paso. "Bill Bowen . . . decided to change to *Cinerama,*" remembered Bill Rast of that city. "It was beautiful. I liked it very much, but Interstate didn't have any *Cinerama.* It (Capri) stayed *Cinerama* a long time."[63] This and other problems notwithstanding, *This is Cinerama* was one of top-grossing films of the 1950s even though it ran in only thirteen theaters in the nation. Later Cinerama motion pictures were *Cinerama Holiday, Seven Wonders of the World, Search for Paradise, South Seas Adventure, How the West was Won,* and *The Wonderful World of the Brothers Grimm.*

Other individuals in Texas thought movies on extremely wide screens would be accepted by the public. They attempted to introduce their own wide-screen process called "Thrill-O-Rama." Lawrence Weldon of Fort Worth worked on the only motion picture ever shot using this process:

[Al] Reynolds and several people in Dallas had made a film called *Thrill-O-Rama Adventures.* It was filmed in the Everglades and all over . . . 1955. Reynolds came up with the idea. He used *Bwana Devil* [3-D] cameras to shoot this stuff.

It was as wide as Cinerama on the screen. He had already done it all over and let the cameras go back. The idea was for you to walk up to the booth with just a can of film and a little attachment on the front . . . with the existing equipment, and you've got Cinerama without installing all this Cinerama equipment and three operators—four operators really.

They had spent too much money on it. He had opened in Houston, and they went to Philadelphia. It got bad reviews because of the angle of projection. . . . What had happened with the *Bwana Devil* cameras . . . they did not take into consideration "keystoning" in a theater. [Keystoning occurs when an on-screen image containing parallel vertical lines becomes distorted because the image is projected at an angle to that screen rather than perpendicular to it. The parallel vertical lines will appear to slant.] If it were shot straight, it would be fine. If you came to the Worth Theater in Fort Worth . . . it spread. Technicolor said that they could straighten it out, but it would cost $10,000 more.

The two guys said, "No more."

Al Reynolds came to me and said, "Could we get those lines out?"

"Yeah, we can get those out; no problem."

I locked two Bolex together. . . . At that time, you could take a good 16mm and come off with a pretty good print on 35mm. I shot film down around the railroad tracks, at San Antonio in Brackenridge Park. . . . We added because it was not long enough. He wanted about thirty more minutes to it.

Later Tom and I went to Maybank; there was an old theater that was closed. We used that for a test theater. We worked on a mirror system that had to be out in front of the projector. It could bring these pictures together and not matter what the angle—the keystoning could be taken care of. The second time around we opened in Brownsville, Texas, and we had to put up the fifty-five-foot screen ourselves. . . . I would round up a crew and put this thing up. It was like Tinkertoys; you could latch it all together. We opened at the Rio Grande in Brownsville and then [went] to Mission. . . . Then came back to Waco . . . at the Orpheum; did real good.

Then we closed it up and never did run it again. The print stayed in Dallas a long time at the Forest Theater. I went over there to get it, and I opened the can and it just about blew my mind it stunk so bad. Could not stay in the room. Closed it up right quick. That's what happens to that film. It had not decomposed, it was just the stench. That's Technicolor; smells like strong vinegar.[64]

Projectionist Scotty Davidson ran Thrill-O-Rama at a Tyler theater. "It was a travel type film, I don't recall much of a story to it. . . . There was a sequence of the Apache Belles in the film." The screen stretched from exit to exit. The feature was scheduled to run for four days; it flopped and closed in two.[65]

Texas Postwar Film Production

The period before, during, and after the Second World War, like the years 1910–30, was an active time of filmmaking in Texas. Just before the war, *The Marching Herd* was filmed twenty-five miles southeast of Cotulla on the La Motta Ranch. Soon after, that location was again used for *The Texan,* a Paramount picture starring Randolph Scott. In 1943, *We've Never Been Licked* was filmed on the Texas A&M University campus. In 1954, Carswell Air Force Base in Fort Worth was the setting for Paramount's *Strategic Air Command* starring James Stewart and

June Allyson. *Indian Paint* starring Johnny Crawford and Jay (Tonto) Silverheels was filmed south of Cleburne near the town of Rio Vista.[66]

In 1955 Charles E. King, a local rancher from Wichita Falls, used a former soap factory as the studio for the filming of *Narcotic Squad,* starring Paul Kelly, Kathy Downs, and Regis Toomey. King's first full-length movie opened at the Queen in that city on July 8, 1955. John Wayne starred in *The Alamo,* which was filmed in Brackettville in 1959. A year later, director John Ford used the same location to film *Two Rode Together,* starring James Stewart, Richard Widmark, Andy Devine, Shirley Jones, and Linda Crystal.[67]

Texas International Productions was formed in 1956 to finance the making of movies in the North Texas area. A $10 million production center was to be situated on 3,000 acres between Fort Worth and Weatherford. In November, Texas International started rehearsing for the Western *Johnnie Ringo.*[68]

In the late 1950s, Gordon McLendon, owner of numerous theaters and radio stations and instigator of the Liberty Broadcasting System, which "recreated" sporting events in a studio, started producing movies. He created the McLendon Radio Pictures Corporation. Cielo Studio, the production center, sat on a five-hundred-acre tract on the shores of Lake Dallas near Denton.

McLendon's first feature was *The Killer Shrews,* starring James Best and Ingrid Goude. The film featured Ken Curtis, later famous as Festus on the television series *Gunsmoke.* McLendon did a cameo role in the film. Cielo's second movie was *The Giant Gila Monster,* which featured disc jockeys from radio station KLIF, McLendon's highly rated, top-forty outlet in Dallas. The movies premiered as a double-feature on June 25, 1959, at the Palace in Fort Worth and the Majestic in Dallas.[69]

In just over five decades, that weak, flickering image that was first presented to Dallas audiences in 1897 evolved into one of the most important entertainment industries in the state—and the world. What became known as "picture sheets" have astonished, amazed, entertained, frightened, motivated, and informed Texans in every city, town, and village where an audience could be gathered.

The first fifty years of motion pictures' evolution were not without struggle. Movies, specifically "talkies," fought for their very existence during the depression. Those years were the first period when the steady growth of the motion picture industry actually stopped and reversed. Hundreds of theaters closed, employees were "let go," and box office receipts dropped sharply. In the end, movies survived in those dismal years because they were good entertainment and satisfying escapism—for only a nickel.

After World War II, motion pictures struggled to keep their position as communicator to the masses. Radio had never been a threat to movies. However, its big brother, television, presented a real and formidable challenge for dominance of mass communications. Started in the late 1940s, this "love/hate" relationship between movies and television has not been resolved. Eventually the two learned to co-exist and now use the strengths of the other to promote their own self-interest. From its very inception, television has always needed motion pictures to "fill-out" its schedule. Today, numerous cable channels run nothing but movies. Just as radio, in too many instances, is nothing but a wireless distribution system for the record industry, television, likewise, is becoming an exhibition system for the film industry.

The motion picture industry utilizes television—as when movie stars conveniently appear as guests on television programs a day or two before their latest film opens. Television has never come close to eliminating or replacing motion pictures as was feared and predicted in the 1950s—and movies have never posed a threat to television. Instead, a kind of informal inter-dependency developed.

In the 1980s movie theaters were challenged by television. Motion pictures rented for home viewing might have eliminated "brick and mortar" theaters—but didn't. Theatrical circuits were constructing mammoth multiscreen theaters. These giants helped

Figure 130. Still doing it the old way! As of 1998, Lambert Little, of Hamilton's Texan Theater, was the only projectionist in Texas still known to be striking carbon arcs, watching for cues, and "changing over" every twenty minutes at the end of each reel of film. Courtesy Lambert Little

keep "movie going" an active part of people's lives. Presently, there is a proposed technical innovation to distribute motion pictures by satellite using high-definition, projection television instead of film. Most surviving drive-in theaters now distribute the movie's soundtrack to the viewers' automobile sound system over stereo, high-fidelity frequency modulation (FM) radio channels broadcast from the projection booth. Motion pictures and broadcasting again have discovered that not only can they make use of each other, but they might have a much more difficult time surviving and growing without the other. The two may be more co-dependent than many realize.

These gargantuan theaters, presently housing thirty or more screens, helped deliver a crippling blow to the already declining single-screen theater market in Texas—but not a death blow. Although most single-screen theaters in the state have closed, a few survive. Fort Worth has the Seventh Street Theater, run by ninety-two-year-old Boyd Milligan and Wills Point the Majestic Theater operated by third-generation family owner, Karl Lybrand. Similar theaters survive in Valley Mills, Hamilton, Canton, and others towns—usually small. In certain locations, as in Pecos, a closed, single-screen theater is making a comeback. Additionally, a small number of single-screen drive-in theaters still survive—like the Sky-View in Lamesa, the Mission in San Antonio, and the Tower in Rule.

Most motion picture establishments located on cities' downtown theater rows before 1960 have closed.

Houston lost all of its downtown theaters including three magnificent grand movie palaces. Dallas saved its Majestic Theater, as did San Antonio. Austin, Waco, and Abilene have preserved a downtown "movie house." Most have been converted into performing arts centers, ironically, *what they were specifically built to be in the 1920s.* The motion picture once "pushed" live performers off the stage of these grand movie palaces, and it is this reverting from motion pictures back to live performances that is now helping these grand old theaters survive.

It is unimaginable that any form of media will ever replace or eliminate the projected, moving image. Inventions and innovations in the future will present challenges, but history seems to indicate that the viewing of moving images projected on a screen is just too vital a social force to go away.

Appendix 1

TEXAS MOTION PICTURE THEATERS

CITY	NAME
Abernathy	Star
Abilene	All State
	Ash Street
	Broadway
	Dixie
	Elmwood Skyline DI
	Gem
	Key City DI
	Linda
	Majestic
	Metro
	Mission
	Near Cross Plains
	Palace
	Paramount
	Park DI
	Pioneer
	Queen
	Ritz
	State
	Texas
	Town and Country
Alamo	Alamo
Alba	Garo
Albany	Aztec
Alice	Queen
	Rialto
	Texas
Alpine	Granada
	Mojave
Alto	Alto
	Majestic
Alvarado	Alvarado
Alvin	Grand
Amarillo	Capitol
	Deandi
	Dreamland
	Esquire
	Fair
	Liberty
	Mission
	Olympic
	Paramount
	Rex
	Rialto
	State
	Texas
	Tower
	Wagon Wheel DI
Amherst	Gem
	Majestic
Ammansville	Lone Star
Anahuac	Rig
Angleton	Angleton
Annona	Annona
Anson	Palace

CITY	NAME
Anson (*cont.*)	Texas
Anton	Spade
Aransas Pass	Rialto
Archer City	Royal
Arlington	Arlington
	Texas
Arp	Liberty
	Rex
Asherton	Nacional
Aspermont	Queen
Atchison	Chris
Athens	Dixie
	Liberty
	Texas
Atlanta	Ritz
Austin	Austin
	Bijou
	Cactus
	Capitol
	Crescent
	Dunbar
	Hancock
	Harlem
	Majestic
	Midget
	Paramount
	Queen
	Ritz
	Skinny's
	State
	Texas
	Varsity
	Yale
Baird	Baird
	Sigal
Ballinger	Palace
	Queen
Balmorhea	Texas
Bartlett	Alamo
Bastrop	Strand
Bay City	Colonial
	Franklin
	State
Baytown	Arcadia
	Palace
Beaumont	Palace
	Circle DI
	Crystal
	East Texas
	Electric
	Gaylyum
	Gem
	Happy Hour
	Imperial
	Jefferson
	Jewel
	Joyland
	Kyle
	Liberty
	People's
	Pyramid DI
	Rex
	Rio
	South Park DI
	Star
	Tivoli
	Verdun
Beeville	Mission
	Rex
	Rialto
	Rio
Bellevue	Bellevue
Bellville	Alamo
	Unique
Belton	Beltex
	Beltonian
Benavides	Empress
Benjamin	Benjamin
Bertram	New
Bessmay	Bessmay
Big Lake	Palace
Big Spring	Lyric

CITY	NAME
	Queen
	Ritz
Bishop	Vest
Blanco	Byars
	Riggs
Blooming Grove	Majestic
	Ritz
Boerne	Cascade
	Sunset
Bogata	Bogata
	Payton
Boling	Boling
	Queen
Bollville	Alamo
Bonham	American
	Best
	Elite
	Queen
Borger	American
	Paramount
	Rex
	Rig
Bowie	Majestic
	Ritz
	Texas
Brackettville	Palace
	Star
Brady	Lyric
	Palace
	Ritz
Breckenridge	Air Dome, Court
	Alhambra
	American
	National
	Palace, New
	Plaza
Brenham	Rex
	Somon
Bridgeport	National
Bronte	Suma
	Texas

CITY	NAME
Brookshire	Brookshire
Brownfield	Rialto
	Rustic
Brownsboro	Palace
Brownsville	Capitol
	Dittman
	Dreamland
	Lyric
	Majestic
	Queen
	Texas
Brownwood	Granada
	Bowie
	Gem
	Lyric
	Queen
	Ritz
	Texas
Bryan	Dixie
	New Dixie
	Palace
	Queen
Buckholts	Queen
Buffalo	B & O
	Leon
Burkburnett	Liberty
	New
	Palace
	Tex
Burkett	Cupid
Burnet	Burnet
Caldwell	Matsonian
Calvert	Queen
Cameron	Cameron
	Milam
Camp Wood	Beck
Canadian	Palace
	Queen
Canton	Plaza
Canutillo	Julimes
Canyon	Olympic

CITY	NAME
Carlisle	Rex
Carrizo Springs	National
	Texan
	Winter Garden
Carrollton	Community
Carthage	Victory
Celina	Queen
	Ritz
Center	Crystal
	Shelby
Childress	Monogram
	Palace
Chillicothe	Strand
	Majestic
	Palace
	Strand
Cisco	Ideal
	Palace
Clarendon	Cozy
	Lem Key
	Mulday
	Pastime
	Queen
Clarksville	Colonial
	Mission
	State
Claude	Gem
Cleburne	Best
	Chief
	Cosy Corner
	Esquire
	Five-Cent Theatorium
	Garden
	Majestic
	Mystic
	Palace
	Rex
	Roosevelt
	Texas
	Yale
Cleveland	Cleveland

CITY	NAME
	Palace
Clifton	Cliftex
	Cub
Clint	Clint
Coleman	Dixie
	Howell
	Oak
College Station	A and M College
Collinsville	Princess
Colorado City	Palace
	Ritz
Columbus	Columbus
	Orphic
	Ritz
Comanche	Majestic
	Ritz
Comfort	Community
Commerce	Air Dome, The
	Barker
	Brigham Blair
	Cupid
	Dreamland
	Hippodrome
	Lilly's DI
	Lyric
	Majestic
	Opera House
	Palace, The
	Star
Conroe	Creighton
	Gem
	Liberty
Coolidge	M. B.
	New Deal
Cooper	Air Dome
	Gem
	Grand
	Lyric
	Spark
Corpus Christi	Agnes
	Aldine

CITY	NAME
	Amuse
	Avalon
	Ayers
	Aztec
	Beach
	Bel-Aire DI
	Boulevard DI
	Buccaneer DI
	Centre
	Chalk Hill DI
	Corpus DI
	Crystal
	Dixie
	Fenix
	Globe
	Grande
	Gulf DI
	Harlem
	Harbor
	Ideal
	Latino Teatro
	Leopard Street
	Liberty
	Lyric
	Majestic
	Melba
	North Beach
	Olympic By-the-Sea
	Osage DI
	Palace
	Palm Garden
	Pan-American Airdome
	Pavilion
	Port
	Queen
	Rio
	Ritz
	Seaside Electric
	Surf DI
	Texas DI
	Thunderbird DI

CITY	NAME
	Tower
	Twin Palms DI
	Viking DI
Corrigan	Corrigan
Corsicana	Grand
	Ideal
	Palace
Cotulla	Junco De La Vega
	Majestic
Crandall	Crandall
Crane	Palace
Crockett	Auditorium
	Texas
Crosby	Crosby
Crosbyton	Crystal
	Queen
Cross Plains	Liberty
Crowell	Rialto
Crystal City	Guild
	Juarez
	Nacional
Cub	Skyview
Cuero	Normana
	Palace
	Rialto
Cumby	Lyric
Cunningham	Universal
Cushing	Crown
Daingerfield	Universal
Daisetta	Daisetta
Dalhart	Mission
Dallas	Air Dome (Ross)
	Arcadia
	Aston
	Astor
	Avenue
	Beckley
	Best
	Beverly Hills
	Big D DI
	Bioscope

CITY	NAME
Dallas (*cont.*)	Bison
	Bluebird
	Bruton Road DI
	Buckner Boulevard DI
	Candy
	Capitan
	Capitol
	Capri
	Casa Linda
	Central
	Century
	Chalk Hill DI
	Circle
	Cliff Queen
	Coliseum
	Colonial
	Columbia
	Coronet
	Crest
	Crystal
	Cycle Park
	Dal-Sec
	Dallas
	Dallas O H
	Delman
	Denton Road DI
	Dixie
	East Grand
	Ella B. Moore
	Empress
	Encore
	Esquire
	Fair
	Fair Park
	Favorite
	Feature
	Folly
	Forest
	Fox
	Gaiety
	Garland Road DI

CITY	NAME
	Garrick
	Granada
	Grand
	Grand Central
	Hampton Road DI
	Happy Hour
	Harlem
	Haskell
	Heights
	Hi-Vue DI
	High School
	Hill
	Hippodrome
	Hope (Capri)
	Ideal
	Inwood
	Jefferson
	Joy
	Jungle Land
	Kaufman Pike DI
	Kessler
	Knox
	Lakewood
	Lawn
	Leo
	Lincoln
	Linda Kay DI
	Lone Star DI
	Lubbock
	Lucus
	Majestic
	Major
	Mammoth
	Maple
	Melba
	Melrose
	Midway
	Mirror
	National
	Newport
	Nickelodeon

CITY	NAME
	Northwest Highway DI
	Old Mill
	Orpheum
	Othello
	Palace (2)
	Pan Americano
	Pantages
	Park
	Parkway
	Peak
	People's
	Plaza
	Pleasuredome
	Preston Royal
	Princess
	Queen
	Rex
	Rialto
	Rio
	Rita
	Ritz
	Roseland
	Rosewin
	South Loop DI
	Star
	State
	Stevens
	Strand
	Sunset
	Telenews
	Texas
	Tower
	Trinity
	Twin DI
	Uptown
	Varsity
	Village
	Vogue
	Washington
	White
	Wilshire

CITY	NAME
	Wynnewood
Damon	Damon
Danyon	Olympic
Dawson	Dawson
	Ritz
Dayton	Texas
Decatur	Majestic
	Ritz
De Kalb	Patriot
Del Rio	Princess
	Strand
De Leon	Liberty
Denison	Dreamland
	Harlem
	Liberty
	Rialto
	Rio
	Star
Denton	College Ind. Arts
	North Texas Teachers College
	Palace
	Ritz
Deport	Deport
Devine	Majestic
Dexter	Playhouse
Dickens	Palace
Dickinson	Dickinson
	Hollywood
Dilley	Anahuac
Dimmitt	Castro
Dodd City	Lone Star
Donna	Chapultepec
	Plaza
Doole	Doole
Doucette	Hoo Hoo
Dublin	Majestic
	Rebel
	Ritz
Dumas	Gem
Eagle Lake	Avalon

CITY	NAME
Eagle Pass	Aztec
East Bernard	Majestic
Eastland	Connelee
	Lyric
	Majestic
Edcouch	Edcouch
Eddy	Nue
Eden	Eden
	Rivas
Edinburg	Aztec
	Citrus
	Grand
	Valley
Edna	Edtex
El Campo	Liberty
	Normana
	Palace
El Paso	Air Dome, American
	Airdome
	Alameda
	Alcazar-SP
	Alhambra
	American
	Ascarate
	Bijou
	Bordertown
	Bronco
	Colon-SP
	Crawford
	Crescent
	Crystal
	Del Norte
	Eden
	El Ideal
	El Paso
	Ellanay
	Empire
	Eureka
	Fiesta
	Grecian
	Hudalgo

CITY	NAME
	Ideal
	Imperial
	Iris
	Liberty
	Lubbock
	Lyric
	Majestic
	Mission
	National
	New Empress
	North Loop
	Palace
	Paris
	Pershing
	Plaza
	Rex
	Rialto
	Smelter
	Star
	State
	Texas
	Texas Grand
	Trail
	Unique
	Valley
	Wigwam
	Yandell
Eldorado	Lone Star
	Ritz
Electra	Crown
	Grand
	Liberty
Elgin	Eltex
	Imp
Eliasville	Palace
Elkhart	Zest
Ellinger	Pastime
Encinal	Encinal
Ennis	American
	Grand
	Lyric

CITY	NAME
	Plaza
Estelline	Pastime
Fabens	Eureka
	Fabens
Fairfield	Iris
Falfurrias	New
Falls City	Royal
Farmersville	Cornes
	Palace
Farwell	Borden
Fayetteville	Prince
Ferris	Queen
Flatonia	Lyric
Flomot	Hightone
Floresville	Arcadia
Floydada	Capada
	Olympic
	Palace
Follett	Criterion
Forney	Star
Fort Stockton	Grand
Fort Worth	Alp
	Arlington
	Avenue
	Azle Avenue
	Belknap DI
	Berry
	Blue Mouse
	Boulevard DI
	Bowie
	Bowie DI
	Capitol
	Circle
	Como
	Cowtown DI
	Crown
	Douglas
	Drive-In
	Fawn
	Forest
	Gateway

CITY	NAME
	Gayety
	Gem
	Grand
	Haltom
	Healy
	Heights
	Hippodrome
	Hollywood
	Home
	Ideal
	Imperial
	Interstate
	Isis
	Jacksboro DI
	Joy
	Kar-vue
	Liberty
	Little
	Lyric
	Majestic
	Mansfield DI
	Marine
	Meadowbrook DI
	Melba
	Morgan
	New Isis
	New Liberty
	New Queen
	Odeon
	Orpheum
	Palace
	Pantages
	Parkaire DI
	Parkway
	Pearl
	Pershing
	Phillips
	Pike DI
	Pix
	Poly
	Rex

CITY	NAME
Fort Worth (*cont.*)	Rialto
	Ridglea
	Ritz
	River Oaks
	Riverside DI
	Rose
	Rosedale
	Roseland
	Savoy
	Seventh Street
	Southside DI
	Standard
	Star
	Stock Yard A M
	Sylvania
	TCU
	Texan
	Texas
	Tivoli
	Tower
	Twin DI
	Varsity
	Village
	Westerner DI
	White
	Worth
Fostoria	Happy Hour
Franklin	Gem
	Robertson
Frankston	Palace
	Strand
Frederickburg	Palace
Freeport	Palace
	Princess
Freer	Rialto
Friona	Capitol
Frisco	Frisco
Frost	Frost
Gadsden (a.k.a. Gadston)	Princess
Gainesville	Air Dome, Electric Park

CITY	NAME
	Bowie
	Chief DI
	Favorite
	Happy Hour
	Lyric
	Majestic
	Major Steward ?
	Queen
	Ritz
	Texan
	Texas
Galveston	Beach Crystal
	Best
	Bookort?
	Casino
	Cozy
	Crystal Majestic
	Crystal One
	Crystal Palace
	Dixie No. 1
	Dixie No. 2
	Dixie No. 3
	Fortuna
	Galvez
	Globe
	Hippodrome
	Isle
	Key
	Leader
	Liberty
	Lincoln
	Lyric
	Majestic
	Martini
	Marvel
	New Martini
	O'Donnell Jacob
	Orpheum
	Palace
	Parisian
	People's

CITY	NAME
	Pershing
	Princess
	Queen
	Rialto
	Rex
	Royal
	Ruby
	Star
	State
	Strand
	Theatorium
	Tremont
	Vaudette
Ganado	Iris
Garland	Crescent
	Gartex
Gatesville	Palace
	Regal
	Ritz
	S&S DI
Georgetown	Aztec
	Gem
	Palace
Giddings	Dixie
Gilmer	Crystal
	Strand
Gladewater	Gregg
	Liberty
	Payne's
	Ritz
Glen Rose	Glentex
	Majestic
Goldthwaite	Melba
Goliad	Goliad
Gonzales	Crystal
	Rialto
Goose Creek	De Luxe
	New Gulf
	Texan
Gorman	Liberty
	New Deal

CITY	NAME
Graford	Texas
Graham	Graham DI
	Liberty
	National
Granbury	Brazos DI
	Palace
	Grand Prairie
	Downs DI
	Texas
Grand Saline	Palace, New
Grandview	Aztec
	Palace
Granger	Alamo
	Tab
Grapevine	Palace
Greenville	(no name given)
	Air Dome
	Colonial
	Crystal
	Dreamland
	Empire, The
	Empress
	Gem
	Greggton
	Hunt DI
	Lyric
	Majestic
	Nickelodeon
	Opera House
	Pastime
	Queen
	Rex
	Rialto
	Rita
	Ritz
	Savoy
	Star
	Texan
	Trail
Greggton	Ritz
Groesbeck	Yale

CITY	NAME
Groveton	Capitol
Gunter	Liberty
Hale Center	Owl
	Ritz
Hallettsville	Cole
Hamilton	Strand
	Texan
Hamlin	Ferguson
	Palace
	Ritz
Harlingen	Arcadia
	Park
	Rialto
Haskell	Texas
Hawkins	Hawk
Hearne	Queen
Hebbronville	Casino
	Texas
Hedley	Dreamland
Hemphill	Palace
Hempstead	Idle Hour
Henderson	Liberty
	Palace
	Strand
	Victory
Henrietta	Dorothy
	Majestic
Hereford	Star
Hico	Palace
Higgins	Alamo
High Island	Swain
Hillsboro	Best
	Hill DI
	Hillsboro Opera House
	Majestic
	Palace
	Ritz
	Texas
Holliday	Palace
Hominy	Pettit
Hondo	Colonial
Honey Grove	(no name given)
	Air Dome, The
	Bon-Ton, The
	Grove
	Happy Hour, The
	Home, The
	Lincoln
	Nickelodeon, The
	State
	Strand
	Topic
Hopkinsville	Princess
Houston	(no name given)
	Air Dome
	Airline DI
	Airway DI
	Alabama
	Alameda
	American
	Avalon
	Aztec
	Azteca
	Bellaire
	Best
	Bluebonnet
	Boulevard
	Broadway
	Capitol
	Centre
	Clinton
	Cozy
	Crescent
	Crown
	Crystal
	Delman
	DeLuxe
	Dixie
	Don Gordon
	Dowling
	Eastwood

CITY	NAME
	Empire
	Epsom DI
	Fulton
	Garden Oaks
	Gem
	Granada
	Happy Hour
	Heights
	Henstead DI
	Hi-Nabor DI
	Horwity
	Houston
	Ideal
	Iris
	Irvington DI
	Isis
	Jesnen
	Jones
	Joy-Tex DI
	Juarez
	Key
	King Center DI
	Kirby
	Lamar
	Leland
	Liberty
	Lincoln
	Lindale
	Loew's Star
	Lyons
	Main
	Majestic #1
	Majestic #2
	Majestic #3
	Market Street DI
	Melba
	Metropolitan
	Midway
	National
	Navaway
	Neighbor

CITY	NAME
	North Main
	North Side
	O S T
	Olympia
	Orpheum
	Palace
	Park
	Pastime
	Post Oak DI
	Prince
	Queen
	Rainbow
	Rex
	Rialto
	Ritz
	River Oaks
	Roxy
	Royal
	Rusk Avenue
	Santa Rosa
	Scenic
	Scott
	Shepard DI
	South Main DI
	St. Elmo
	Star
	State
	Strand
	Stude
	Sunset
	Texan
	Texas DI
	Theato
	Tower
	Trail DI
	Travis
	Union
	University
	Uptown
	Vaudette
	Vendome

CITY	NAME
Houston (*cont.*)	Venus
	Village
	Vogue
	Washington
	Wayside
	Westheimer
	Winkler DI
	Yale
	Zoe
Hubbard	Crystal
	Uptown
Hughes Springs	Movie Town
	Strand
Humble	Lidell
	Star
Huntsville	Avon
	Dorothy
	Life
	Pines DI
Idalou	Sunset
Ingleside	Rialto
	Texas
Iowa Park	Pickwick
	Ritz
Iraan	Dixie
	Texas
Irving	Irving
Italy	Ilk
Itasca	Pastime
Jacksboro	Mecca
	Opera House
Jacksonville	Dorbandt
	Palace
	Rialto
Jasper	Lone Star
Jayton	Palace
Jefferson	Lyric
Johnson City	Blue Bonnett
Joinersville	Dixie
Josephine	Paramount
Jourdanton	Royal

CITY	NAME
Junction	Texas
Karnes City	Joyland
	Karnes
Kaufman	Plaza
	Uptown
Kemp	Kemp
	Rex
Kenedy	Grand
	Rialto
Kerens	Majestic
	Navarro
Kerrville	Arcadia
	Dixie
Kilgore	Crim
	Dixie
	Ritz
	Strand
	Texas
Killeen	Texas
Kingsville	Atenas
	Rex
	Rialto
Kirbyville	Palace
Kirkland	Kirkland
Knox City	Texas
Kosse	Palace
La Feria	Bijou
La Grange	Cozy
La Porte	Broadway
Ladonia	Rolaine
Lamesa	Majestic
	Palace
	Sky-Vue DI
Lampasas	(no name given)
	Air Dome
	Bailey
	Hannah Springs O H
	Le Roy
	Rio
Lancaster	Criterion
	Grand

CITY	NAME
Laredo	Azteca
	Empire
	Fernand Garcia
	Juarez
	Rialto
	Royal
	Tivoli
Lawn	King
Leakey	Price's
Leander	Leanshaw
Lefors	Rialto
Leonard	Liberty
	Texas
Levelland	Wallace
Lewisville	Liberty
Liberty	American
Linden	Capitol
	New
Littlefield	Palace
	Ritz
Livingston	Fain
Llano	Lantex
	Opera House
Lockhart	Baker's
	Obrero
Lockney	Isis
Lometa	Cozy
	Lyric
London	Majestic
Lone Oak	Lone Oak
	Palace
Longview	Arlyne
	Grand
	Liberty
	Park
	Rembert
	Rita
	Ritz
	Strand
Loraine	Best
	Loraine

CITY	NAME
Lorenzo	Crystal
Lott	Gem
Lubbock	Broadway
	Cactus
	Circle
	Golden Horseshoe DI
	Lyric
	Midway
	New Lindsey
	Palace
	Red Raider DI
	Rex
	Texan
	Texas
	Trail DI
	Westerner DI
Lufkin	Lincoln
	Pines
	Ritz
	Texan
Luling	Princess
	Queen
Mabank	Matex
	Royal
Madisonville	New Rex
Malakoff	Ritz
Malone	Queen
Manning	Manning
Mansfield	Farr Best
Marathon	Marathon
Marble Falls	Riggs
Marfa	Palace
	Texas
Marlin	Air Dome, Majestic
	Drive-In
	Palace
	Rex
	Strand
Marshall	Grand
	Palace
	Paramount

CITY	NAME
Marshall (*cont.*)	Strand
Mart	Martex
	Queen
Mason	Edeon
Matador	Majestic
	Rogue
Mathis	Mathis
	Ritz
McAdoo	McAdoo
McAllen	Aztec
	El Rey
	Palace
	Queen
	Valley DI
McCamey	Grand
	Palace
McGregor	Curtis
	Dixie
	McLendon
	Opera House
	Ritz
	Texas
McKinney	Arcadia
	Pope
	Ritz
	Texas
McLean	American
	Avalon
Medina	Medina
Megargel	Texas
Melvin	Leedja
Memphis	Gem
	Palace
	Ritz
	Texas
Menard	Mission
Mercedes	Capitol
	Empire
	Mercedes
Meridian	Bosque
	Capital
	Circle
	Meridian
	Riverside DI
Merkel	Palace
	Queen
Mertens	Queen
Mesquite	Palace
Mexia	American
	National
	Palace
Miami	Pastime
Midland	Grand
	Idle Hour
	Palace
	Ritz
	Yucca
Midlothian	Crystal
Miles	Aztec
	State
Millersview	Gem
Mineola	Alamo
	Select
Mineral Wells	Grand
	Palace
Mingus	Opera House
Mirando City	Trinity
Mission	Concordia
	Electric
	Mission
Mobeetie	Mobeetie
Monahans	Palace
	Pen-ell
	Texas
Moody	Palace
Moran	Moran
Morton	Wallace
Moulton	New
	Olympia
Mount Calm	Ritz
Mount Enterprise	Texan
Mount Pleasant	Jones

CITY	NAME
	Martin
	Palace
	Titus
Mount Vernon	Franklin
	Joy
	Queen
Muenster	Palace
Muleshoe	Palace
Munday	Roxy
Nacogdoches	Austin
	Rita
	SFA
	Stone Fort
Naples	Morris
Navasota	Dixie
	Miller's
	Queen
Nederland	Nederland
Needville	Alcove
New Boston	Grand
New Braunfels	Brauntex
	Capitol
	Opera House
	Rialto
Newcastle	Star
Newgulf	Texas
Newark	Newark
Newton	Pastime
Nixon	Arcadia
	Nixon
Nocona	Majestic
	Millstone
Nordheim	Cozy
Normangee	Payne
North Zulch	Community
O'Donnell	Lynn
	Ritz
Odell	Odell
Odem	Palace
Odessa	Ector
	Lyric

CITY	NAME
	Odessa
	Palace
	Scott
	State
Oglesby	New
Olney	Olney
	Palace
	Princess
Olton	Melba
Orange	American
	Gem
	Liberty
	Starland
	Strand
Orange Grove	Cozy
Ovalo	Lone Star
Overton	Gem
	Strand
Ozona	Ozona
	Palace
Paducah	Palace
	Zana
Paint Rock	Crystal
Palacios	Queen
Palestine	Best
	Pal
	Palace
	Queen
	Ritz
	Star
	Texas
Pampa	Crescent
	La Vista
	Lanora
	Rex
	State
Panhandle	Panhandle
	Rex
Paris	271 DI
	Air Dome
	Airport DI

CITY	NAME
Paris (*cont.*)	Alhambra
	Arena
	Cozy
	Dime
	Dixie
	Grand
	Grand Lyric
	Jewel
	Lamar
	Little Dixie
	Lyric
	Main
	Majestic
	Nickelodeon
	North Star
	Palace
	Parisian
	Peterson
	Plaza
	Queen
	Rex
	Texas Grand
Peacock	Peacock
	Juarez
	Monterey
	Rialto
	Rio
Pecos	Grand
	Palace
Pelly	New Gulf
Perryton	American
	Ellis
Petersburg	Petersburg
Petrolia	Petrolia
Pettus	Cozy
Pharr	Cactus DI
	Texas
	Valencia
Pilot Point	Queen
Pineland	People's
	Pineland

CITY	NAME
Pittsburgh	Crystal
Plainview	Granada
	Olympic
	Palace
	Plainview
	Texas
Plano	Palace
	Plano
Pleasanton	Ples-Tex
Port Arthur	Elks
	People's
	Strand
	Dreamland
	Majestic
	Pearce
	Texan
Port Lavaca	Amuse
	Rex
Port Neches	Lyric
Post	Palace
Poteet	Robinson's
Poth	Princess
Prairie View	Auditorium
Presidio	Ritz
Putnam	Palace
Pyote	Circle
	Palace
Quanah	Court
	Texan
Quemado	Palace
Quinlan	Capitol
	Dixie
Quitaque	Queen
Quitman	Gem
	Quitman
Ralls	Crystal
Ranger	Arcadia
	Columbia
Raymondville	Delta De Oro
	Raymon
Razor	Community

CITY	NAME
Realitos	Duval
Red Rock	Liberty
Refugio	Loew's
	Rialto
Rhome	Lyric
Richards	Cozy
Richland	Richland
	Gem
Richmond	Queen
Rio Grande City	Dreamland
	Juarez
Rising Star	Liberty
Roanoke	Roanoke
Roaring Springs	Texan
Robert Lee	Alamo
	Robert Lee
Robstown	Obrero
	Palace
Roby	Roby
Rochester	Rochester
Rocksprings	O & S
Rockdale	Dixie
Rockport	Rio
Rockwall	Empress
Rogers	Strand
Roma	Roma
Ropesville	Wallace
Roscoe	Majestic
Rosebud	Gem
Rosenberg	Liberty
Rotan	Majestic
Roxton	Magnolia
Royse City	Crystal
	Palace
	Tower DI
Rule	Rule
	Tower
Rusk	Aston
	Texas
Sabinal	Majestic
Saint Jo	Majestic

CITY	NAME
San Angelo	Angelus
	Angelista
	Atomic DI
	Belvue DI
	Cecilia
	Concho
	Crystal
	Crystal Air Dome
	Jet DI
	Lyric
	Mission
	Orpheum
	Palace
	Parkway
	Plaza
	Princess
	Rex
	Ritz
	Rocket
	Roxy
	Royal
	Star
	Texas
	Theatorium
	Vendome
San Antonio	Alameda
	Alamo
	Alhambra
	Aztec
	Big Tent
	Bijou
	Broadway
	Cozy
	Crescent
	Dixie
	Eagle
	Electric
	Empire
	Gem
	Grand
	Greentree

CITY	NAME
San Antonio (*cont.*)	Harlandale
	Harling
	Highland
	Hippodrome
	Ideal
	Imperial
	Jewel
	Lyric
	Majestic
	Marvel
	Mexico
	Mission DI
	Nacional
	New Empire
	New Strand
	Newman's
	Obrero
	Orpheum
	Palace
	Pearl
	Picture Show
	Pike
	Plaza
	Prince
	Progreso
	Queen
	Rialto
	Ritz
	Rivoli
	Royal
	Sam Houston
	Star
	State
	Strand
	Sunset
	Texas
	Union
	Uptown
	Venus
	Washington
	Wigwam #1

CITY	NAME
	Wigwam #2
	Wonderland
	Woodlawn
	Zaragoza
San Augustine	Augus
San Benito	Juarez
	Palace
	Rivoli
San Diego	Palace
	Rio
San Juan	Rex
	San Juan
San Marcos	Hays
	Palace
	Plaza
San Saba	Palace
Sanderson	Princess
Sanger	Texan
Santa Anna	Queen
Santa Rosa	Queen
Santo	Santo
Saragosa	Community
	Texas
Schulenberg	Cozy
Seadrift	Palace
Seagoville	Seago
Seagraves	O. Kay
Sealy	Texas
Seguin	Austin
	Palace
	Texas
Seymour	Queen
	Ritz
	Texas
Shamrock	Liberty
	Texan
Sherman	Air Dome, Empire
	Air Dome, Jungle Land
	Andrews
	Gem

CITY	NAME
	Grand
	Grayson
	Jewel
	King
	Lyric, Empire
	Plaza
	Queen
	Rialto
	Ritz
	Royal
	Texan
	Texas
	Travis
	Washington
Shiner	Palace
Sierra Blanca	Sierra Blanca
Silsbee	Palace
Silverton	Legion
	Palace
Sinton	Rialto
Slaton	Palace
	State
	Texas
Smiley	Smiley
Smithville	Star
	Texas
Snyder	Palace
	Ritz
	Tiger
Somerville	Majestic
Sonora	Las Vista
	Valencia
Sour Lake	Crescent
Southland	Princess
Spearman	Lyric
Spur	Lyric
	Palace
	Rex
	Ritz
Stamford	Alcove
	Palace

CITY	NAME
	Ritz
	S & S DI
Stanton	Crystal
Stephenville	Majestic
	Palace
Sterling	Sterling
Stockdale	American
	Dale
Stratford	Roxy
Strawn	Strawn
Sudan	Garden
Sugarland	Auditorium
Sulphur Springs	Air Dome
	Broadway
	Buford
	Carnation
	Hi-Vue DI
	Lyric
	Mission
	Palace
Sunray	(no name given)
Sweetwater	Lyric
	Midway
	Palace
	Ritz
	Rocket
	Texas
Taft	Roberta
Tahlequah	Sequovah
Tahoka	English
Talf	Rialto
Tatum	Rae
Taylor	Colonial
	Howard
	Star
Teague	Star
Temple	Arcadia
	Bell
	Gem
	Little
	Texas

CITY	NAME
Terrell	Iris
	Lyric
	Rocket DI
Texarkana	Hardin?
	Hippodrome
	Little Princess
	Midway
	Paramount
	Perot
	Sanger
	Strand
Texas City	Jewel
Texon	Texon
Thorndale	Gem
Three Rivers	Rialto
Throckmorton	Texan
Thurber	Opera House
Timpson	Palace
Tomball	Ritz
Trenton	Queen
Trinity	Queen
Troup	Texas
	Troup
Truscott	Truscott
Tulia	Grand
Turkey	Gem DI
	Midway Drive-In
Tuscola	Cupid
Tyler	Air Dome, Lamkin's
	Arcadia
	Bluebird
	Broadway
	Crest DI
	Electric Palace
	Empire
	Grand Opera House
	Hippodrome
	Joy
	Liberty
	Lincoln
	Lyric

CITY	NAME
	Majestic
	Palace
	Plaza
	Queen
	Rapeeds
	Roller Rink, Tyler
	Theatorium
	Tyler
	Tyler Electric
	White Star
Utopia	Community
Uvalde	Ritz
	Strand
Valentine	Star
Valley Mills	Lyric
	Royal
	Valley
Van	Victor
Van Alstyne	Lyric
	Ritz
Van Horn	(no name give)
	Community
	Hernandez
	Sage (2)
Vega	Vega
Venus	New
	Venus
Vernon	Majestic
	Pic
	Pictorium
	Plaza
	Vernon
Victoria	Princess
	Queen
	Rita
	Uptown
	Victoria
Waco	25th Street
	Air Dome
	Air Dome, Royal
	Alamo

CITY	NAME
	Alpha
	Auditorium
	Belmead
	Capri
	Circle DI
	Cozy
	Crystal
	Dixie
	Elm Street
	Elmo
	Fox
	Gayety
	Gem
	Grand
	Hippodrome
	Huaco
	Ideal
	Imperial
	Joy
	Joy DI
	Kintoscope Parlor
	La Vega
	Lake Air DI
	Little Gem, Nickelodeon
	Lyric
	Majestic
	Melrose
	National
	Nickel
	Oak Lawn DI
	Orpheum
	Palace
	Rex
	Rivoli
	Royal
	Strand
	Sunset
	Texas
	Theatorium, Nickelodeon

CITY	NAME
	Trefoil DI
	Vendome
	Victory
	Waco
	Waco DI
	Washington
	Westview DI
Waelder	Cove
Walnut Springs	Palace
Waskom	Rex
Waxahachie	Dixie
	Empire
	Lincoln
Weatherford	Palace
	Princess
Weimar	Palace
Weinert	Rex
Wellington	Rialto
	Ritz
Weslaco	Capitol
	National
	Ritz
	Wesmer DI
West	Best
West Columbia	Queen
Wharton	Queen
	Rio
Wheeler	Rogue
White Deer	State
Whitesboro	Princess
	Roosevelt
Whitewright	Palace
Whitney	Opera House
Wichita Falls	Airdome Lamar Street
	Airdome Plaza
	Alamo
	Casino
	Colonial
	Dorothy
	Empress
	Fall DI

CITY	NAME
Wichita Falls (*cont.*)	Folly
	Garden
	Gem
	Grant
	Happy Hour
	Linda
	Lydia Margaret
	Lyric
	Majestic
	Mission
	Monroe
	Noble
	Olympia
	Palace
	Park Airdome
	Princess
	Queen
	Ritz
	Roxy
	Ruby
	Scottie
	Seymour
	St. Elmo
	State
	Strand
	Texan
	Tower
	Victoria
CITY	NAME
	Wichita
Wiergate	Vim
Wilie	Palace
Willow Springs	Avalon
	Ritz
Wills Point	Home
	Majestic
	Ritz
	Wednesday Book Club Opera House
Wink	Rex
	Rig
Winnsboro	Amuse
Winters	Lyric
	Queen
Wolfe City	Palace
Woodsboro	Arcadia
Woodville	Crescent
Wortham	Palace
Yoakum	Grand
	Ritz
Yorktown	L'Arcade
Youens	Humble
Ysleta	International
	Ysleta
Zapata	Iris

Appendix 2

TEXAS MOTION PICTURE STARS

Starting around 1910, Texas has furnished a large number of movie stars for the nation's industry. Tom Mix from El Paso owned a circus about 1928 and toured the state before becoming a Hollywood Western star. Jennifer Jones was the daughter of Philip Isis of Fort Worth who owned theaters in Dallas, Houston, etc. Dale Evans of Uvalde, later wife of Roy Rogers, sang on *The Early Birds* radio show on WFAA in Dallas before she went to Hollywood. Harry James played in the house band at radio station WRR in Dallas and KFDM in Beaumont before he "broke into" motion pictures. William Boyd, later known in Westerns as Hopalong Cassidy, started in 1928 singing with a group called *The Cowboy Ramblers* on radio station WRR in Dallas.

"Ginger Rogers watched movies at the Majestic in Fort Worth. She always sat in the exact same seat. . . . The manager would tell ushers, 'You be sure and hold Ginger's seat. . . . Don't let nobody sit in it.' She sat on the back row, first seat . . . left aisle, middle section. Rogers got her start when she won a Charleston contest at that theater."[1]

Other stars included Gene Autry from Tioga; Cyd Charisse and Bill Patton from Amarillo; Bebe Daniels, James Hall, Francellia Bilington, Catherine Moylan, Robert I. Payne, William Saal, Edwin L. Traver, Dorothy Janis, Spanky McFarland, Constance Moore, Linda Darnell, Dorothy Malone, and Don Castle from Dallas; Dad Taylor from Brownsville; Pat Boone from Denton; Mary Hay from Fort Bliss; Gale Storm, Joyce Reynolds, Ann Miller, Nan Grey, James Craig, Florence Vidor, Howard Hughes, Elliott Dexter, Ted Healy, Hope Hampton, Louise Cotton, and Don Barry from Houston; Ann Sheridan, Imogene Stanley, Joan Blondell, and Nancy Gates from Denton; Mary Brian from Corsicana; Guinn Williams from Decatur; Evelyn Pierce from Del Rio; Dorothy Devore and Zachary Scott from Fort Worth; Joan Crawford, Anne Gwynne, Ann Harding, Jacqueline Logan, Allene Ray, Lucien Littlefield, Lucille Powers, Harry G. Stein, Malcyn Arbuckle, and Florence Bates from San Antonio; Dana Andrews from Huntsville; Faye Emerson and Helen Vinson from Beaumont; Sara Haden, Beatrice Burnham, Eileen Josie, Greta Yoltz, Julian Rivero, and Edward Sedgewick from Galveston; John Arledge from Crockett; Jo-Carroll Denison from Tyler; Chill Wills from Seagoville; King Vidor from Galveston; Arthur Edmond Carewe from Gainesville; John Boles and Audie Murphy from Greenville; Bessie Love from Midland; Ken Maynard from Mission; Tom Foreman from Mitchell City; Neil Neely from Moody; Eve Southern from Ranger; Corinne Griffith from Texarkana; Alice Terry from Nashville; Texas Guinan from Waco; Carl Miller from Wichita County; Sharon Lynn and Mary Martin from Weatherford; Lynn Baggett from Cameron; Nell

O'Day from Prairie Hill; Edward S. Oldsmith from Paris; Jack Pepper from Palestone; Ruth Renick from Colorado; Mel Riddle from Granbury; Henry Roquemore from Marshall; Harold Shumate from Austin; Martha Lee Sparks from Floydada; J. B. Underwood from Holland; Fess Parker from San Angelo; Harold E. Wertz from Denison; Madge Bellamy from Hillsboro; and Will Whitmore from Lockhart. Richard Alexander, Nancy Nash, Charlotte Walker, and Ted Wells were Texans from undetermined locations.[2]

Appendix 3

PIONEERS OF THE TEXAS MOTION PICTURE THEATER INDUSTRY

There have been many individuals responsible for the growth and development of the motion picture industry in Texas. Will Horwitz owned and operated approximately fifteen theaters in the state and the Houston area. Fred V. Cannata managed theaters for Horwitz. Vaudeville star Eddie Foy, Jr., owned many theaters in Dallas. J. S. Phillips showed the first moving image in Fort Worth and built several nickelodeons and theaters there. E. J. Lamkin brought the first movies to Greenville and built and operated theaters in Northeast Texas. In Abilene, Wally Akin managed the Majestic, Queen, Palace, Paramount, and Park Drive-In for Interstate. A. W. "Jack" Lilly owned and operated theaters in Northeast Texas including Sulphur Springs, Greenville, Commerce, Winnsboro, Mount Pleasant, Clarksville, Honey Grove, Alba, and Wolfe City. George Kenneth Jorgensen started early nickelodeons in Houston and Galveston and by the 1930s owned and operated numerous theaters around the state. Clifford Lindsey owned and operated theaters in the Lubbock area. Besserer and Marshall owned and operated the Bes-Mar, Casino, Texas, and Princess in Austin. Lone Star Theaters owned numerous movie houses and drive-ins. For forty-two years Al Lever managed twenty-one Interstate Theaters in Houston. Until 1933, Harry and Simon Ehrlich managed theaters in Texarkana, Marshall, and Houston. Motion pictures in Waco revolved around Louis Jacobs, Abe Levy, J. P. Harrison, and J. A. Lemke. B. R. McLendon and son Gordon owned nineteen theaters in Oklahoma, Louisiana, and Texas. Philip Isis of Fort Worth owned theaters in Dallas, Houston, etc.[1]

L. N. Crim's East Texas Theaters operated the Liberty in Fort Worth and numerous theaters around the state. Victor, Frank, and Otto Wojtek operated theaters in West Texas including the Alamo in Robert Lee and the Texas in Bronte. B. R. Lucky had theaters in Goliad, Nixon, and Karnes City. Boyd Milligan owned theaters in Fort Worth. Harold Robb and Ed Rowley, R & R Theaters, operated over a hundred movie houses in the state. Interstate Circuit, Inc., the creation by Karl Hoblitzelle, ran over a hundred theaters in Texas and the nation, and built grand movie palaces in Austin, Abilene, Houston, Dallas, and San Antonio. William O'Donnell managed the Interstate Circuit, Inc. John Eberson designed many grand movie palaces, especially the "atmospheric" theaters, which were first used by Hoblitzelle. Underwood and Ezell operated drive-ins in Dallas, San Antonio, Fort Worth, Houston, Waco, Pharr, Port Arthur, Austin, and Beaumont. W. Scott Dunne was architect of many theaters in Texas including the Texas in Dallas and others in Corpus Christi, San Antonio, Big Spring, Sherman, and Palestine.[2]

Clifford Edge of Robstown recalled other theater circuits in the state and their owners:

> August Kruth was a lumber man out of Diboll. He decided to get into the theater business. His flagship theater was the Jefferson in Beaumont which was the Jefferson Amusement Company in that area. It was in towns like Longview, Lufkin, Nacogdoches, Jacksonville, Henderson, Marshall, all up in that area. The house architect was Able Wheel who did most of the things for the Saenger Circuit in the deep South.
>
> Jesse Jones (of Houston) built everything for everybody—leased it. He owned many of the buildings that were leased to those theaters. Out in West Texas you had Skeet-Noret Theaters—Levelland and lot of the smaller towns in West Texas. Blankenship Theaters were also out in West Texas almost overlapping Skeet-Noret. Mrs. Blankenship's name was Rose and there were many Rose Theaters out there in West Texas. The biggest one in this part of the state was Hall Industries centered in Beeville.[3]

Appendix 4

THEATER CIRCUITS IN TEXAS IN THE 1930S

H. H. Cluck
Home office: Belton
Number of theaters: 5
Theaters were the Beltonian in Belton; Lyric in Brady; Colonial in Clarksville; Palace in Georgetown; and LeRoy in Lampasas.

Cole's Chain Theaters
Home office: Rosenberg
Number of theaters: 9
Theaters were the Avalon in Eagle Lake; Cole in Hallettsville; Alcove in Needville; Queen in Richmond; Liberty in Rosenberg; Dreamland in Wallis; Grand in Yoakum; Angleton in Angleton; and Texas in Sealy.

Federated Theaters, Inc.
Home office: Dallas
Number of theaters: 7
Theaters were the American and Best in Bonham; Rialto, Colonial, and Rita in Greenville; Palace in Seguin; and National in Graham.

Frels' Theaters
Home office: Victoria
Number of theaters: 6
Theaters were the L'Arcade in Yorktown; Victoria and Uptown in Victoria; Normana in El Campo; Orphic in Columbus; and Alamo in Bellville.

H. & H. Theater Company
Home office: Abilene
Number of theaters: 11
Theaters were the Queen and Lyric in Winters; Ritz and Alcove in Stamford; Lyric in Odessa; Ritz and Grand in Midland; Queen in Merkel; Queen and Palace in Ballinger; and Palace in Anson.

Hall Industries Theaters
Home office: Beeville
Number of theaters: 11
Theaters were the Rialto in Sinton; Rialto and Rex in Kingsville; Rialto in Kennedy; Rialto and Palace in Cuero; Rialto and Mission in Beeville; Rialto in Aransas Pass; and Rialto and Queen in Alice.

Interstate Circuit, Inc.
Home office: Dallas
Number of theaters: 22
Theaters were the Tremont and Queen in Galveston; Paramount, Queen, and Hancock in Austin; Queen, Kirby, Metropolitan, and Majestic in Houston; State, Aztec, Texas, and Majestic in San Antonio; Majestic, Palace, Hollywood, and Worth in Fort Worth;

Old Mill, Capitol, Melba, Palace, and Majestic in Dallas.

Jefferson Amusement Co., Inc.
Home office: Beaumont
Number of theaters: 14
Theaters were the Queen in Victoria; Texas and Palace in Seguin; People's, Pearce, Palace, and Majestic in Port Arthur; Strand in Orange; Gem and Rita in Greenville; People's, Tivoli, Liberty, and Jefferson in Beaumont.

East Texas Theaters, Inc.
Home office: Beaumont
Number of theaters: 19
Theaters were the Queen and Palace in Bryan; Gregg in Gladewater; Texas in Goose Creek; Arcadia in Baytown; Liberty in Conroe; Austin in Nacogdoches; Paramount and Palace in Marshall; New Gulf in Pelly; Pines in Lufkin; Strand and Rembert in Longview; Crim and Strand in Kilgore; Palace in Jacksonville; Strand and Palace in Henderson; and Payne in Gladewater.

A. W. Lilly Circuit
Home office: Greenville
Number of theaters: 6
Theaters were the Mission and Broadway in Sulphur Springs; Titus and Palace in Mount Pleasant; and Lyric and Palace in Commerce.

O. K. Theaters
Home office: Dallas
Number of theaters: 11
Theaters were the Princess in Sanderson; Palace in Post; Grand in Pecos; Plainview and Granada in Plainview; Grand in McCamey; Palace in Marfa; Grand in Fort Stockton; Palace in Crane; Palace in Canadian; and Granada in Alpine.

Paschall-Texas Theaters, Inc.
Home office: Dallas
Number of theaters: 54
Theaters were the Gem, Strand, State, and Majestic in Wichita Falls; Ritz in Weslaco; Strand, Orpheum, and Waco in Waco; Vernon and Pictorium in Vernon; Queen, Majestic, and Arcadia in Tyler; Gem, Bell, and Arcadia in Temple; Palace and Ranger in San Benito; Columbia and Arcadia in Ranger; Grand and Plaza in Paris; Palace and National in Mexia; Capitol in Mercedes; Queen and Palace in McAllen; Rialto and Arcadia in Harlingen; Wigwam, Ellanay, and Palace in El Paso; Lyric in Eastland; Dreamland and Palace in Denton; Star and Rialto in Denison; Arcadia in Dallas; Ideal and Palace in Corsicana; Gem and Lyric in Brownwood; Queen and Capitol in Brownsville; Palace and National in Breckenridge; Rialto, Paramount, Mission, and Fair in Amarillo; and Palace, Majestic, Queen, and Paramount in Abilene.

Publix Theaters
Home office: New York City
Number of theaters: 22
Same Texas theaters as Interstate Circuit, Inc.

Robb & Rowley Theaters, Inc.
Home office: Dallas
A few years earlier this circuit owned 150 theaters, but, as of 1933, all theaters in Texas had been sold.

Rockett Bros. Co.
Home office: Waxahachie
Number of theaters: 4
Theaters were the Crystal in Midlothian; Pastime in Itasca; Elk in Italy; and Queen in Ferris.

Saenger Theaters, Inc.
Home office: New Orleans
Number of theaters: 16
Texas theaters were the Strand and Old Saenger in New Saenger; Hippodrome in Texarkana; Strand in Orange; Strand and State in McComb; Gaiety in

Kingston; Liberty and Isis in Houston; Old Mill, Circle, and Capitol in Dallas; Tivoli, Palace, Liberty, and Kyle Opera House in Beaumont.

Texas Consolidated Theaters, Inc. (Dent Circuit)
Home office: Dallas in the Majestic Theater
Number of theaters: 61
Texas theaters were the Capitol in Brownsville; Strand, Palace, Majestic, State, and Gem in Wichita Falls; Ritz in Weslaco; National, Waco, Strand, Rivoli, and Orpheum in Waco; Vernon, Queen, and Pictorium in Vernon; Queen, Majestic, and Arcadia in Tyler; Gem, Bell, and Arcadia in Temple; Columbia and Arcadia in Ranger; Plaza, Lamar, and Grand in Paris; Palace and National in Mexia; Capitol in Mercedes; Queen and Palace in McAllen; Rialto and Arcadia in Harlingen; Wigwam, Plaza, Palace, Ellanay, and American in El Paso; Lyric in Eastland; Palace and Dreamland in Denton; Star, Rialto, Denison, and Arcadia in Dallas; Palace, Ideal, and Grand in Corsicana; Lyric and Gem in Brownwood; Gem, Palace, and National in Breckenridge; Rialto, Paramount, Mission, and Fair in Amarillo; and Queen, Paramount, Palace, and Majestic in Abilene.

Texas Federated Theaters
Home office: Dallas
Number of theaters: 15
Theaters were the L'Arcade in Yorktown; Victoria and Princess in Victoria; Palace in Seguin; Palace and Grand in San Marcos; Texas in Sealy; Rialto and Colonial in Greenville; Goliad in Goliad; Palace in El Campo; Orphic in Columbus; Best and American in Bonham; and Alamo in Bellville.

Universal Chain Theaters Corp.
Home office: New York City
Number of theaters: 11
Texas theaters were the Tex and Rig in Wink; Ritz and Rialto in Wellington; Rex in Panhandle; Rex, State, and La Nora in Pampa; Lyric in Dallas; and Rig and Rex in Borger.[1]

The armed services had a circuit of theaters on posts around Texas in 1933. There were theaters at Fort Bliss, El Paso; Brooks Field, Fort Sam Houston, Kelly Field, and Randolph Field in San Antonio; Fort Clark, Brackettville; Fort Crockett, Galveston; and Fort Ringgold, Rio Grande City.[2]

Notes

Introduction

1. David Chesire, *The Book of Movie Photography,* pp. 18–19.
2. Brian Coe, *The History of Movie Photography,* pp. 9–29, 39–51.
3. Q. David Bowers, *Nickelodeon Theatres,* p. 2; Ron Tyler, ed., *The New Handbook of Texas,* p. 998.

Chapter 1. Storefronts to Nickelodeons: The Beginnings to 1914

1. "From the Beginning, Waco a Movie Town," *Waco Tribune-Herald,* July 16, 1967; Bowers, *Nickelodeon Theatres,* p. 2.
2. "From the Beginning"; Bowers, *Nickelodeon,* p. 6.
3. Bowers, *Nickelodeon,* p. 1.
4. Tyler, *The New Handbook of Texas,* p. 998; "From the Beginning"; A. Morton Smith, *The First 100 Years in Cooke County,* pp. 148–49; Coe, *The History of Movie Photography,* p. 112.
5. Stanley Babb, "Moving Pictures Reached Galveston Exactly 50 Years Ago This Month," *Galveston Daily News,* Apr. 10, 1947.
6. Ibid.
7. *Chronicles of Smith County, Texas* 6:1 (spring, 1967): 46.
8. Ibid.; Billy Holcomb, "The Great Movie Palaces of Honey Grove," undated article from Hall-Voyer Foundation.
9. "First S.A. Moving Pictures Used Bedsheet for a Screen," *San Antonio Express-News,* Sept. 26, 1965.
10. A. W. Neville, "Backward Glance," *Paris News,* Mar. 6, 1940.
11. Paul Hochuli, "Former Mayor Says Houston's First Movie House Dates Back to 1898," *Houston Press,* June 10, 1948.
12. "Owner of First Movie House Here Recalls Rock-Tossing Days," *Houston Post,* Apr. 14, 1940.
13. Louis Wolfin, 1988 interview in the Southwest Collection, Texas Tech University, Lubbock.
14. "Cineograph Show," *El Paso Daily Herald,* May 10, 1900.
15. Tyler, *New Handbook of Texas;* Jack Gordon, "Cowtown Seen (?) 100 Years Hence," *Fort Worth Press,* July 13, 1949.
16. Jack Gordon, "Storm Shook Theater—and John Cranked," *Fort Worth Press,* May 28, 1957.
17. Winston O. Sparks, interview by author, typewritten notes, in author's possession, Fort Worth, Dec. 23, 1996.
18. "Jews in West Texas: Runnels County," undated article from the West Texas Collection, Angelo State University, San Angelo; "Watch For Opening of White City," *Ballinger Banner-Leader,* Mar. 5, 1909; *The Permian Historical Annual,* Dec., 1969, p. 7.
19. W. Walworth Harrison, "Greenville's Early Movie Theatres," *Greenville Morning Herald,* May 9, 1950.
20. Ibid.
21. Ibid.
22. "Movie Shows Held Many Locations in Early Days," *Wichita Falls Times,* May 12, 1957; "Giddings Casino Hall," *Giddings 100th Souvenir Book,* undated article from the Institute of Texan Cultures.
23. "Southern Talking Machine Co," undated article from Texas/Dallas History and Archives Division, Dallas Public Library.
24. Bowers, *Nickelodeon,* p. 5.
25. "Majestic Theatre," *Dallas Morning News,* Feb. 4, 1910.
26. Bowers, *Nickelodeon,* pp. 1–8.
27. Maggie Valentine, *The Show Starts on the Sidewalk,* pp. 23–24.

28. Ibid.; Bowers, *Nickelodeon,* p. 43.
29. Map of theater from the Galveston Public Library; Patrick McInroy, "Military Epics in S.A.," *San Antonio Light,* May 30, 1976; Bowers, *Nickelodeon,* pp. 1–8.
30. "First S.A. Moving Pictures."
31. "Airdome Packed for the Opening," *El Paso Herald,* May 28, 1906; "Airdome a New Summer Resort For the Citizens of El Paso," *El Paso Herald,* May 30, 1906.
32. Mildred Stockard, "Houston's 'Flicker' Houses," *Houston Chronicle,* Nov. 11, 1956; Mildred Stockard, undated article from the Texas Room.
33. "Movies Now Are Ranked Over Stage," *Houston Chronicle,* Feb. 22, 1938.
34. Ibid.
35. Arthur F. Sanders, "George K. Jorgensen, Crystal Palace Operator, Established First Motion Picture Show Here in 1907—Recalls Early Days of Industry," *Galveston Tribune,* Jan. 21, 1933.
36. Ibid.
37. "Two 'Country Boys' Operate R & R Circuit," undated article from the Corpus Christi Public Library.
38. *Chronicles of Smith County* 24, no. 2 (Winter, 1985), pp. 19–26; Frank Wagner, "Early Moviehouses in Corpus Christi," undated article from the Corpus Christi Public Library.
39. Harrison, "Greenville's Early."
40. "Lybrands Celebrates 43rd Anniversary in Theatre Business in Wills Point," files of Karl Lybrand; Karl Lybrand, interview by author, typewritten notes, in author's possession, Wills Point, Mar. 13, 1996.
41. George Turner, "Early Movie House Victim of Flaming Film," *Amarillo Globe-News,* Jan. 16, 1974.
42. Ibid.
43. "Movie Shows Held Many Locations."
44. D' Anne McAdams Crews, ed., *Huntsville and Walker County, Texas,* pp. 163–64.
45. "First Waco Movie Flashed on Bedsheet Screen at North 4th Majestic Theater," *Waco Tribune-Herald,* Oct. 15, 1961; "Bedsheet Used for Screen To Show First Movies in Waco," undated article from the Texas Collection; Betty Johnson, "Flashback—Wacoan Recalls Development of Burgeoning Film Industry," *Waco Tribune-Herald,* Sept. 21, 1980.
46. Valentine, *The Show Starts,* p. 23; "First Waco Movie"; "Bedsheet Used for Screen."
47. "Early-Day Stage And Movie Highlights Here Recalled," *Lubbock Avalanche-Journal,* July 26, 1959.
48. Bowers, *Nickelodeon,* p. 11; Francis Raffetto, "58 Years of Magic Shadows," *Dallas Morning News,* Apr. 19, 1970.
49. Virginia Cooper, "When The Movies Came to Dallas," undated article from the Texas/Dallas History and Archives Division.
50. Jack Gordon, "Every Movie Should Have Such a Fan," *Fort Worth Press,* Feb. 15, 1965.
51. Jack Gordon, "Last of City's Nickelodeons Shuts Doors," *Fort Worth Press,* Mar. 31, 1960.
52. Jack Gordon, "When Main Was City's Movie Row," *Fort Worth Press,* May 1, 1969.
53. Oliver Knight, *Fort Worth—Outpost on the Trinity,* 1953 edition, p. 168; Gordon, "Cowtown Seen"; Dave Kehr, "The big canvas," *Chicago Tribune,* Mar. 27, 1988.
54. "Glory of Texas Theater worth another showing," files of Glenn Carr; "Smith Built First Plane Ever Flown In San Angelo," *San Angelo Standard-Times,* Aug. 29, 1954.
55. Jonnie Elzner, *Lamplights of Lampasas County, Texas,* p. 131.
56. Jack Gordon, "Everlasting? Ancient Theater Lamp Burns on into 43rd Year," *Fort Worth Press,* Aug. 2, 1951.

Chapter 2. Nickelodeons to De Luxe Theaters: 1908 to 1921

1. Tyler, *New Handbook of Texas,* p. 998; Don Graham, *Cowboys and Cadillacs,* p. 11.
2. Tyler, *New Handbook of Texas.*
3. Graham, *Cowboys.*
4. Frank Thompson, *The Star Film Ranch; Texas' First Picture Show,* p. 23; "Hatless Men are Chasing through Business Streets of El Paso," *El Paso Herald,* Nov. 19, 1909; "Would Locate Motion Picture Plant Near City," *El Paso Herald,* Aug. 26, 1914.
5. Tony Rimmer, "Austin's first filmmakers," *Daily Texan,* Nov. 29, 1976; Marj Wrightman, "Golden Age Is No More," files of James Buchanan.
6. Rimmer, "Austin's first."
7. James R. Buchanan, "Early Pioneers Of Silent Films in Texas," *FilmTexas,* Sept., 1972.

8. Rimmer, "Austin's first."
9. Wrightman, "Golden Age."
10. Rimmer, "Austin's first."
11. Ibid.; "New Industry to Spread Austin's Fame over Globe," files of James Buchanan.
12. Rimmer, "Austin's first."
13. Ibid.
14. Thompson, *The Star Film,* pp. 12, 15; Ibid., p. 15, citing *Film Index,* Jan. 22, 1910.
15. Ibid., pp. 26–56; McInroy, "Military Epics"; Gerald Ashford, "Early filmmaking recalled," *San Antonio Express-News,* Sept. 26, 1971.
16. Thompson, *The Star Film.*
17. David Middleton, "We're going Hollywood," undated article from the San Antonio Air Logistics Center; Ashford, "Early filmmaking"; James R. Buchanan, "Movie-Making in Texas," pp. 343–45, files of James Buchanan.
18. "Movie Studio May Come Here," *El Paso Herald,* Dec. 30, 1915; Graham, *Cowboys,* p. 13.
19. "Movie Camera Hit by Girl Aviator," *San Antonio Express,* May 14, 1915; F. A. Schmidt, "Hollywood in San Antonio," pp. 2–5, undated article from the Center for Western Cultures, University of Texas at Austin.
20. "In Old El Paso," *El Paso Herald,* June 30, 1942; "In Old El Paso," *El Paso Herald,* June 26, 1942.
21. "El Paso Valley Selected For Motion Picture Making," *El Paso Herald,* July 20, 1920.
22. Ibid.; "Company to Make Films in El Paso," *El Paso Herald,* Feb. 15, 1921.
23. Graham, *Cowboys,* p. 14.
24. "A. AND M. BOYS TO APPEAR IN MOVIES," *The Eagle,* May 29, 1913; John H. Lopez, "The History of Old Movie Houses of Galveston, Texas," undated article from the Galveston Public Library.
25. *The Handbook of Commerce, Texas, 1872–1985,* pp. 156–57.
26. Harrison, "Greenville's Early."
27. Jack Maguire, "Talk of Texas," *Beaumont Enterprise,* Jan. 17, 1971.
28. "To Make Moving Pictures of El Paso Wednesday," *El Paso Herald,* Jan. 25, 1915; "Film Drama to Boost El Paso," *El Paso Herald,* Oct. 18, 1915; "Plenty of Work Getting Warm Welcome For Film Tourists," *El Paso Herald-Post,* Jan. 31, 1940.
29. Alice Reese, "1920 film production had a real local flavor," *Greenville Herald Banner,* Dec. 13, 1994.
30. "Light-Texas Movie is Showing," *San Antonio Light,* Feb. 19, 1928.
31. Undated newspaper clipping from the Louise Kelly Collection; Bob Darden, "An Old Bit of Waco Discovered," *Waco Tribune-Herald,* Apr. 22, 1983.
32. Margaret Smith, interview by author, typewritten notes, in author's possession, McGregor, Mar. 14, 1995.
33. Ibid.
34. "Movies Now Are Ranked Over Stage," *Houston Chronicle,* Feb. 22, 1938.
35. Lawrence Birdsong, interview by author, typewritten notes, in author's possession, Longview, Feb. 19, 1995.
36. "The Alhambra to have Initial Opening Tonight," *El Paso Herald,* Aug. 1, 1914; Jack Gordon, "Ex-Traveling Man to Open New Parkaire Theater Tomorrow," undated article from the Fort Worth Public Library; Gordon, "Storm Shook"; Gordon, "Ex-Traveling."
37. Gordon, "Ex-Traveling."
38. Ibid; files of the Walker County Historical Commission.
39. "R & R Early History," *The 24 Sheeter,* Aug. 21, 1946, pp. 2–3; Bud McDonald, "Old movie memories jogged by conversation," *San Angelo Standard-Times,* Apr. 24, 1980.
40. John H. Rowley, interview by author, typewritten notes, in author's possession, Dallas, Aug. 13, 1998.
41. Martha B. Steimel, "Movie Projectionists Enjoy Work of Lifetime," *Wichita Falls Times,* Feb. 14, 1965.
42. Raffetto, "58 Years."
43. Felix Sanchez, "Projectionist smooth operator," *Corpus Christi Community Life Central,* Dec. 7, 1978; Felix Sanchez, "Like father, like son," *Corpus Christi Caller-Times,* Dec. 7, 1978.
44. "Machinists of Make-Believe," *Southwest Scene,* Sept. 23, 1973.
45. Donna M. Lestage, "A Career In Movies—Behind The Camera," undated article from the Smith County Historical Society.
46. Scotty Davidson, interview by author, typewritten notes, in author's possession, Tyler, Jan. 28, 1997.
47. James Dear, interview by author, typewritten notes, in author's possession, Mineola, Aug. 21, 1997.
48. Raffetto, "58 Years."
49. Lestage, "A Career"; "Crawford to Offer 'Movies,'" *El Paso Herald,* July 13, 1916.

Chapter 3. Grand Movie Palaces: 1921 to 1929

1. Buchanan, "Movie-Making"; Schmidt, "Hollywood in San Antonio," p. 4.
2. "Benroy Motion Pictures," *Dallas Express,* June 3, 1922.
3. Buchanan, "Movie-Making."
4. Schmidt, "Hollywood in San Antonio," p. 6.
5. "Film Company Locates Here," undated article from the Institute of Texan Cultures; Middleton, "We're going Hollywood"; Jack Alicoate, ed., *The 1934 Film Daily Year Book of Motion Pictures,* p. 557, files of John Rowley; Frank Thompson, *Alamo Movies,* p. 117.
6. "Grand Old Woman of Trail Driving Days to be Featured in Picture Soon to be filmed by Paramount at 'La Motta,'" undated article from the Institute of Texan Cultures; "S.A. Will have Movie of Its Own," undated article from the Institute of Texan Cultures; Buchanan, "Movie-Making."
7. Kehr, "The big canvas."
8. Ibid., p. 5; Buchanan, "Movie-Making"; James R. Buchanan, "Location: San Antonio," *Texas Parade* 31 (Apr., 1971): 24–27.
9. Hart Stilwell and Slats Rodgers, *Old Soggy No. 1,* pp. 145–46.
10. Ibid., pp. 149–50; *The History of Johnson County, Texas,* p. 145; Harold Scarlett, "First to fly the skies of Houston," *Tempo,* Sept. 21, 1969.
11. Buchanan, "Location: San Antonio."
12. Gerald Ashford, "The Movie-Makers of San Antonio," *San Antonio Express,* Sept. 26, 1965.
13. "Wings," undated article from the San Antonio Air Logistics Center; An undated, untitled history from the San Antonio Air Logistics Center.
14. Ashford, "The Movie-Makers"; An undated history from the San Antonio Air Logistics Center.
15. *The Permian Historical Annual,* Dec., 1969, p. 7.
16. Assembled from city directories, phone books, and files of author.
17. Three ads from the *Dallas Express,* Jan. 8, 1921.
18. Jeff Millar, "The Lincoln—city's oldest operating theater," *Houston Chronicle,* Sept. 11, 1977.
19. Alma Braudirick, "Honey Grove Theaters," undated article from the Hall-Voyer Foundation.
20. Birdsong interview.
21. Robert Prince, *Dallas—From a Different Perspective,* p. 79.
22. Wagner, "Early Moviehouses."
23. Nicolas Kanellos, *A History of Hispanic Theatre in the United States: Origins to 1940,* pp. 72–85.
24. Map of Elm Street from the Texas/Dallas History and Archives Division.
25. Birdsong interview.
26. "Houston had 25 Theaters Two Decades Ago, 15 on 5 Blocks of Main Street," undated article from the Texas Room, Houston Public Library.
27. Map of theaters from the Galveston Public Library.
28. Jerry Bradbarry, interview by author, typewritten notes, in author's possession, Cleburne, Jan. 31, 1995.
29. Bob and Dorothy Phillips, interview by author, typewritten notes, in author's possession, Sulphur Springs, Feb. 4, 1995.
30. Cooper, "When the Movies."
31. Conover Hunt Jones, "The New Majestic Theatre," files of John H. Rowley.
32. Jackson Davis, "A History of Professional Theater in Dallas, Texas, 1920–1930," Ph.D. diss., Louisiana State University, 1962, pp. 15, 16, 40.
33. William Edward Mitchell, interview by author, typewritten notes, in author's possession, Dallas, Aug. 26, 1998; Steve Blow, "Theater mogul recalls glamour of days gone by," *Dallas Morning News,* Mar. 25, 1998.
34. Jones, "The New Majestic"; Davis, "A History of Professional Theater."
35. Ibid; Undated article from the Texas/Dallas History and Archives Division.
36. Ibid.
37. Jones, "The New Majestic."
38. Jane Preddy, "John Eberson and the Greater Majestic Theatre San Antonio, Texas," Dec., 1989, pp. 2–3, from the Texana Collection, San Antonio Public Library.
39. Undated article from the Texas/Dallas History and Archives Division.
40. Jones, "The New Majestic."
41. Undated article from the Texas/Dallas History and Archives Division; William A. Payne, "Palace Full Of Memories," *Dallas Morning News,* Nov. 29, 1970.
42. Lynn Ashby, "A Fitting Name . . . Majestic," undated article from the Texas Room.
43. Josie Weber, "Majestic," *Houston Chronicle,* Mar. 8, 1970.

44. Ashby, "A Fitting Name."
45. Weber, "Majestic."
46. Ben M. Hall, *The Best Remaining Seats,* p. 167.
47. Weber, "Majestic"; Ink Mendelsohn, "Movie palaces, like Houston's Majestic, were designed to transport patrons to another world," *Houston Chronicle,* Aug. 28, 1983.
48. Louis B. Parks, "60 years ago, Loews chain opened Houston's stately movie theater," *Houston Chronicle,* Oct. 21, 1987.
49. "Loew's State is One of Most Beautiful Theaters on Circuit," *Houston Post,* Oct. 2, 1927.
50. W. G. Roberts, "Loew's State Theatre," *Marquee* 10:1 (first quarter, 1978): 10.
51. Jeff Millar, "It's a Heckuva Way to Have to End an Era," *Houston Chronicle,* Oct. 15, 1972.
52. Judith Singer Cohen, "When the Worth, Hollywood and Palace Ruled 7th Street," *Fort Worth News-Tribune,* Feb. 12, 1988.
53. Preddy, "John Eberson," pp. 3–13; Don Dailey, "The Lady Majestic," undated article from the Daughters of the Republic of Texas Library, San Antonio.
54. Preddy, "John Eberson."
55. Barbara Lau, "Her Majesty Reigns in San Antonio," *Texas Highways* 37:11 (Nov., 1990): 18; Preddy, "John Eberson."
56. Eric E. Brendler, interview by author, typewritten notes, in author's possession, San Antonio, Mar. 9, 1999.
57. Susan McAtee Monday, "At the Aztec," *San Antonio Light,* Mar. 16, 1991; "Exotic Aztec Theater may dazzle audiences once again," *The Medallion,* Sept./Oct., 1992, pp. 4–5; A written description of the Aztec Theater from the Center for Western Cultures.
58. Birdsong interview.
59. Ibid.; Hall, *The Best Remaining,* pp. 187, 196.
60. Hall, *The Best Remaining,* pp. 184–87.
61. Earl McDonald, interview by author, typewritten notes, in author's possession, Dallas, Dec. 10, 1995.
62. Boyd and Mike Milligan, interview by author, typewritten notes, in author's possession, Fort Worth, Jan. 30, 1995.
63. Sparks interview.
64. Paul Rosenfield, "He's Looking Over Your Shoulders," *Dallas Morning News,* Jan. 27, 1963.
65. Davidson interview.
66. Ibid.
67. Ibid.
68. Smith interview.

Chapter 4. "Talkies"—Motion Pictures Learn to Speak: 1928 to 1941

1. Wrightman, "Golden Age."
2. Davis, "A History of Professional Theater," pp. 435–39.
3. Bowers, *Nickelodeon,* p. 91.
4. Ibid.; Hall, *The Best Remaining,* pp. 243–44.
5. Harrison, "Greenville's Early."
6. Neville, "Backward Glances."
7. Bill Walraven, "Step right up to Corpus Christi," undated article from the Corpus Christi Public Library; Bud McDonald, "Old movie memories jogged by conversation," *San Angelo Standard-Times,* Apr. 24, 1980.
8. Sanders, "George K."
9. Frank Wagner, "Early Moviehouses in Corpus Christi," undated article from the Corpus Christi Public Library.
10. Frederic Oheim, "First Movies in New Braunfels Shown in Tent on Market Plaza," *New Braunfels Herald,* Mar. 1, 1973.
11. Tyler, *New Handbook of Texas;* "Talking-Motion Pictures," *Austin American-Statesman,* Apr. 25, 1915.
12. Wagner, "Early Moviehouses"; "Houston Had 25 Theaters."
13. John C. Tibbetts, *The American Theatrical Film,* p. 35; "Veteran Operators, E. T. Pool and W. C. Shaver, Like Projection Room," *Wichita Daily Times,* Nov. 29, 1939; "Talking Movie Production for Amarillo," *Amarillo Daily News,* Mar. 17, 1928; Davis, "A History of Professional Theater," pp. 435–39.
14. "Bedsheet Used for Screen"; Rowley interview.
15. Davis, "A History of Professional Theater," pp. 435–39.
16. Davidson interview.
17. "The Majestic rose as a Mediterranean 'palace' in the heart of downtown S.A.," *San Antonio Light,* Feb. 1, 1970.
18. Earl Moseley, "Date Books Trace Life of Small Town Theater," *Amarillo Globe-Times,* Jan. 12, 1976.

19. Kanellos, *A History of Hispanic*, pp. 72–85; Elzner, "Lamplight of Lampasas"; "Majestic Theatre Opens Monday Night With Talking Pictures," *Canton Herald,* Dec. 6, 1929.
20. *Chronicles of Smith County;* Davis, "A History of Professional Theater," pp. 435–39.
21. Birdsong interview.
22. Kenneth Ragsdale, interview by author, typewritten notes, in author's possession, Austin, Mar. 10, 1999.
23. Ibid.
24. Valentine, *The Show Starts,* p. 92.
25. "Talking Movie Productions."
26. An undated article from the Texas/Dallas History and Archives Division.
27. Rowley interview.
28. Mack Williams, "The Movie That Became a Bank," undated article from the Fort Worth Public Library; "Texas's Sound-Proofed Cry Room Solves One of Mom's Problems," and "Smoking Room to be Feature of Texan Theater," *Hamilton Herald-News,* Feb. 24, 1950; Mary Wynn, *Fort Worth Star-Telegram,* Dec. 8, 1937, undated article from the Fort Worth Public Library.
29. "History of the Paramount," undated history from the Abilene Public Library; Todd Martin, "Dreams of past glory, uncertain future haunt sleeping Texas Theatre," undated article from the San Angelo Public Library; Robin B. Jackson, "The Yucca Theatre: History Here to Stay," *Advantage,* Jan.–Feb., 1984, p. 11.
30. Sparks interview; Dorothy Phillips, Allen Barker, and Brad Davis, interview by author, typewritten notes, in author's possession, Sulphur Springs, Feb. 4, 1995; Jones, "The New Majestic"; "Old Fair Theater Opened Doors Seventeen Years Ago," undated article from the Amarillo Public Library.
31. Birdsong interview.
32. Mitchell interview.
33. Glen Carr, interview by author, typewritten notes, in author's possession, San Angelo, Sept. 15, 1997.
34. William Rast, interview by author, typewritten notes, in author's possession, El Paso, Mar. 6, 1999.
35. Dear interview.
36. Birdsong interview.
37. "Fit for a Screen," *Texas Highways,* Sept., 1998, p. 54.
38. Wilber Myres, interview by author, typewritten notes, in author's possession, Sulphur Springs, Feb. 4, 1995.
39. Ibid.
40. "Wally Akin, 'showman,' dead at 89," undated article from the Abilene Public Library; "Fit for a Screen," p. 53.
41. Ibid; Jeanne Mabey, "The History of WBAP-TV," Feb., 1970, pp. 1–2, from the files of WBAP; Gene Fowler and Bill Crawford, *Border Radio,* pp. 104–107.
42. Josie Weber, undated article from the Texas Room; Jeff Millar, undated article from the Texas Room.
43. Rowley interview.
44. Valentine, *The Show Starts,* p. 97.
45. "Bicentennial Heritage Profile," files of Craig Edge; "Speaking of Texas," *Texas Highways* 37:1 (Jan., 1990): 39.
46. Mark Sanders, "Abandoned Spanish Theater Rich in local history," *Kingsville Record,* July 5, 1981.
47. "Lydia Mendoza: A Family Autobiography," files of Craig Edge; Gloria Bigger, "Teatro Carpa Used to be entertainment spot, Many Celebrities Performed in Kingsville," *Kingsville Record,* Apr. 12, 1972.
48. Carr interview.
49. *Chronicles of Smith County;* Davidson interview; Johnson, "Flashback—Wacoan Recalls."

Chapter 5. War to Wide Screens: 1941 to 1960

1. Mitchell interview; Valentine, *The Show Starts,* p. 166.
2. Rick Smith, "Picture Show—Perfect Image," *San Angelo Standard-Times,* Aug. 9, 1992.
3. Milligan interview.
4. Ibid; Dear interview.
5. Mitchell interview.
6. Lawrence Weldon, interview by author, typewritten notes, in author's possession, Fort Worth, Apr. 10, 1995.
7. Smith interview.
8. Philip Wuntch, "Wilshire rings down curtain on final movie," *Dallas Morning News,* Apr. 24, 1978.
9. Mitchell interview.
10. Wuntch, "Wilshire rings down."
11. Mitchell interview; Valentine, *The Show Starts,* p. 166.
12. McDonald interview.
13. Valentine, *The Show Starts,* pp. 171–72; Jones, "The New Majestic."
14. Milligan interview.
15. Mitchell interview.

16. "Movies Now Are Ranked."
17. Smith interview.
18. Weldon interview.
19. William Stanford, personal history mailed to author.
20. Dear interview.
21. Weldon interview.
22. Mitchell interview.
23. Rowley interview.
24. Dear interview.
25. Lybrand interview.
26. Weldon interview.
27. "Machinists of Make-Believe."
28. Paul Adair, interview by author, typewritten notes, in author's possession, Dallas, Feb. 14, 1995.
29. Stanford history.
30. Carr interview.
31. McDonald interview.
32. Adair interview.
33. McDonald interview.
34. Weldon interview.
35. Myers, Phillips, Barker, and Davis interviews.
36. "Construction To Start This Week on New Harlem Theatre," *Corpus Christi Caller-Times,* Jan. 26, 1941; "Open Movie House for Negroes on Alameda," *El Paso Herald-Post,* Jan. 23, 1941; Laura West Knoll, "An insider's look at an old theater," *The River City Free Press,* Apr. 6, 1979.
37. Lybrand interview.
38. Myers, Phillips, Barker, and Davis interviews.
39. Rast interview.
40. Dear interview.
41. Weldon interview.
42. G. William Jones, *Black Cinema Treasures,* pp. 31–35, 174–78.
43. "Black Film Restoration Draws Overflow Crowd," undated article from the Smith County Historical Society.
44. Don and Susan Sanders, "The Last Picture Show," *Dallas Morning News,* Oct. 4, 1998; Don and Susan Sanders, *The American Drive-In Movie Theatre,* p. 19; Two advertisements in the *Houston Chronicle,* Apr. 21 and June 7, 1940; "Patrons May View Motion Pictures In Comfort of Car," undated article from the Corpus Christi Public Library.
45. Weldon interview; Sanders, *The American Drive-In,* p. 39; Stanford, personal history.
46. "Largest Texas Drive-In Movie is Opened on E. Lancaster," *Fort Worth Star-Telegram,* Oct. 26, 1947; "New $225,000 Drive In Theatre on South Port Opens Next Week," *Corpus Christi Caller-Times,* Jan. 15, 1949; Valentine, *The Show Starts,* pp. 169–70.
47. Sanders, "The Last Picture."
48. Sam Kirkland, interview by author, typewritten notes, in author's possession, Lamesa, Mar. 3, 1999.
49. "Panhandle's First Fly-In Movie Open at Spearman," undated article from the Amarillo Public Library; Sanders, *The American Drive-In,* p. 62.
50. Weldon interview.
51. Ibid.
52. Ibid.
53. Sanders, *The American Drive-In,* p. 65.
54. Rowley interview; Weldon interview; "'The House of Wax' Real Advance in 3-Dimension," *Fort Worth Star-Telegram,* Apr. 12, 1953.
55. Coe, "The History of Movie," pp. 156–58; Paul Adair, "Everything You Wanted To Know About 3-D But Were Ashamed To Ask," files of Paul Adair.
56. Adair interview.
57. Carr interview.
58. Eleanor Wilson, "Texas to be Testing Ground for MGM on 3-D or Flat Production, Schary Says," *Fort Worth Star-Telegram,* Sept. 26, 1953.
59. Dear interview.
60. Coe, "The History of Movie," pp. 144–48.
61. Dorothy Adler, "Cinerama Southwest Premiere Attracts Capacity Audience," *Fort Worth Star-Telegram,* July 2, 1954.
62. Adair interview.
63. Rast interview.
64. Weldon interview.
65. Lestage, "A Career in Movies."
66. "'Marching Herd' to be one of 1938' Big Productions," and "'A Texan' Gets a Light," undated articles from the Institute of Texan Cultures; Ida Belle Hicks, "'We've never Been Licked' Passes its Severest Test Before A&M Audience," undated article from Fort Worth Public Library; Dorothy Adler, "James Stewart Spends Entire Day Trying 'to Enter' Carswell Base," *Fort Worth Star-Telegram,* Apr. 6, 1954; Pete Kendall, "Esquire was youngster among Cleburne movie houses," *Cleburne Times-Review,* Jan. 9, 1991.
67. Frank X. Tolbert, "On Wichita Falls 'Going Hollywood,'" *Wichita Falls Daily News,* June 15, 1955; Elmer Kelton, "Filming Scheduled To Begin

Today For New Brackettville Movie Epic," *San Angelo Standard-Times,* Oct. 17, 1960.

68. "$10,000,000 Movie Making Center Planned Near Here," *Fort Worth Star-Telegram,* Nov. 21, 1956.
69. Ronald Garay, *Gordon McLendon,* files of Dennis Harp.

Appendix 2. Texas Motion Picture Stars

1. Milligan interview.
2. Undated article from Special Collections Division, University of Texas at Arlington Libraries, Arlington; undated article from University of Texas; *Dallas Morning News,* May 26, 1946; *Dallas Morning News,* Mar. 11, 1943.

Appendix 3. Pioneers of the Texas Motion Picture Theater Industry

1. William Whitaker, "Wally Akin, 'showman,' dead at 89," undated article from the Abilene Public Library; "Jack Lilly in Show Business Here 21 Years," *Greenville Morning Herald,* Sept. 1, 1940; "Austin's Moving Picture Industry," *Austin Daily Statesman,* Jan. 19, 1913; Zarko Franks, "To Al Lever It's Perpetual Spring and He's Stepping Down Smartly," *Houston Chronicle,* Apr. 2, 1967; Barbara Overton Chandler and J. Ed Howe, *History of Texarkana and Bowie and Miller Counties,* p. 166; "B. R. McLendon Started Theatre Chain in Idabel," undated article from the Texas/Dallas History and Archives Division, Dallas Public Library.
2. Jack Gordon, "Liberty's Dead, As a Theater; Opened in 1924," *Fort Worth Press,* July 17, 1956; Smith, "Picture Show"; Lindwood Broyles, interview by author, typewritten notes, in author's possession, Fort Worth, Jan. 29, 1996; "Two 'Country Boys'" and "Large Group Employed by Local Shows," undated articles from the Corpus Christi Public Library; "New $225,000 Drive In Theatre On South Port Opens Next Week," *Corpus Christi Caller-Times,* Jan. 15, 1949.
3. Clifford Edge, interview by author, typewritten notes, in author's possession, Robstown, Sept. 12, 1997.

Appendix 4. Theater Circuits in Texas in the 1930s

1. Jack Alicoate, ed., *The 1934 Film Daily Year Book,* pp. 853–76, files of John Rowley.
2. Ibid., p. 849.

Bibliography

Interviews Conducted by Author

Adair, Paul. Dallas, February 14, 1995.
Baker, Allen. Sulphur Springs, February 4, 1995.
Baker, Garnell. Cleburne, January 31, 1995.
Birdsong, Lawrence. Longview, February 19, 1995.
Bradbarry, Jerry. Cleburne, January 31, 1995.
Brendler, Erik E. San Antonio, March 9, 1999.
Broyles, Lindwood "Curly." Fort Worth, January 29, 1996.
Carr, Glen. San Angelo, September 15, 1997.
Creasy, Florence. Houston, January 19, 1999.
Davidson, "Scotty" Littleton. Tyler, January 28, 1997.
Davis, Brad. Sulphur Springs, February 4, 1995.
Dear, James. Mineola, August 21, 1997.
Edge, Clifford. Robstown, September 12, 1997.
Kirkland, Sam. Lamesa, March 3, 1999.
Lybrand, Karl. Wills Point, March 13, 1996.
McDonald, Earl. Dallas, December 10, 1995.
Milligan, Boyd and Mike. Fort Worth, January 30, 1995.
Mitchell, William Edward. Dallas, August 26, 1998.
Myers, Wilber T. Sulphur Springs, February 4, 1995.
Phillips, Bob. Sulphur Springs, February 4, 1995.
Phillips, Dorothy. Sulphur Springs, February 4, 1995.
Ragsdale, Kenneth. Austin, March 10, 1999.
Rast, William C. El Paso, March 6, 1999.
Rowley, John H. Dallas, August 13, 1998.
Smith, Margaret. McGregor, March 14, 1995.
Sparks, Winston O. Fort Worth, December 23, 1996.
Weldon, Lawrence. Fort Worth, April 10, 1995.

Archival Materials and Collections

Abilene Public Library.
Adair, Paul, Files.
Amarillo Public Library.
Armstrong, John J., Files.
Buchanan, James, Files.
Carr, Glen, Files.
Center for Western Culture, University of Texas at Austin.
Corpus Christi Public Library.
Daughters of the Republic of Texas Library, San Antonio.
Edge, Craig, Files.
Fort Worth Public Library.
Galveston Public Library.
Hall-Voyer Foundation, Honey Grove.
Harp, Dennis, Files.
Institute of Texan Cultures, San Antonio.
Louise Kelly Collection, Wichita County Archives, Wichita Falls.
Lybrand, Karl, Files.
Mitchell, William E., Files.
Rowley, John H., Files.
San Antonio Air Logistics Center, Office of History, Kelly Air Force Base, San Antonio.
Smith County Historical Society, Tyler.
Southwest Collection, Texas Tech University, Lubbock.
Special Collections Division, University of Texas at Arlington Libraries, Arlington.
Stanford, William, personal history mailed to author.
Texana Collection, San Antonio Public Library.
Texas/Dallas History and Archives Division, Dallas Public Library.
Texas Collection, Baylor University, Waco.
Texas Room, Houston Public Library.
Walker County Historical Commission, Huntsville.
WBAP-TV, files at KXAS-TV, Fort Worth.
West Texas Collection, Angelo State University, San Angelo.
Wolfin, Louis, from the Southwest Collection, Texas Tech University, Lubbock.

Books and Articles

"$10,000,000 Movie Making Center Planned Near Here." *Fort Worth Star-Telegram,* November 21, 1956.

The 24 Sheeter. 3:24 (August 21, 1946): 2–3.

"A. AND M. BOYS TO APPEAR IN MOVIES." *The Eagle,* May 29, 1913.

Adler, Dorothy. "Cinerama Southwest Premiere Attracts Capacity Audience." *Fort Worth Star-Telegram,* July 2, 1954.

———. "James Stewart Spends Entire Day Trying 'to Enter' Carswell Base." *Fort Worth Star-Telegram,* April 6, 1954.

Advertisements on Motion Picture Theaters, *Houston Chronicle,* April 21 and June 7, 1940.

Advertisements on Motion Picture Theaters, *Dallas Express,* January 8, 1921.

"Airdome a new summer resort for the citizens of El Paso." *El Paso Herald,* May 30, 1906.

"Airdome Packed for the Opening." *El Paso Herald,* May 28, 1906.

"The Alhambra to Have Initial Opening Tonight." *El Paso Herald,* August 1, 1914.

Ashford, Gerald. "Early filmmaking recalled." *San Antonio Express-News,* September 26, 1971.

———. "The Movie-Makers of San Antonio." *San Antonio Express,* September 26, 1965.

"Austin's Moving Picture Industry." *Austin Daily Statesman,* January 19, 1913.

Babb, Stanley. "Moving Pictures Reached Galveston Exactly 50 Years Ago This Month." *Galveston Daily News,* April 10, 1947.

"Benroy Motion Picture." *Dallas Express,* June 3, 1922.

Bigger, Gloria. "Teatro Carpa Used to be Entertainment Spot, Many Celebrities Performed in Kingsville." *Kingsville Record,* April 12, 1972.

Blow, Steve. "Theater mogul recalls glamour of days gone by." *Dallas Morning News,* March 25, 1998.

Bowers, Q. David. *Nickelodeon Theaters.* Vestal, N.Y.: The Vestal Press, 1986.

Buchanan, James R. "A Look at the Texas Film Industry." *Texas Business Review* 46:1 (January, 1972): 8–15.

———. "Early Pioneers of Silent Films in Texas." *FilmTexas,* September, 1972.

———. "Location: San Antonio." *Texas Parade* 31 (April, 1971): 24–27.

Chandler, Barbara Overton, and J. Ed Howe. *History of Texarkana and Bowie and Miller Counties.* Shreveport: J. Ed Howe, 1939.

Cheshire, David. *The Book of Movie Photography.* New York: Alfred A. Knopf, 1979.

Chronicles of Smith County, Texas 6:1 (spring, 1967): 46.

Chronicles of Smith County, Texas 24:2 (winter, 1985): 19–35.

"Cineograph Show." *El Paso Daily Herald,* May 10, 1900.

Coe, Brian. *The History of Movie Photography.* Westfield, N.J., Eastview Editions, 1981.

Cohen, Judith Singer. "When the Worth, Hollywood and Palace Ruled 7th Street." *Fort Worth News-Tribune,* February 12, 1988.

"Company to Make Films in El Paso." *El Paso Herald,* February 15, 1921.

"Construction to Start This Week on New Harlem Theatre." *Corpus Christi Caller-Times,* January 26, 1941.

"Crawford to Offer 'Movies.'" *El Paso Herald,* July 13, 1916.

Crews, D' Anne McAdams, ed. *Huntsville and Walker County, Texas.* Huntsville: Sam Houston State University Press, 1976.

Darden, Bob. "An old bit of Waco discovered." *Waco Tribune-Herald,* April 22, 1983.

Davis, Jackson. "A History of Professional Theater in Dallas, Texas, 1920–1930." Ph.D. diss. Louisiana State University, Baton Rouge, 1962.

"Drive-In Theatre Opens Tonight." *Houston Chronicle,* June 7, 1940.

"Early-Day Stage And Movie Highlights Here Recalled." *Lubbock Avalanche-Journal,* July 26, 1959.

Elliott, Carolyn. "Movies Took Time Out for 'Amos and Andy.'" *San Antonio Light,* June 25, 1978.

"El Paso Valley Selected for Motion Picture Making." *El Paso Herald,* July 20, 1920.

Elzner, Jonnie. *Lamplights of Lampasas County, Texas.* Austin: Firm Foundation Publishing House, 1951.

"Exotic Aztec Theater may dazzle audiences once again." *The Medallion,* September/October, 1992, pp. 4–5.

"Film Drama to Boost El Paso." *El Paso Herald,* October 18, 1915.

"Finishing Up the El Paso Film Drama; Actors Busy." *El Paso Herald,* December 13, 1915.

"First S.A. Moving Pictures Used Bedsheet for a Screen." *San Antonio Express-News,* September 26, 1965.

"First Waco Movie Flashed on Bedsheet Screen at North 4th Majestic Theater." *Waco Tribune-Herald,* October 15, 1961.

"Fit for a Screen." *Texas Highways.* September, 1998, pp. 50–56.

Fowler, Gene, and Bill Crawford. *Border Radio.* Austin: Texas Monthly Press, 1987.

Franks, Zarko. "To Al Lever It's Perpetual Spring and He's Stepping Down Smartly." *Houston Chronicle,* April 2, 1967.

"From the Beginning, Waco a Movie Town." *Waco Tribune-Herald,* July 16, 1967.

Gordon, Jack. "Cowtown Seen (?) 100 Years Hence." *Fort Worth Press,* July 13, 1949.

———. "Everlasting? Ancient Theater Lamp Burns on into 43rd Year." *Fort Worth Press,* August 2, 1951.

———. "Every Movie Should Have Such a Fan." *Fort Worth Press,* February 15, 1965.

———. "Last of City's Nickelodeons Shuts Doors." *Fort Worth Press,* March 31, 1960.

———. "Liberty's Dead, As a Theater; Opened in 1924." *Fort Worth Press,* July 17, 1956.

———. "Storm Shook Theater—and John Cranked." *Fort Worth Press,* May 28, 1957.

"When Main Was City's Movie Row." *Fort Worth Press,* May 1, 1969.

Graham, Don. *Cowboys and Cadillacs.* Austin: Texas Monthly Press, 1983.

Granberry, Mike. "The Last of the Last Picture Shows." *Dallas Morning News,* September 25, 1977.

"Grand Central Theatre." *Dallas Express,* January 8, 1921.

Griffith, Richard, and Arthur Mayer. *The Birth of the Movies.* New York: Simon & Schuster, 1957.

Hall, Ben M. *The Best Remaining Seats.* New York: Bramhall House, 1961.

The Handbook of Commerce, Texas, 1872–1985. Wolfe City: Henington Publishing Company, 1985, pp. 156–57.

Harrison, W. Walworth. "Greenville's Early Movie Theatres." *Greenville Morning Herald,* May 9, 1950.

———. *History of Greenville and Hunt County, Texas.* Waco: Texian Press, 1977, pp. 285–93.

"Hatless Men are Chasing Through Business Streets of El Paso." *El Paso Herald,* November 19, 1909.

Hawley, Douglas. "Uncle Lou Bessinger at Helm of Queen Theater for 32 Years." *Dallas Morning News,* April 30, 1945.

Hays, Lavern. "Olympic featured silent films." *Canyon News,* March 4, 1982.

History of Johnson County, Texas. Dallas: Curtis Media Corporation, p. 145.

Hochuli, Paul. "Former Mayor Says Houston's First Movie House Dates Back to 1898." *Houston Press,* June 10, 1948.

Holloway, Bill. "Illusions of Grandeur." *Texas Monthly* 10:10 (October, 1982): 150–57.

"'The House of Wax' Real Advance in 3-Dimension." *Fort Worth Star-Telegram,* April 12, 1953.

Howard, Katherine. "Orchestra Ready for Castle Movie." *Fort Worth Star-Telegram,* March 31, 1939.

"In 1907, Galveston's first motion . . . ." *Galveston News,* May 31, 1953.

"In Old El Paso." *El Paso Herald,* May 10, 1940; June 26 and June 30, 1942.

"Jack Lilly In Show Business Here 21 Years." *Greenville Morning Herald,* September 1, 1940.

Jackson, Robin B. "The Yucca Theatre: History Here to Stay." *Advantage,* January–February, 1984.

Johnson, Betty. "Flashback—Wacoan Recalls Development of Burgeoning Film Industry." *Waco Tribune-Herald,* September 21, 1980.

Johnson, Lori K. "A sequel for Texas Theatre." *Dallas Morning News,* November 11, 1990.

Jones, G. William. *Black Cinema Treasures.* Denton: University of North Texas Press, 1991.

Kanellos, Nicolas. *A History of Hispanic Theatre in the United States: Origins to 1940.* Austin: University of Texas Press, 1990.

Kehr, Dave. "The big canvas." *Chicago Tribune,* March 27, 1988.

Kelton, Elmer. "Filming Scheduled To Begin Today For New Brackettville Movie Epic." *San Angelo Standard-Times,* October 17, 1960.

Kendall, Pete. "Esquire was youngster among Cleburne Movie houses." *Cleburne Times-Review,* January 9, 1991.

Knight, Oliver. *Fort Worth—Outpost on the Trinity.* Norman: University of Oklahoma Press, 1953; reprint, Fort Worth: Texas Christian University Press, 1990.

Knoll, Laura West. "An insider's look at an old theater." *River City Free Press,* April 6, 1979.

"Largest Texas Drive-In Movie Is Opened on E. Lancaster." *Fort Worth Star-Telegram,* October 26, 1947.

Lau, Barbara. "Her Majesty Reigns in San Antonio." *Texas Highways* 37:11 (November, 1990): 18–25.

"Light-Texas Movie is Showing." *San Antonio Light,* February 19, 1928.

"Loew's State is One of Most Beautiful Theaters on Circuit." *Houston Post,* October 2, 1927.

"Machinists of Make-Believe." *Southwest Scene,* September 23, 1973.

Mack, Jerry. "Almanac." *San Angelo Standard-Times,* August 14, 1983.

"The Majestic rose as a Mediterranean 'palace' in the heart of downtown S.A." *San Antonio Light,* February 1, 1970.

"Majestic Theatre." *Dallas Morning News,* February 4, 1910.

"Majestic Theatre Opens Monday Night With Talking Pictures." *Canton Herald,* December 6, 1929.

"The Mammoth." *Dallas Express,* January 8, 1921.

Mendelsohn, Ink. "Movie palaces, like Houston's Majestic, were designed to transport patrons to another world." *Houston Chronicle,* August 28, 1983.

McDonald, Bud. "Old movies memories jogged by conversation." *San Angelo Standard-Times,* April 24, 1980.

McGuire, Jack. "Talk of Texas." *Beaumont Enterprise,* January 17, 1971.

McInroy, Patrick. "Military Epics in S.A." *San Antonio Light,* May 30, 1976.

Millar, Jeff. "The Lincoln—city's oldest operating theater." *Houston Chronicle,* September 11, 1977.

———. "It's a Heckuva Way to Have to End an Era." *Houston Chronicle,* October 15, 1972.

Monday, Susan McAtee. "At the Aztec." *San Antonio Light,* March 16, 1991.

Moseley, Earl. "Date Books Trace Life of Small Town Theater." *Amarillo Globe-Times,* January 12, 1976.

"Movies Now are Ranked Over Stage." *Houston Chronicle,* February 22, 1938.

"Movie Camera Hit by Girl Aviator." *San Antonio Express,* May 14, 1915.

"Movie Shows Held Many Locations in Early Days." *Wichita Falls Times,* May 12, 1957.

"Movie Studio May Come Here." *El Paso Herald,* December 30, 1915.

Neville, A. W. "Backward Glance." *Paris News,* March 6, 1940.

"New $225,000 Drive In Theatre on South Port Opens Next Week." *Corpus Christi Caller-Times,* January 15, 1949.

North, Joe. "City Story an Angelo Industry Film." *San Angelo Standard-Times,* May 3, 1957.

Oheim, Frederic. "First Movies in New Braunfels Shown in Tent on Market Plaza." *New Braunfels Herald,* March 1, 1973.

"Open Movie House for Negroes on Alameda." *El Paso Herald-Post,* January 23, 1941.

"Owner of First Movie House Here Recalls Rock-Tossing Days." *Houston Post,* April 14, 1940.

"Palace Theatre." *Dallas Express,* January 8, 1921.

Parks, Louis B. "60 years ago, Loew's chain opened Houston's stately movie theater." *Houston Chronicle,* October 21, 1987.

Payne, William A. "Palace Full of Memories." *Dallas Morning News,* November 29, 1970.

The Permian Historical Annual. Odessa, Tex.: Permian Historical Society, December, 1969.

"Plenty of Work Getting Warm Welcome for Film Tourists." *El Paso Herald-Post,* January 31, 1940.

Prince, Robert. *Dallas—From a Different Perspective.* N.p.: Nortex Press, 1933.

"R & R Early History." *The 24 Sheeter* 3:24 (August 21, 1946): 2–3.

Raffetto, Francis. "58 Years of Magic Shadows." *Dallas Morning News,* April 19, 1970.

Reese, Alice. "1920 film production had a real local flavor." *Greenville Herald Banner,* December 13, 1994.

Rimmer, Tony. "Austin's first filmmakers." *Daily Texan,* November 29, 1976.

Roberts, W. G. "Loew's State Theatre." *Marquee* 10:1 (first quarter, 1978): 10.

Rosenfield, John. "Linda, Ginger and Ann . . . Three Daughters of the Dallas Area." *Dallas Morning News,* May 26, 1946.

Rosenfield, Paul. "He's Looking Over Your Shoulders." *Dallas Morning News,* January 27, 1963.

Sanchez, Felix. "Like father, like son." *Corpus Christi Caller-Times,* December 7, 1978.

———. "Projectionist Smooth Operator." *Corpus Christi Community Life Central,* December 7, 1978.

Sanders, Arthur F. "George K. Jorgensen, Crystal Palace Operator, Established First Motion Picture Show Here in 1907—Recalls Early Days of Industry." *Galveston Tribune,* January 21, 1933.

Sanders, Don and Susan. *The American Drive-In Movie Theater.* Hong Kong: Motorbooks International Publishers, 1997.

———. "The Last Picture Show." *Dallas Morning News,* October 4, 1998.

Sanders, Mark. "Abandoned Spanish Theater Rich in Local History." *Kingsville Record,* July 5, 1981.

Smith, A. Morton. *The First 100 Years in Cooke County.* San Antonio: The Naylor Company, 1976.

Smith, Rick. "Picture Show—Perfect Images." *San Angelo Standard-Times,* August 9, 1992.

"Smith Built First Plane Ever Flown In San Angelo." *San Angelo Standard-Times,* August 29, 1954.

"Smoking Room to Be Feature of Texan Theater." *Hamilton Herald-News,* February 24, 1950.

"Speaking of Texas." *Texas Highways* 37:1 (January, 1990): 39.

Steimel, Martha B. "Movie Projectionists Enjoy Work of Lifetime." *Wichita Falls Times,* February 14, 1965.

Stilwell, Hart, and Slats Rodgers. *Old Soggy No. 1.* New York: Julian Messner, Inc., 1954.

Stockard, Mildred. "Houston's 'Flicker' Houses." *Houston Chronicle,* November 11, 1956.

"Talking-Motion Pictures." *Austin American-Statesman,* April 25, 1915.

"Talking Movie Productions for Amarillo." *Amarillo Daily News,* March 17, 1928.

Tanco, Burton. "Wichita Falls Youngsters Starred in Movie About Dope Addiction." *Abilene Reporter-News,* July 3, 1955.

Temple, Georgia. "Since 1917, movie theaters flicker, changed, endured." *Midland Reporter Telegram,* July 4, 1985.

"Texas's Sound-Proofed Cry Room Solves One of Mom's Problems." *Hamilton Herald-News,* February 24, 1950.

"Theatre Boom Stimulates So. Side Progress." *Dallas Express,* February 27, 1937.

Thompson, Frank. *Alamo Movies.* Plano: Wordware Publishing, Inc., 1991.

———. *The Star Film Ranch: Texas' First Picture Show.* Plano: The Republic of Texas Press, 1996.

"Three-Dimension Feature Climaxes 25 Years of Work." *Fort Worth Star-Telegram,* January 8, 1953.

Tibbetts, John C. *The American Theatrical Film.* Bowling Green: Bowling Green State University Popular Press, 1985.

Tolbert, Frank X. "On Wichita Falls 'Going Hollywood.'" *Wichita Falls Daily News,* June 15, 1955.

"To Make Moving Pictures of El Paso Wednesday." *El Paso Herald,* January 25, 1915.

Turner, George. "Early Movie House Victim of Flaming Film." *Amarillo Globe-News,* January 16, 1974.

———. "Interstate: 70 Years of Community Service." *Amarillo Globe-Times,* March 20, 1975.

Tyler, Ron, ed. *The New Handbook of Texas.* Austin: Texas State Historical Association, 1996.

Valentine, Maggie. *The Show Starts on the Sidewalk.* Hong Kong: Everbest Printing Company, 1994.

"Veteran Operators, E. T. Pool and W. C. Shaver, Like Projection Room." *Wichita Daily Times,* November 29, 1939.

"Watch For Opening of White City." *Ballinger Banner-Leader,* March 5, 1909.

Weber, Josie. "Majestic." *Houston Chronicle,* March 8, 1970.

Williams, Rosemary. "Family Adventures at the Drive-In." *Texas Highways* 44:9 (September, 1997): 24–31.

Wilson, Eleanor. "Texas to Be Testing Ground for MGM On 3-D or Flat Production, Schary Says." *Fort Worth Star-Telegram,* September 26, 1953.

"Would Locate Motion Picture Plant Near City." *El Paso Herald,* August 26, 1914.

Wuntch, Philip. "Wilshire rings down curtain on final movie." *Dallas Morning News,* April 24, 1978.

Index

Note: Pages with illustrations are indicated by italics.

Abilene, 94–97, 105

Adair, Paul: interest in movies at age seven, 125–26; on projection booth fire, 127; shows *This is Cinerama,* 142–43; on 3-D movies, 140–41

Aggie Theater (Arlington), *115*

Agriculture and Mechanical College of Texas at College Station, 37

air conditioning, 59, 66–67, 106; at Loew's State, 69

Air Dome (Mineola), *25*

air domes, 8, 9, *10,* 13, 20, 25, *25,* 43, 55, 132; in San Angelo, 42–43; in Waco (1908), 20–21

Air Dome (San Angelo), 42–43

Air Dome (Waco), 20–21

Airline Drive-In (Houston), *132*

Akin, Wally, 105, 175

Alamo, The, 31, 34

Alamo, The, 145

Amarillo, 19–20, *29,* 78, 100; first projected image (1890s), 8; first sound movie, 86

Amos 'n' Andy, 65, 131

Anderson, G. M. "Broncho Billy," 29

Arcadia Theater (Ranger), *120*

Around the World in Eighty Days, 121

"atmospheric" theaters, 61–72, *66, 72,* 97, *111. See also* grand movie palaces

Austin, *12, 16, 17, 24, 124;* first projected image (1900), 8; Majestic Theater, 61; sound for silent movies, 84; Tilley Brother's film production, *30, 31,* 31–33; town-booster films (1915), 38

automatic player-piano. *See* piano(s)

Autry, Gene, 107, 173

aviation in motion pictures, 35, 51–54

Aztec Theater (San Antonio), 72

Baker, Bob, 22, 43; on projection booth fire, 46–47

Ballinger, 9

ballyhoo, 97–107; in Corpus Christi, *98, 99;* in Greenville's first theater, 9–11; in nickelodeons, 13, 17; in Waco, *79, 80, 100, 101,* 101–104, *102, 103, 104, 105*

Bara, Theda, 25

Belleville, 51–52

Benny, Jack, 67

Benroy Motion Pictures Corporation (Dallas), 48–49

Berle, Milton, 67

Bernhardt, Sarah, 33

Berrymore, John, 84

Big Springs, 17–18, 41, 83

Bijou Nickelodeon (Austin), *16*

Biograph, 6, 16, 28, 32

Birdsong, Lawrence: Grand Theater (Longview), 40; on his first projector, 40–41; on organs with sound movies, 89–91; on promotion on theater row (Dallas), 100; on promotion at theaters, 100, 104; on theater organs, 73; on theater row (Dallas), 57-59

Bitzer, G. W. "Billy," 28

black tops, *3*

Blood of Jesus, The, 131

booking movies, 92, 118–23; for nickelodeons (1907), 16; in the 1910s, 41

Bow, Clara, 53

Bowie Theater (Brownwood), *114*

Bowie Theater (Fort Worth), 94

box office. *See* ticket office

Brendler, Erik, 71–72

Brenon-Alvares Productions (El Paso), 36

Bronte, 110

Brownsville, 112, 144

Bunny, John, 16

buying films for nickelodeons, 14. *See also* booking movies

Bwana Devil, 139, *139,* 140, 142

Byer's Opera House (Fort Worth), 26

Cactus Drive-In (Pharr), *133*

Camp Stanley. *See Wings*

Cantinflas, 107
Canton, 120
Canyon, 89
Capitol Theater (Dallas), 100–101, 113, *114*
Capri Theater (El Paso), 143
carbide light, 9, 11
Carr, Glen: interest in movies as a child (1946), 126; promotion in theaters, 101; Spanish theaters (San Angelo), 108; 3-D movies, 141
Carter, Amon G., 117
Cassidy, Hopalong, 173
Central Shipping, 121
Chaplin, Charlie, 22, 83
chaptered movies. *See* serials
checkers, theater, 123–25
Childress, 45
Cielo Studio, 145
Cinerama, 110, 142–43
Cisco, 126
Cleburne, 52, 59
Cliff Queen Theater (Dallas), 77
Clough, Roy, 30
Cohen, Bernie, 90–91
color movies, 16, 18–19, 25, 46, 51
Columbia Theater (Ranger), *125*
Commerce, 38
concession stands, 116–17, *117*
Concho Theater Group, 25. *See also* Robb, Harold and Ed Rowley
Cooper, 25
Corpus Christi, 44, 129, *74, 98, 99;* first drive-in theater in, 132–33; Gulf Drive-In in, 134; promotional material in, 104; silent movie operators in, 43–47; sound for silent movies in, 83; sound for Spanish movies in, 84; Spanish-language theaters in, 57
Cozy Nickelodeon (Waco), *20*
Crawford, Jesse, 74
Crawford Theater (El Paso), 47
Crescent Nickelodeon (Austin), *24*
Crystal Nickelodeon (Dallas), 43, *44*
Crystal Nickelodeon (Waco), *19*
Cyclone Pete's Matrimony, 33

Dallas, 44, 92, *93, 94, 95, 114,* 129; Benroy Motion Pictures Corporation in (1922), 48–49; Bob Baker in, 43; Cliff Queen Theater in, *77;* Crystal Nickelodeon in, *44;* desegregation of Majestic in, 57, 65; Earl McDonald in, 126–27; early film exchanges in, 16, 29; early movie operators in, 43–47; first movies at Majestic in (1907), 11; first projected image in (1897), 4; first sound movie in, 84–87; Harlem and (Grand) Central Theaters in, *55,* 55–57; Interstate Theaters applying for a television license (1946), 115, *116;* Interstate Theaters on Elm Street in, 113; jackrabbit theaters in, 59; *Jazz Singer, The,* shown in (1928), 84–87; Knox Theater in, *94;* Lawn Theater in, *95;* Majestic Theater in, 57, 61–65, *62, 63, 64,* 92, 100, *109;* minority theaters in (1921), 55–57; neighborhood theaters in, 77, *92,* 92–94; nickelodeons in, *21,* 21–23; obtaining equipment during WWII, 112; organ at Majestic in, 74; organ at Palace in, 74, 75, 116; organ with sound movies, 89–91; Palace Theater in, 58–59, 65–66, 100; Paul Adair of, 125; projection booth fires in (1915), 46–47; Sack Amusement Enterprises in, 130, 131; silent movie operators in, 43–47; staging aviation crashes for movies in, 51; theater row in, 57–59, *58,* 100–101; Washington Nickelodeon in, 21–23, *21,* 43; working at Palace in, 76; Wylie York of, 44
Davidson, "Scotty," 144; on joining operator's union (1920s), 76–78; on learning to be a projectionist (1919), 45–46; on projection booth fires, 47, 78; on seeing and showing sound movies, 86–89; on seeing first movie as child (1914), 45; on showing *Gone With The Wind,* 108–109
Dear, James: on booking movies, 119; on promotion, 104; on special balcony for blacks, 130; on theater checkers, 123–24; on 3-D movies, 141; on war tax, 112; on working at theater in Mineola, 46
Del Rio, Delores, 107
de luxe theaters, 38–43, *39,* 54–55, *58, 60, 61, 62, 63, 64, 66, 67, 68, 69, 70, 71, 72, 74, 77, 79, 80, 85, 86, 90, 93, 94, 95, 96, 97, 98, 101, 102, 112, 114, 115, 117, 118, 119, 120, 122, 123, 124, 125, 129, 130, 132, 133, 134, 139, 140;* list of, 54–55
De Mille, Cecil B., 33
Denison, 131
depression and the movies, the, 44, 82, 92–106
Dirty Gertie From Harlem, 131
Dixie Nickelodeon (Houston), *12,* 59
Don Juan, 84
Dorothy Theater (Huntsville), 41
Dove, Billy, 46
Drive-In Short Reel Theater (Galveston), 132
drive-in theaters, 124–25, 126, 129, *132,* 132–39, *133, 134;* list of, 134, 138–39
Duncan Movie Posters, 126

Eberson, John, 61–72; and Majestic (Austin), 61; and Majestic (Dallas), 61–65, *62, 63, 64;* and Majestic (Houston), 66–68, *66, 67;* and Majestic (San Antonio), 69–72, *71, 72*
Edge, Clifford, 176

Edison, Thomas A., 4, 5, 8, 11, 28; and first attempts at movie sound (1890s), 82, 83
El Paso, 13–14, 41, *74*, 129, *129*, *142*, 143; Brenon-Alvares Productions in (1920), 36; early film production in (1915), 35; Essanay Film in (1909), 29–30; first projected image in (1900), 8; Pasograph Company in (1918), 36; projection booth fires in, 47; Service Film Company in (1921), 36; *This is Cinerama* shown in, 143, *142;* town-booster films in (1915), 38; Ziegfeld Cinema Corporation in (1918), 36
El Rey Theater (El Paso), *129*
equipment for early movie production, 11
Essanay Studios (El Paso), 16, 29–30
Evans, Dale, 173
Excel Fotoplay Company (San Antonio), 35

Fair Theater (Amarillo), 100
Fields, W. C., 67
film delivery companies, 119, 121
Film Forward Agency, 119
film production, *29; Alamo, The,* 145; Benroy Motion Pictures Corporation (1922), 48–49; Biograph Company (1900), 28; *Blood of Jesus, The,* 131; Brenon-Alvares Productions (1920), 36; *Dirty Gertie From Harlem,* 131; Essanay Film Manufacturing Company (1909), 29–30; Excel Fotoplay Company (1915), 35; films by Spencer Williams, 131–32; fire during production, 49, *50; Giant Gila Monster, The* 145; *Indian Paint,* 145; *In The Hot Lands,* 34; Jester Comedy Company (1918), 36; *Juke Joint,* 131; *Killer Shrews, The,* 145; King Vidor, 30; *Marching Herd, The,* 51, 144; movies made during WWII for black audiences, 131; *Narcotic Squad,* 145; National Pictures Gulf Coast Studio, 49–51; Out West Pictures (1926), 49; in the Panhandle (1916), 35; Pasograph Company (1918), 36; San Antonio Photo Plays Studio, 35; San Antonio Pictures Corporation (1923), 48; Service Film Company (1921), 36; Shamrock Photoplay Corporation (1917), 35; Siege and Fall of the Alamo Motion Picture Corporation (1911), 35; staged aviation crashes, 51–52; Star Film Ranch (1910), 33–35, *34; Strategic Air Command,* 144–45; Sunset Picture Corporation (1917), 35–36, *36, 37; Their Lives by a Slender Thread,* 32–33; Tilley Brothers (1910), *30, 31,* 30–33; town-booster films, 37–38; *Two Rode Together,* 145; *Warrens of Virginia, The* (1923), 49, *50; We've Never Been Licked,* 144; *Wings* (1926), 52–54, *52, 53, 54;* Ziegfeld Cinema Corporation (1918), 36
fires in projection booths, 20, 46–47, 78–80, 127–28; in film production, 49, *50;* in nickelodeons (1910), 15
Flanagan, Weldon, 116
flick(er)s, 3
Fort Sam Houston: during filming of *Wings* (1926), 52–54, *52, 53, 54;* Tilley Brother's film production of, 30
Fort Worth, 75–76, *96, 97,* 97–98, 124–25, 128, 129, *132,* 133; attending Isis Theater in, 75–76; first all-black theater in (1937), 94, *96;* first movie theater in the stockyards in (1904), 8–9, *42;* first projected image in (1903), 8–9; Isis Theater opening in (1914), 41, *42;* long-burning theater light bulb in, 26, *26;* Meadowbrook Drive-In in, 136–38; nickelodeons in, *22, 23,* 23–25; Pike Drive-In in, 134; Pix Theater during the war in, 111–12; Poly Theater and Amon G. Carter in, 117; River Oaks Theater during WWII in, 112; sound movies in, 81–82; Texas' largest drive-in in (1947), 134; 3-D movies in, 139; Worth Theater in, 69
Foster and Lincoln Studios, 55

Gainesville, 4
Galveston, 14, *60, 61,* 83; early film production in (1900), 28, 30; first drive-in theater in (1938), 132; first projected image in (1897), 4–5; nickelodeons in (1907), 13, 15–17; theater row in, 59; town-booster films in (1915), 37–38
Gayety Theater (Fort Worth), *97*
Giant Gila Monster, The, 145
Giddings, 11
Gladewater, 40
Gone With The Wind, 108–109, *109*
Graham, 104
(Grand) Central Theater (Dallas), 21, 49, 55, 58
grand movie palaces, 59–72; Aztec, 72; built during the depression, 94–96; Loew's State, 68–69, *70;* Majestic (Dallas), 61–65, *62, 63, 64;* Majestic (Houston), 66–68, *66, 67;* Majestic (San Antonio), 69–72, *71, 72;* Metropolitan, 68, *68, 69;* Palace (Dallas), 65-66; Paramount, 94, 97; Texas (San Angelo), 94, *111;* Worth, 69; Yucca, 94, 97
Grant, Kathryn, 107
Great Train Robbery, The, 8, 9, 25, 26
Greenville, 25, 55; early nickelodeons in, 18–19; first projected image in, 9–11; sound for silent movies in, 83; town-booster films in, 38
Gulf Drive-In (Corpus Christi), 134

Hamilton, 129, *146*
Harden, Johnny, 112
"hardtops." *See* grand movie palaces
Harlem Theater (Dallas), 55, *55,* 56, 58
Harlingen, 112
Harling Theater (San Antonio), *119*
Harrison, W. Walworth, 38; on early movies (Greenville), 9–11; on films shown in nickelodeons, 18–19; on sound for silent movies, 83

Hart, William S., 22
Highland Theater (San Antonio), *123*
Hippodrome (Waco), *15,* 79–80, *79, 80*
Hoblitzelle, Karl, 59–72, *109,* 115, 121; and concessions stands, 117; and Interstate's applying for a television license (1945), 115, *116;* and Interstate during WWII, 112–13; and Majestic (Dallas), 61–65, *62, 63, 64;* and Majestic (Houston), 61, 66–68, *66, 67;* and Majestic (San Antonio), 69–72, 71, 72
Hogg, James S., 48
Holly, Buddy, 136
Honey Grove, 6, 55
Horwitz, Will, *85,* 105–106, 175
House of Wax, The, 139, *140*
Houston, *40,* 52, *86, 90,* 92, *132,* 186; first de luxe theater in (1913), 40; first drive-in in, 133; first projected image in (1898), 7–8; Interstate Circuit in, *66,* 66–68, *67;* Loew's State in, 68–69, *70;* Majestic Theater in, 61, *66,* 66–68, *67;* Metropolitan Theater in, 68, *68, 69;* nickelodeon fire in (1910), 15; nickelodeons in (1906), *12,* 14, 55, *56;* Pastime Theater in, 55, *56;* sound for silent movies in, 84; theater row in, 59; Tilley Brothers in, 30; Will Horwitz of, *85,* 105–106
Hughes, Howard, 92–94
Humanuva Sound System, 83
Humphries, Paul, 76
Huntsville, 20, 41, 92–94

illustrated songs, 13, 14, 18–19
Immortal Alamo, The, 34
Indian Paint, 145
International Alliance of Theatrical Stage Employees and Motion Picture Machine Operators Union, 43, 46, 76–78
Interstate Circuit, 100–101, 109, *109,* 110, 113, *114,* 117–18; applying for a television license (1945), 115, *116;* booking movies, 121; concessions stands, 117; during WWII, 112–13, 115; grand movie palaces, 59–72, *62, 63, 64, 66, 67, 71, 72. See also* Hoblitzelle, Karl
Iris Theater (Houston), *85,* 106
Isis Theater (Fort Worth), 41, *42,* 75–76
Isis Theater (Houston), 40, *40, 90*
It Came From Outer Space, 140

jackrabbit theaters, 59, 92
Jackson, Thomas Jefferson "Stout," 107–108
James, Harry, 173
Jazz Singer, The, 86–87
Jessel, George, 81–82
Jester Comedy Company (San Antonio), 36
Jolson, Al, 86, 87
Jones, John D., 25, 170
Jorgensen, George K.: on nickelodeons in Galveston (1907), 15–17; on nickelodeons in Houston (1906), 14; on sound for silent movies, 83
Joy Drive-In (Cisco), 126
Juke Joint, 131

Kaufman Pike Drive-In (Dallas), 138
Keeler, Bill, 89
Kelly Field (San Antonio), 52–53, *52, 53, 54*
Kier, H. W., 49–51
Killer Shrews, The, 145
Kinetograph. *See* Edison, Thomas A.
Kinetoscope, 4
King of Kings, 86
Kirkland, Sam, 135–36
Knox Theater (Dallas), *94*
KRLD (Dallas), 115

Lamesa, 135–36
Lampasas, 25–26
Lawn Theater (Dallas), *95*
Leonard, Marian, 15
LeRoy Theater (Mineola), 130
Liberty Freight Line, 119
Liberty Nickelodeon (Fort Worth), *23*
Lights of New York, The, 87
Lilly, A. W., 38, 105, 175
Lincoln Theater (El Paso), 129
Lincoln Theater (Honey Grove), 55
Lincoln Theater (Houston), 55
Little, Lambert, 129, *146*
Loew's State (Houston), 68–69, *70*
Longoria, Frank, 43–44
Longview, 40, 55, 104, 120
Lubbock, 21, 107
Lybrand, Karl, 19; on special balcony for blacks, 129; on theater checkers, 124. *See also* Wills Point
Lyric Theater (San Antonio), *42*

Majestic Family Theatre (Waco), 4, *5*
"Majesticland," 65
Majestic Theater (Austin), 61
Majestic Theater (Dallas), 58, 61–65, *62, 63, 64,* 74, 113, 115, 121; desegregating at, 57, 65; first movies shown at (1907), 11; first sound movie at, 86; surviving the depression, 92, 100
Majestic Theater (Fort Worth), 75, 94
Majestic Theater (Houston), 66–68, *66, 67*

Majestic Theater (San Antonio), 69–72, *71, 72;* closing during the depression, 92; first sound movie at, 89
Majestic Theater (Wills Point), 129
Mammoth (Dallas), 55
Mansfield, Martha, 49, *50*
Marching Herd, The, 51, 144
marquees, *39,* 61–62, *62,* 70, *70, 93, 94,* 101, 106–107, *132, 133, 134,* 138, *139;* at Maybank, 144
McAllen, 112
McAvoy, May, 53
McDonald, Earl: interest in movies at age sixteen, 126–27; organ at Palace (Dallas), 75, 116; on projection booth fires, 127–28
McGregor, 39, *39,* 40, 114–15, 118–19
McLendon, Gordon, 145
Meadowbrook Drive-In (Fort Worth), 128, 136–38
Melba Theater (Dallas), 113, *139,* 142
Melies, Georges, 33, *34*
Merchants Fast Motor Lines, 119
Metropolitan Theater (Houston), *68, 69*
Michaeux, Oscar, 55
Mickey Mouse Club officers (Palace Theater, Corpus Christi), *99*
"mid-nite rambles," 130–31, *131, 132*
Milligan, Boyd, 117; on getting job in theater (1926), 75; on opening Pix Theater during WWII, 111–12
Mineola, *25,* 46, 104, 112, 119, 120, 130, 141
minority audiences, theaters, and film production, 55–57, *96, 97,* 129–32, *129, 131, 132;* and Benroy Motion Pictures Corporation (1922), 48–49; in Corpus Christi, 129; desegregating Majestic (Dallas), 57, *62;* Foster and Lincoln Studios, 55; at LeRoy Theater, 130; at Lincoln Theater (El Paso), 129; at Lincoln Theater (Honey Grove), 55; at Lincoln Theater (Houston), 55; and list of theaters, 55; and Oscar Michaeux, 55; at Pastime, 55, *56;* at Plaza Theater (El Paso), 129; in San Angelo, 108; at Spanish language theaters (Corpus Christi), 57; at Spanish language theaters (San Antonio), *56,* 57, *57, 58, 90;* at Texas Theater (McGregor, 1912), 39–40; at Texas Theater (San Antonio), 129; and theaters in Dallas, *55,* 55–57; and Thomas Jefferson "Stout" Jackson, 107–108
Mission, 144
Mission Drive-In (San Antonio), *134*
Mistletoe Film Delivery Company, 119, 121
Mitchell, Bill: on booking movies, 121; on Interstate's demonstration of television (1946), 115, *116;* on Karl Hoblitzelle, 61, *109;* on promotional fronts for theaters, 100–101; on theater's declining popularly after WWII, 110, 117–18; on working at Interstate during WWII, 112–13
Mix, Tom, 107, 173
Morgan, Gerald, *42*
Morgan Film Truck Lines, 121
movie stars from Texas. *See* Appendix II
Movietone, 84–86, *85, 86*
Movie-Tone, 84
music in nickelodeons, 16–17, 22–23, *73. See also* organ(s); piano(s)

names for movies and theaters, 3–4
Narcotic Squad, 145
National Pictures Gulf Coast Studio (San Antonio), 49–51
National Screen Service, 101, 103
National Theater (Graham), 104
Native Americans in movies, 29, 35
New Braunfels, 84
New Liberty Theater (Fort Worth), 94, *96*
newsreels, 32, 113; in 1911, 14
nickelodeons, 11–26, 97; in Austin, *12, 16, 17, 24;* in Dallas, *21,* 21–23; early music in, 16–17; fire in 1910, 15; in Fort Worth, 23–25, *22, 23;* in Galveston, 13, 83; in Houston, *12,* 14–15, *55;* in San Antonio, 13; in Tyler, 18; in the United States, 13; in Waco (1907), *19,* 20, *20*
nitrate film, 46–47, 78–80, 111, 119, 127–28, 131–32. *See also* fires in projection booths
Noret, "Skeet," 135
North Main Historical Society Museum, 26, *26*

Odem Theater (Fort Worth), 75
Odessa, 9, 54
"Old Soggy No. 1," 52
operators, projection booth, 43–47, 75–80, 125–29
Orange, 5
orchestra(s), 69, 70, 82; at Aztec, 72; at Majestic (Houston), 67; in nickelodeons, 73; at Palace (Dallas), 65, 66; at Queen (Houston), 40. *See also* organ(s); piano(s)
organ(s), 22, 69, 73–75, *74,* 76, 82, 89–91, 116; at Palace (Dallas), 65, 66, 116; at Queen (Houston), 40. *See also* orchestra(s); piano(s)
Orpheum Theater (Waco), 86
Out West Pictures Corporation (San Antonio), 49

Palace Theater (Corpus Christi), *98, 99*
Palace Theater (Dallas), 58–59, 65–66, 74, 75, 76, 77, 100, 113, 116; working there, 76–77
Palace Theater (El Paso), 129
Palace Theater (Fort Worth), 26
Palace Theater (San Antonio), *122*
Palestine, 75
Paramount Theater (Abilene), 94, 97
Paris, 83; first projected image, 7

Pasograph Company (El Paso), 36
Pastime Nickelodeon (Houston), 55, *56,* 59
Pathé, 16, 51, 52; newsreels from (1911), 14
Perils of Pauline, The, 36
Perry, Harry, 53–54, *53*
Phillips, Joe S., 81–82; and first projected image (Fort Worth, 1903), 8; and nickelodeons (1910), 22, 25
Phillip's Egyptian Nickelodeon (Fort Worth), 22. *See also* Phillips, Joe S.
piano(s), 39, 73–75, 76, 82, 136; during silent serials (chaptered movies), 46; in nickelodeons, 13; at Washington Nickelodeon, 22–23, 73. *See also* organ(s)
Pickford, Mary, 15, 22
Pike Drive-In (Fort Worth), 134
Pioneers of Texas motion picture theaters. *See* Appendix III
Pix Theater (Fort Worth), 111
Poly Theater (Fort Worth), 117
Pool, E. T., 86
Port Arthur, 30
Princess Theater (Dallas), 46–47
promotion, *15, 79, 80, 90,* 92–106, *98, 99, 100, 102, 103, 104, 105*
Pyle, Charles, 32

Queen Theater (Dallas), 58–59, *58,* 113
Queen Theater (Galveston), *60, 61*
Queen Theater (Houston), 40

"race movies," 1910s, 48–49
Ragsdale, Kenneth, 91–92
Ranger, *120, 125*
Rast, William, *104, 114, 142,* 143; on promotion in Waco, 101–104; on special balcony for blacks in El Paso, 129–30
Ray, Allene, 51
Rio Grande Valley, 112, 144
Ritz Theater (Corpus Christi), *98, 99*
Ritz Theater (Houston), *86*
Ritz Theater (Longview), 55
Ritz Theater (Wesleco), *122*
River Oaks Theater (Fort Worth), 112
Robb, Harold and Ed Rowley (R & R Theaters), 25, 41–43, *43, 74, 98,* 106, 126; and booking movies, 121–23; and first nickelodeon (San Angelo), 18; and relations with Howard Hughes, 92–94
Robb, Harold and Yuill: and first nickelodeon, 17–18; and sound effects during silent movies, 83
Robstown, 107
Rodgers, "Slats," 51–52
Rogers, Buddy, 53
Rogers, Ginger, 173
Rogers, Roy, 136
Roland, Ruth, 51
Roosevelt, Teddy, 30, 52
Rowley, John, 86; on booking movies for Robb and Rowley theaters, 121–23; on his father starting Robb and Rowley Theaters, 41–43, *43;* on Robb and Rowley's relations with Howard Hughes, 92–94. *See also* Robb, Harold and Ed Rowley
Russell, Martha, 32

Sack Amusement Enterprises (Dallas), 130, 131
San Angelo, 25, 94, 101, 108, *111,* 126, 141; first nickelodeons in, 18; Robb's and Rowley's formation (1916), 43
San Antonio, *42, 88,* 89, *112, 117, 118, 119,* 129, 130, *130, 134;* Aztec Theater in, 72; early film exchanges in, 29; Excel Fotoplay Company in (1915), 35; filming chaptered movies in (1916), 51; first projected image in (1898), 6–7; Jester Comedy Company in (1918), 36; Majestic Theater in, 69–72, *71, 72,* 92; minority theaters in, *56,* 57, *57, 58, 90;* National Pictures Gulf Coast Studio in, 49–51; nickelodeons in (1911), 13; Out West Pictures Corporation in (1926), 49; San Antonio Photo Plays Studio in, 35; San Antonio Pictures Corporation in (1923), 48; Satex Film Company in, 30–33, *30;* Shamrock Photoplay Corporation in (1917), 35; Siege and Fall of the Alamo Motion Picture Corporation in (1911), 35; Star Film Ranch in (1910), 33–35, *34;* Sunset Picture Corporation in (1917), 35–36, *36, 37;* Tilley Brothers film production in (1910), 30–31, *30;* town-booster film in (1928), 38; unnamed movie studio in, 49, 51; *Warrens of Virginia, The* (1923), 49, *50;* Wigwam Nickelodeon in, 13; *Wings* (1926), 52–54, *52, 53, 54. See also* Satex Film Company
San Antonio Photo Plays Studio, 35
San Antonio Pictures Corporation, 35
Santa Anna, 127
Satex Film Company, 30–33, *30, 31. See also* Tilley, W. Hope and Paul
Sealy, 51–52
Secret Kingdom, The, 51
serials, 46, 51
Service Film Company, The, 36
Shamrock Photoplay Corporation (San Antonio), 35
Shaver, W. C., 43, 128
sheets or picture sheets, 3, 4, 6, 7–8, 11, 13, 14, 19, 25
Siege and Fall of the Alamo Motion Picture Corporation, The, 35
silent movie operators: Bob Baker, 43, 46–47; Frank Longoria, 43–44; "Scotty" Davidson, 45–46, 47; W. C. Shaver, 43; Wylie York, 44
Sky-Vue Drive-In (Lamesa), 135–36
slides in silent movies, 18, 23, 39, 46, 76, 91

Smith, Margaret, 39–40; on booking movies, 118–19; on operating a theater during WWII, 114–15; on projection booth fire, 79–80
Snow, Marguerite, 16
sound effects for silent movies, 83. *See also* Harrison, W. Walworth; Robb, Harold and Yuill
"Sound in the Ground" drive-in movie sound system, 134
sound motion pictures, 81–92, *85, 86, 88;* patrons attitude about, 82
Sparks, Winston O., 97–100; on first attending movies in Fort Worth, 75–76; on first movies in Fort Worth stockyards (1904), 8–9
Spearman, 136
special accommodations for patrons, 94
special balcony. *See* minority audiences, theaters, and film production
stage(s), *64, 68, 70, 72, 74, 80, 95, 115, 125*
Stanford, Bill, 119; interest in movies (1939), 126; on Waco Drive-In, 134
Star Film Ranch, The (San Antonio), 33–35, *34*
Star Theater (San Antonio), *118*
State Theater (Fort Worth), *132*
Stinson, Marjorie, 35
storefront theaters, 3, 6–11; in Dallas (1905), 21–23
Storey, Edith, *33, 34*
Strategic Air Command, 144–45
Sulphur Springs, *10,* 105, 128, 129
Sunset Picture Corporation (San Antonio), 35–36, *36, 37*
"Supers." *See also* grand movie palaces, 61–72

talkies, 4, 81–92, *85, 86*
Tarzan, 46
Teatro Carpas, 107–108. *See also* Jackson, Thomas Jefferson "Stout"
Teatro Nacional (San Antonio), 89, *90*
Teatro Obrero (San Antonio), *57*
Teatro Progreso (San Antonio), *58*
Teatro Zaragoza (San Antonio), *56*
Telenews Theater (Dallas), 58, 113
Ten Commandments, The, 121
Texan Theater (Hamilton), 94, 129, *146*
Texas Drive-In Theater (Corpus Christi), 132–33
Texas Drive-In Theater (Houston), 133
Texas Nickelodeon (Austin), *17*
Texas Tex, 29
Texas Theater (Austin), *124*
Texas Theater (Dallas), 92–94
Texas Theater (McGregor), *39,* 39–40, 106, 118–19
Texas Theater (San Angelo), 94, *111*
Texas Theater (San Antonio), 54, 120, *130*
Texas Theater (Seguin), 127
theater circuits: Interstate, 59–72; Robb and Rowley (1916), 41–43. *See also* Appendix IV
theater row (Dallas), 57–59, *58*
theater row (Galveston), 59
theater row (Houston), 59
theater rows, 57–59, *58,* 97, 100
theaters: Aggie, *115;* Airdome (Mineola), *25;* Airdome (Sulphur Springs), *10*: Airline Drive-In, *132;* Arcadia, *120;* Aztec, 72; Bijou Nickelodeon, *16;* Bowie (Brownwood), *114;* Bowie (Fort Worth), 94; Cactus Drive-In, *133;* Capitol, 100–101, 113, *114;* Capri running *This is Cinerama,* 143; Circle in Dallas showing sound movies, 84–85; Cliff Queen, *77;* Columbia, *125;* Cozy Nickelodeon, *20;* Crawford, 47; Crescent Nickelodeon, *24;* Crystal Nickelodeon (Dallas), 43, *44,* 58; Crystal Nickelodeon (Waco), *19;* desegregating Majestic (Dallas), 57, *62,* 65; Dixie Nickelodeon, *12;* Dorothy, 41; Drive-In Short Reel Theater, 132; El Rey, *129;* Fair, 100; Fort Sam Houston Theater (San Antonio), *112;* Gayety, *97;* Grand (Longview), 40; Gulf Drive-In, 134; Harlem (Dallas), 55, *55,* 56, 58; Harling, *119;* Highland, *123;* Hippodrome, *15,* 79–80, *79, 80;* Iris, *85,* 106; Isis (Fort Worth), 41, *42,* 75–76; Isis (Houston), 40, *40, 90;* Kaufman Pike Drive-In, 138; Knox, *94;* jackrabbit theaters, 59; Lawn, *95;* LeRoy, 130; Liberty Nickelodeon, *23;* Lincoln (El Paso), 129; Lincoln (Honey Grove), 55; Lincoln (Houston), 55; list of de luxe theaters, 54–55; list of drive-ins theaters in operation (1999), 138–39; list of minority theaters, 55; Loew's State, 68–69, *70;* Lyric, *42;* Majestic (Austin), 61; Majestic (Dallas), 57, 58, 61–65, *62, 63, 64,* 100, 113; Majestic (Fort Worth), 75; Majestic (Houston), 61, 66–68, *66, 67;* Majestic (San Antonio), 69–72, *71, 72;* Mammoth, 55; Meadowbrook Drive-In, 128, 136–38; Melba, *139,* 142; Melba shows *This is Cinerama,* 142; Metropolitan, *68, 69;* minority theaters after WWII, 128–32; minority theaters in Dallas, 55–57, *55;* minority theaters in Houston, 55, *56;* Mission Drive-In, *134;* New Liberty, 94, *96;* Nickelodeon (Austin), *12;* Odem, 75; Palace (Corpus Christi), *74, 98;* Palace (Dallas), 58–59, 65–66, 76, 77, 100, 113; Palace (San Antonio), *122;* Paramount, 94, 97; Pastime Nickelodeon, 55, *56,* 59; Payne's Palace (Gladewater), 40; Phillip's Egyptian Nickelodeon, *22;* Pike Drive-In, 134; Pix (Fort Worth), 111–12; Poly (Fort Worth), 117; Princess (Dallas), 46–47; Queen (Dallas), *58,* 58–59, 113; Queen (Galveston), *60, 61;* Queen (Houston), 40; Ritz (Corpus Christi), *98, 99;* Ritz (Houston), *86;* Ritz (Longview), 55; Ritz (Weslaco), *122;* River Oaks, 112; Sky-Vue Drive-In, 135–36; Spanish-language theaters (San Antonio), 57, *56, 57,*

theaters (*cont.*)
58, 90; Star, *118;* State, *132;* Teatro Nacional, 89, *90;* Teatro Obrero, *57;* Teatro Progreso, *58;* Teatro Zaragoza, *56;* Tele-news, 58, 113; Texas (Austin), *124;* Texas (Dallas), 92–94; Texas (Hamilton), 129, *146;* Texas (McGregor), 39–40, *39,* 106; Texas (San Angelo), 94, *111;* Texas (San Antonio), 54, 120, 129, *130;* Texas (Seguin), 127; Texas Drive-In (Corpus Christi), 132–33; Texas Drive-In (Houston), 133; Texas Nick-elodeon, *17;* theater row (Dallas), 57–59, *58;* theater row (Galveston), 59; theater row (Houston), 59; Tyler Theater (Tyler), *117;* Upton, *117;* Village, *93;* Waco Drive-In, 134; Waco Theater, *100, 101, 102, 103, 104, 105;* Wagon Wheel Drive-In, 136; Washington Nickelodeon, *21,* 21–23, 43, 58, 73; Wednesday Book Club Opera House, *18;* Wigwam, 13; Wilshire, 115, *116;* Worth, 69; Yale Nickelodeon, *24;* Yucca, 94, 97. *See also* Appendix I
Their Lives by a Slender Thread, 32
This Is Cinerama, 142–43, *142*
Thomas, Lowell, 143
Three-Dimensional (3-D), 110, 139–42, *139, 140*
Thrill-O-Rama, 143–44
ticket office, *58, 63,* 68, 69, *71,* 72, 129, 138
Tidball, L. C., 9; on booking movies (1910s), 41; on opening Isis Theater (Fort Worth, 1914), 41, *42;* on promotion during the depression, 97–100; on ticket sales at Isis Theater (Fort Worth, 1923), 41
Tilley, W. Hope and Paul, 30–33, *30, 31,* 82
town-booster films, 37–38
Trevino, Frederico, 57
Turner, Florence, 15
Two Rode Together, 145
Tyler, *6, 7,* 101, 108–109, *117;* early nickelodeons in (1906), 18; first projected image in (1898), 5–6, *6, 7;* "Scotty" Davidson of, 45–46, 78; sound for silent movies in, 84

union of projection booth operators, 46, 76–78. *See also* International Alliance of Theatrical Stage Employees and Motion Picture Machine Operators Union
Uptown Theater (San Antonio), *117*
ushers, 63, 67–68, 71–72, *113*

Velez, Lupe, 107
Vidor, King, 30, 33, 49
Village Theater (Dallas), *93*
Vitagraph, 15, *15,* 33
Vitaphone, 35, 81–82, 84–89, *85, 86, 88*
Vitascope, 4; in Dallas (1897), 4; in Galveston (1897), 4–5; in Tyler (1898), 5–6, *6, 7*

Waco, 3, 4, *5, 15, 20,* 79, 126, 144; first drive-in theater in, 134; first projected image in (1897), 4; *Gone With The Wind* shown in, 108–109; *Jazz Singer, The* shown in (1928), 86; minority theaters in, 56–57; nickelodeons in (1908), *19,* 20–21; promotion during the depression in, *79, 80, 100, 101,* 101–104, *102, 103, 104, 105;* town-booster film in (1956), 38
Waco (Hippodrome) Theater (Waco), *79, 80, 100, 101, 102, 103, 104, 105*
Wagon Wheel Drive-In (Spearman), 136
war. *See* World War II
Warrens of Virginia, The, 49, *50*
war tax, 112
Washington Nickelodeon (Dallas), *21,* 21–23, 43, 58, 73
WEAY (Houston), 106
Wednesday Book Club Opera House (Wills Point), *18,* 19
Weldon, Lawrence: on booking movies, 120–21; on filming *Thrill-O-Rama,* 143–44; on managing the Meadowbrook Drive-In, 136–38; on projection booth fire, 128; on sound in drive-in theaters, 133; on special balcony for blacks, 131; on theater checkers, 124–25; on theater managers, 113
Wellman, William, 52–54, *52*
Westerns, 17, 22, 29–30, *31,* 33–35, *34,* 36, 45, 49, 51, 55, 91, 92, 112, 113, 118, 119
We've Never Been Licked, 144
Wheelan-Loper Film Company, 16, 29
White, Pearl, 51
Wichita Falls, 145: first projected image in (1904), 11; first sound movie in, 86; nickelodeons in (1907), 20; silent movie operators in, 43; town-booster film in (1922), 38
Wigwam Nickelodeon (San Antonio), 13
Williams, Spencer, 131–32
Wills Point, *18,* 19, 89, 124, 129
Wilshire Theater (Dallas), 115, *116*
Wings, 52–54, *52, 53, 54*
WOAI (San Antonio), *88*
Wojtek, Ronda, 110
Wolf City, 59
World War II, 110–18
Worth Theater (Fort Worth), 69, 139
Wright Brothers, 30
Wurlitzer Organs, 74, 75. *See also* organ(s)

Yale Nickelodeon (Austin), *24*
York, Wylie, 44
Yucca Theater (Midland), 94, 97

Ziegfeld Cinema Corporation (San Antonio), 36